M000043022

"Mary Joye has written courses for DailyOM that have helped many people in their quest for a body/mind/spirit connection to recovery. Her work in this book continues to help those with codependency in a holistic and engaging way."

—**Madisyn Taylor**, co-founder and editor-in-chief of DailyOM

"Mary Joye has been an instrumental influence in my own journey to becoming a mental health counselor, and she has remained a source of inspiration and consultation, both as a colleague and a friend. I am honored to be able to count Mary as one of my connections, and I am excited that she is sharing her wealth of knowledge and expertise with the entire literary world.

In her book, Mary approaches codependency from a holistic, well-rounded perspective that enables people to intentionally choose a path of empowerment and enlightenment. I have no doubt that through this book, Mary will continue to inspire and guide colleagues in the mental health field, as well as individuals struggling with codependency and any and all readers who choose this book for their next read."

—**Jesse Williams**, MS, LPC/MHSP, NCC, CCH

"Using neuroscience, psychology, and spirituality, Mary Joye shares how to conquer old habits of feeling the need to rescue loved ones and friends. In this compelling book you can free yourself and learn that living well and giving well can occur naturally."

—**Dr. Laurie Nadel**, author of *The Five Gifts: Discover Hope, Healing, and Strength When Disaster Strikes*

"If you are feeling stuck in unhealthy codependent patterns, this book offers support and guidance on how to 'tear up the old outline of your life and write a new one,' using insights, meditations, affirmations, and other exercises that can begin to rewire the patterning of the brain and the nervous system."

—**Dr. Jodie Skillicorn**, holistic psychiatrist, author of *Healing Depression without Medication: A Psychiatrist's Guide to Balancing Mind, Body, and Soul*

Codependent
DISCOVERY AND
Recovery
2.0

A Holistic Approach to Healing and Freeing Yourself

Mary Joye, LMHC

Health Communications, Inc.
Boca Raton, Florida

www.hcibooks.com

**Library of Congress Cataloging-in-Publication Data
is available through the Library of Congress**

© 2021 Mary Joye

ISBN 13: 978-0-7573-2409-3 (Paperback)
ISBN 10: 0-7573-2409-6 (Paperback)
ISBN 13: 978-0-7573-2410-9 (ePub)
ISBN 10: 0-7573-2410-X (ePub)

The material in this book is intended for education. It is not meant to take the place of diagnosis and treatment by a qualified medical practitioner or therapist. No expressed or implied guarantee of the effects of the use of the recommendations can be given or liability taken.

All identifying characteristics, including names, have been changed to protect the privacy of the individuals described.

HCI, its logos, and marks are trademarks of Health Communications, Inc.

Publisher: Health Communications, Inc.
1700 NW 2nd Ave.
Boca Raton, FL 33432–1653

Cover design by Larissa Hise Henoch
Interior design by Larissa Hise Henoch, formatting by Lawna Patterson Oldfield

DEDICATION

This book is dedicated in memory of
Shirley "Ann" Cunnen, whose years of loving friendship
and gift of therapy are why I'm a therapist today,
and to Beverly "Bear" Powell for her loving
kindness and mentorship.

CONTENTS

Chapter 3 • The Neuroscience of Codependency • 81

Chapter 4 • Family Secrets and Inner Child Healing • 97

Chapter 5 • Higher, Happier, and Healthier Relationships • 115

Chapter 11 • Continuing to Establish Independent
and Interdependent Abundance • 249

ACKNOWLEDGMENTS

I am grateful to those mentioned here who have acted as alchemists in my life. All are golden threads woven together who made this book possible.

Thank you to Ruth Boggs, who I met in the backstage parking lot of a Willie Nelson concert when we were bringing food for the tour bus. She helped me through a horrible divorce with her wonderful friendship. Ruth later invited me to go to Wyoming to a writer's retreat, where I met authors and instructors Tina Welling and Janet Hubbard. They assisted me in writing about parts of my life I was hesitant to share. My gratitude for their mentorship is as immense as the ranch where we gathered. I appreciate Janet's encouragement and for introducing me to literary agent Lisa Hagan, with whom I am *sympatico*. I appreciate Lisa's tenacity and integrity and for leading me to HCI Books. I am grateful to Christine Belleris of HCI for believing in this work and giving it harbor. Camilla Michael of HCI has been a wonderful editor and navigator. You have this book because of these very strong links in this chain of professional encouragers.

To Leslie Dougherty Reed and her husband Billy Reed, I give thanks for being the best of friends for decades. Leslie taught me the gift of making memories and I have immense gratitude for all the Doughertys for making me part of their loving family. I can't imagine how my life would be without them all and their unswerving support and loving kindness.

To Michael Powell, a friend and brother in spirit of over forty years, thank you for making my life more beautiful with your friendship and paintings. His mother Beverly "Bear" Powell is one of two to whom this book is dedicated. To Danny DeCastro, who, with Michael, has made me "ohana." Thank you for including me in your global adventures. No matter where we go, it always feels like home because you are there.

Thanks to Alexander Gimon, PhD for being my supervisor while I became a counselor and for mentoring me to keep writing.

I thank Madisyn Taylor, co-founder of DailyOM, for being one of the first to believe in me as an e-course author and for publishing my works on trauma, relationships, and codependency.

And last, but not least, sincere gratitude to Tommy Laymon, my partner in life, who gave me wings to travel and encouraged me to enjoy life, to self-care, and who taught me how to invest in myself on many levels. He drove me to Sedona, Arizona where we stayed in a beautiful home for forty days so I could recover from a family death which forced me to examine my codependency. This book began as a journal on that journey. To Ace and Jet, our two little rescue dogs, who have been patient companions at my side for every word written here. They and I hope you are rescued from your codependency with this book.

FOREWORD

When you write songs with someone over a long period of time, you get to know them pretty well through all the discussions that take place in songwriting sessions. Those discussions usually include life, love, family, past hurts, losses, funny stories, politics, religion, sad stories, and so forth, and it's no wonder that songwriting is almost like a therapy session set to music. And, as I said, you get to know your cowriters pretty well, but in looking back, I realize also how much we all hide from those around us. It's amazing how much we don't see about the other person—even though the clues are all right in front of our faces.

I had been friends with MJ (Mary Joye) and her husband prior to my time as a writer for their company and had always seen them as a fun-loving, happy couple. However, as I began writing regularly with MJ, I could see that things were not perfect in Camelot, but I was so caught in my own world of anxiety disorders and the related addictions that I didn't notice how well she was hiding her pain. MJ's husband was a very strong-willed man and basically "rode herd" over just about everyone in his circle to the point of being a bully, so I can only imagine what he put her through.

Thinking back on how MJ would look many times when we were writing, I am reminded of a line in a song that I wrote with David Leone called "Woman with a Past." The first line says, "There's a certain sadness in her smile," and it is now as clear as day to me, even though I didn't recognize it then. I do know that music has played a huge part in helping MJ get through the tough times, just as it has helped me. I am glad we could share that time together writing, even though we didn't really realize we were helping each other to cope through writing songs (at least I didn't realize!).

Reading now what MJ is doing to help herself and others is a great testament to her faith in God and to the truth that a person can get to the other side of just about anything in life with help from beside and above. I am very proud to see that my friend is using her recovery from things that were meant to take her out to help others find their own freedom!

—**Bobby E. Boyd**
January 2021

INTRODUCTION

I t is said that your greatest strength is also your greatest weakness. As a codependent, your greatest strength may be compassion because you probably have a genuine desire to care for others and help them solve their problems. This is an admirable and noble trait, but if your compassion turns into a compulsion to help others while neglecting or exhausting yourself, or you have a hidden underpinning of resentment or anger when you do, you may be codependent. Have hope because you can learn to say no to others and yes to yourself, guilt free.

Many of those for whom you care might cause you to believe that they are dependent on you, and some of them may be, but some are not. Most everyone, at one time or another, will have an actual dependent of some sort. These people are your responsibility, such as children, the elderly, a disabled adult, or anyone in your immediate family who needs you and lacks the ability to reciprocate. This is genuine, compassionate caregiving, not codependence. Yet in this context, you may still burn out easily because of reticence to ask for assistance while caring for others or from doing too much for too many for too long.

Caring about and for others who treat you badly is another dynamic entirely. It can also lead to an early demise from a lack of self-care and a false sense of over-responsibility or guilt. If you cringe when you receive a phone call from one of these people or organizations, you might want to examine your motives for saying yes when you mean no. This can also occur in your own home with addicted relatives, mooching roommates, or those who make you feel guilty by accessing your empathy through manipulating your feelings. If there are people in your life like this, it can cause you to give all your resources to stop them from asking and to relieve your anxiety. However, you are really giving until you give out—and this can be mentally, emotionally, and physically overwhelming. Over the long haul of your life, giving can render you the most in need with no one to help you.

Most models of codependency rely heavily on a twelve-step addiction model and this is understandable but not quite comprehensive enough. This book is holistic and structured from eclectic and evidential viewpoints. It is built to teach you to learn how to live and give well in a supportive way to the body/mind/spirit trinity within you.

1. Your mind can change your thoughts.
2. Your spirit can help you believe in the possibility of change.
3. You will take physical action to achieve your goals.

The premise to the aforementioned addiction recovery model is that someone is dependent on a substance and you have become codependent with them and are *enabling* them in some way. In truth, you have actually *disabled* them from becoming responsible for themselves. You will learn much more about how you no longer have to take the blame for anyone's addiction here. My mother was a food addict, and if I didn't buy her copious amounts of chocolate, she would find it online or by phone. If an addict needs a drink or anything else, they do not need you to get it. There is always someone ready, willing, and able to deliver whatever substance suits their fancy. They will find a way to get what they need whether you "enable" them or not.

An addict does need someone to be responsible and stable to cover for them, and this is what a codependent does well. Needing to be needed is the addiction of the codependent, and this is an extremely simplified view. You are about to go on a customized journey of discovery to see how complex and clandestine codependency can be and how it may be operating in your life or the lives of people you care about. Codependency is much more than an addict/enabler relationship, but it can be part of it and may be for you as it has been for me at different times throughout my life. You will learn that you want to attract a person *of* substance, not a person addicted *to* substances. You will also learn it's not your job to make sure an addict is cured. That will make you very ill if you try, and this may be where you are as you read this. It is no way to live your life, but you can get your life back. However, a broader view outside the addiction model of the components of codependency can insidiously extend into every facet of your life, sometimes without you having insight or foresight. It is in hindsight that you may see you gave up your life or identity to become a champion or savior for others, and this can leave you feeling lonely and used.

This is exactly the opposite of what you are seeking by doing so much for others in an effort to stay connected through their need for you. It is a flawed relationship because it's one-sided, and those taking from you make it feel like it's all your fault for not helping them enough. Selfish people can twist their words to make the codependent feel selfish by imposing false guilt on them. Not feeling like you have done enough is the cry of every codependent.

I will never forget, prior to a serious reconstructive surgery in my teens, that I had type O negative blood, which is known as the "universal donor." I had to donate my own blood for myself. I can give blood to anyone but can only receive from myself or someone else with O negative. I'm glad my mother wasn't in the lab because I said to the tech, "How fitting! I can give to everyone and receive from little to no one." Even at seventeen, I was acutely aware of the metaphor of codependency without even knowing

I was a codependent. Donating blood was something I did for a long time as I felt obligated because of the need for O negative, until one day the Red Cross turned me away, saying I was anemic. I was only in my late twenties, so it was one of many wake-up calls I had about giving until there was nothing left of me. I was allowing a false sense of responsibility to quite literally extract the life out of me. A codependent has a difficult time knowing when enough is enough when it comes to giving. Challenging the purported person to take some steps to help themselves is wiser and enables them to care for themselves.

As a mental health counselor and a recovering codependent, I had to take a good, hard look at my life and take ownership for feeling over-responsible for others in my family and in all my relationships. It could not be done without asking for help. I had to devise a way out of a mindset that seemed hardwired but was actually forced upon me from my family system. No two codependents are alike, but they share a basic commonality in how they present themselves to the world through being attentive to the needs of others.

A codependent person can become completely overextended and will say "I'm fine" when they're clearly not. "I'm fine" or "I'm sorry" are mantras of codependents, and they say it with a smile, even if their heart is breaking. Many of my clients come to me to get help for someone else who doesn't want it. They want to know what to do to make people get help, and this motive seems pure to them, but it will exhaust them to come to therapy to fix someone else. They often express anger toward me when we explore the possibility of their codependence and the inevitability of what will happen if they don't learn to self-care and allow the addict, abuser, or narcissist to suffer consequences. When you give to others without receiving or resting yourself, your quality of life is impaired, and counterintuitive to codependent thinking, you have less to give to people who really need you when they actually want your assistance. They realize they are trying to change someone who doesn't want to change, and it is to stay connected and to reduce their driving fear of abandonment. You can't force change in anyone but yourself, nor can you become less codependent without the desire from within.

This book is not about changing your personality; making you feel greedy, selfish, or narcissistic; or telling you to withhold things from those who have sincere needs. More than anything, it will enlighten you on how to give generously while living well and prosperously. You'll discover much more than just learning to say "No" to others. You'll learn how to say "Yes!" to yourself independently and interdependently and to form healthy, reciprocal relationships.

Don't beat yourself for not recognizing your codependency until now. These could-have, should-have, and would-have ruminations can be calmed with enlightenment. You can change your codependent drives with independent thinking and accomplish interdependent, healthy relationships, and learn that doing everything for everyone or rescuing anyone who asks something from you isn't a sustainable way to live. You may be in codependent crisis on the brink of collapse, and if so, it's time to rest, reset, and restore. Knowing, accepting, and having self-compassion is the place to begin.

One of my graduate school supervisory professors, Dr. S., a neuropsychologist, pulled me aside after class and told me I was codependent. I asked, "What is that?"

She explained and admonished, "Clients will eat you alive and walk all over you if you don't get a grip on your boundaries."

"I'm just trying to be nice," I said with polite but ruffled defensiveness.

I was unaware that this self-justifying, prickly feeling was really a defense mechanism and a cover-up for my people-pleasing and a need to be needed ingrained in me from youth. In truth, I felt like I had to be an extension of my family image. I was a psychiatrist's daughter and worked in my father's practice and had witnessed him helping many alcoholics detox and assisting them in recovery. I also went on house calls with him back in the day, witnessed horrific events and deaths, and saw how he attempted to rescue everyone, and I thought it was what I was supposed to do too. It didn't seem to take a toll on him then, but it showed up later in his life. I know it took a toll on me because we couldn't save them all, and this haunted me.

Dr. S. was the daughter of an alcoholic, so she knew what I went through in my youth and also what I was getting into as a counselor. I had to learn the hard way and am grateful for her required and excellent supervision. Dr. S. also was aware I was about to go into an internship in a drug and alcohol rehab and was not in recovery myself as I had to be the picture of health in my prior career. She knew I was transitioning from my former people-pleasing career as a professional singer/songwriter and told me performers have boundary issues because people ask and expect so much of them. "The show must go on" is a work ethic of most performers. They set their needs aside and compartmentalize any problems they have so others can be entertained.

I had to learn to accept that and be glad Dr. S. knew these things about me. She was absolutely correct about clients taking advantage of my ability to believe the best in people. One client got me to believe tales of toothaches and damaged his own gums so he could get a release to the dentist and for pain pills. A funny counselor swiped my shoulders, saying, "You've been snowed by your own sympathy." I didn't get in trouble because this is what internships are for: to learn and lean on the expertise of those with more experience. That is what this book is for, not to correct you, but to protect and redirect you.

Every day, then and now, I have some revelation of how codependency could ruin my ability to enjoy life. The reason I went back to school in the first place was because my soon-to-be ex-husband was an abusive and controlling man and had made our financial lives a shamble from his addiction to lifestyle "needs." These were much like my mother's needs, and there were pieces I had to put together or I would fall apart. An epiphany was necessary, and accepting I was codependent and no longer wanted to be was essential to my recovery—and it is to yours too.

How many stories do we hear about a wife putting a husband through medical or law school and then being dumped when he begins working, and she inherits half the student loan and none of the fruits of her labor? What if she had gone to medical school or followed her dreams? What about your dreams? Go for them or some best version of them. Do not be stymied for the rest of your life by helping others to enjoy theirs. Everyone needs to receive before they give, and there is a reason for the saying, "You can't give what you don't have," which is a difficult concept for a codependent. If a person wants something and a codependent doesn't have it, the codependent will find a way to get it at their own expense. I did this many times, so I know it is true, and it's also debilitating.

Because of this compulsion to meet the needs of others while neglecting themselves, codependents seldom live up to their potential as they run out of time to achieve or do what they want. With self-awareness, you can correct the course of your life, and the sooner the better. Time is the most precious and unrenewable commodity on the planet. If anyone could find out how to manufacture and sell time, they would be the richest person on the planet. Codependents "lend" a hand to others so often they sacrifice this precious gift, but you can recondition yourself.

You can only help people who desire to be helped, and this is true of codependents too. Codependency is treated like addiction because it causes reactivity in the body that keeps you clinging to the false belief that if you do enough, you can save others. Sadly this couldn't be further from reality. Though there are medications for addiction, there is not a pill for the desire to get better, and nothing you can do as a codependent can make someone get help if they do not want it. The same is true of you. If you want to get help for the maladaptive effect codependency has on you, then you will seek your truth and emerge from this introspective book, armed with the tools to help you help others. This will only work as much you are willing to work on yourself.

Establishing boundaries is essential to living an abundant life, and you can learn to say no without guilt or fear. You don't have to fear abandonment or being alone anymore. You can enjoy helping others from a place of peace, motivated by kindness, and not compelled by a need to feel better about yourself by giving "tirelessly" to others. You don't have to be tired, resentful, or exhausted anymore. You no longer have to self-judge or compare yourself to others or deny yourself care in order to be used or be of benefit to others. The "I'm-not-good-enough-unless-I-do-enough" loop in your head can be edited by realizing you are enough just as you are.

As you will soon learn, codependency is not a diagnosable disorder, but it can wreak havoc on your life. You have been giving your resources, power, and kindness away for a long time and you may even be a covert codependent who appears to be independent but is still exhausted from caring for everyone else but yourself. This book is titled *Codependency Discovery and Recovery 2.0* because there is much more to this condition of the heart than you may think. Your mind, body, and spiritual life have much to do with how you came to be codependent. You can use this book as a compass to get back on course in your life and no longer lose your identity or desires by acquiescing to everyone else. You can get into a flow state of receiving and giving.

By changing your thinking through meditation, guided imagery exercises, and insightful Life Lists, your journal at the end of each chapter will help guide you to be self-aware and self-caring. The Life Lists will culminate at the end of the book and act as a ceremonial takeaway that you can keep for the future.

Go at your own pace and recognize resistance along the way. It's good to question your motives in the context of this book, and in doing so, you may learn how to better serve others by understanding their motives. When we pay attention to ourselves and how our bodies and minds are speaking to us through our spiritual nature, we can see where we need to make adjustments. We can set healthier intentions when we are enlightened and allow our subconsciousness to fully integrate with our consciousness. We are no longer driven by an invisible force when we do this, and what seemed like natural choices in the past will become more self-nurturing in the future.

You can learn to overcome past conditioning and enjoy an abundant future through the process of becoming independent and interdependent. You will transcend into a happier and healthier life where you are authentically and powerfully able to keep giving to others while living well yourself.

CHAPTER 1

....

Overview of the
Root Causes of Codependency

We are made wise not by the recollection of our past,
but by the responsibility for our future.

—George Bernard Shaw

B roadly defined, codependency is a loss of self while caring for others
more than you do for yourself. Another description is that how
you feel about yourself depends on how you perceive others feel
about you. The roots of codependency are born of a subconscious fear of
abandonment. Other roots of codependency are more complex.

Many people are simply born more empathic and sympathetic. Sometimes perfect families teach us everyone can be trusted and to look for the

good in people. You may become too good for your own good because you have been taught to overlook negative traits in others. Think of how this may have come about for you, and as each chapter unfolds, discover any innate, learned, or conditioned traits you may have. You will be able to use these key moments to unlock what has been holding you secretly hostage so you can enjoy your life for the better.

Codependents live in an invisible prison of fear of loss of connection. You are hardwired simultaneously for connection but also for fear, and both are meant to keep you safe. When you get mixed messages in your brain from outside influences, you can care much for people who care too little for you, and this causes a disconnect with self. Feelings of self-worth and authentic identity become occluded or diluted by trying to make everyone happy, but you are subconsciously trying to keep yourself happy, calm, and connected. It attracts you to people who say they need you, but they are nowhere to be found if you need them. This is not a coincidence; it's codependence.

Defining the unique ways your codependency manifests is the first revelatory step to healing. You can be more specific about how you're allowing yourself to become overextended. A personal journal will help you with specific discoveries, and make sure it is one you love. Be lavish in choosing your journal because it will be a highly personalized self-reference guide to keep you on course for the rest of your life. The meditations, affirmations, and Life Lists are progressive building blocks. At the conclusion, you will find a tangible way to ceremoniously release the negative side of the bullet-point lists and keep the positive ones.

You can revisit the guided imagery exercises and Life Lists as guides when you feel you may be relapsing into codependent behaviors. Recognition of your motivations and intentions is key to maintaining your well-being.

Recognition of the Attrition

We can only break patterns after they are formed through repetition and recognized in hindsight. *Attrition* is a barely noticeable erosion process. The wearing down can be so slow you may not realize it until you are at rock bottom. Think of yourself like the Grand Canyon, in layers and layers of erosion by soft water cutting through hard rock. Codependents acquiesce or give in to others incrementally and subconsciously. Neural pathways form like this: little by little, you can feel overexposed and overwhelmed, wondering where your life has gone.

Recognition requires retrospection. Try to note any codependent relationship patterns that may have played out in your life with the same or similar types of people. The list below is a good beginner's guide to recognizing many codependent traits. You can add more of your own. Any one of these may impair your life.

- Approval-seeking or people-pleasing
- Fear of being alone or abandoned
- Feeling selfish or guilty for not meeting the needs of others
- Feeling not good enough, or "too much" or "too little"
- Diminishing yourself to lift others
- Being everyone's "go-to" person
- Getting caught in others' trauma and drama
- Rescuing or fixing others
- A need to be needed or feeling a rush of excitement when asked to do things for others
- Giving ultimatums or nagging to keep others out of trouble
- Covering for or taking a fall for others
- Enduring unhealthy relationships to avoid loneliness
- Giving of your finances and other resources to depletion
- Having an addict, user, abuser, or narcissist in your life
- Having self-limiting or self-sabotaging beliefs

- Helping others to your detriment
- Over-responsibility or doing more than your fair share
- Believing the best in the worst of people and getting taken advantage by them
- Apologizing by beginning sentences with, "I'm sorry," or asking permission like a child
- Giving unsolicited advice or getting upset if someone doesn't act on your advice
- Extreme empathy for others and lacking it for yourself
- Lack of self-care and burnout
- Sense of false guilt or shame that results in self-deprivation
- Finding it difficult to ask for or receive help
- Perfectionism that prevents you from relaxing or enjoying your life
- Coming from a "perfect" family with beliefs about helping others to extremes
- Oversharing
- Over-caring
- Difficulty making decisions without reassurance from others

This is not an exhaustive list, but it is exhausting to read and more so to do it. You are a human being, not a human doing.

Many overextended codependents say, "I can't take anymore!"

What they mean is, "I can't *give* anymore!"

It does not have to be this way.

Think of codependence like reverse narcissism. Narcissists are self-absorbed with getting their needs met, and they can't be alone. Codependents are absorbed in meeting the needs of others and don't want to be alone. Narcissists use other people to feel better about themselves. Codependents allow people to use them so they will feel better. Both extremes are twisted and dysfunctional systems. A narcissist loves to subversively bend others to their will, and a codependent is a subconsciously willing participant. A narcissist loves you just like you *aren't,* and codependents love to accommodate the wishes of others to prove themselves worthy of affection. There will be more on this later, and it's important to recognize how you may be feeding the very monster today who may destroy you tomorrow. You can break codependent patterns by learning how to receive and give in healthy cycles and flow. We have heard in many cultures it is better to give than to receive. It's a wonderful concept, but it's impossible to give without receiving first.

You don't have to appease or please people anymore. You can unapologetically be yourself and allow others to be themselves. You no longer have to cave in to emotional extortion out of fear, obligation, or guilt, nor do you have to try to fix or rescue anyone who doesn't want your help. You have the power to find out what you really want and to go for it without any input from anyone. The outcome will surprise you when you let go of what you think you "have" to do or "must do" and get into the nirvana flow state of simultaneous receiving and giving.

When you get gut honest about taking responsibility for the part you played in allowing others to breach your boundaries, it will catapult you onto a healing path. Bitterness of the past will not overtake you anymore, and the trajectory of your life will change for the better. As a therapist, it's my job to help people listen to themselves. It's time for you to listen to yourself, and your internal dialogue will reveal what drives your codependency. It will also show you how to stop for a moment and, like a GPS, recalculate toward a new direction of joyful living and loving.

Analysis of the Roots

The nature/nurture debate has long been around, and it's no different with codependency. Your roots may be in enculturation, you may have been born this way, traumatized, or had spiritual upbringings or belief systems at work singly or simultaneously. Uncovering all the layers of what drives you with a sense of anxious urgency will help you separate what is healthy from unhealthy giving and living. The programming from all the aforementioned sources has a profound effect on how your codependency began and how it currently manifests.

Repetition of unhealthy reactivity is the way these patterns took up residence in your psyche, and repetition of healthy responses is how to repair the damage. Psychoanalysis relies heavily on how things that occurred in childhood are roles perpetuated in adulthood. There are numerous ways psychoanalytical theorists have adapted this model but all have concluded what happened in our past had a direct correlation to our present and will determine our future if we haven't made the connection.

There is biology to codependency, and there is much more to your need to be needed than receiving an emotional boost. "Feel-good" chemicals release when you help someone, and you may even get an adrenaline rush when you rescue someone. Ask any first responder, and they will tell you it feels good to rescue. You might think people who need to be rescued seem to "show up" in your life. It's not a coincidence; it may be codependence. You may subconsciously be attracting these people.

You may have been born with greater empathy or be more highly sensitive or intuitive than others. The empathic response is often an invisible root of codependency. When you feel *with* someone, it's far more chemically and energetically involved than if you feel *for* someone. Empathy helps people out, but over-sympathizing can suck you into a trap of the trauma and drama of others. You will be learning how important it is to pay attention to how you feel. In helping other people, you may subconsciously be relieving your false guilt or pain for feeling *with* them instead of *for* them. When you feel sorry for someone it hurts, and when you relieve their pain, yours is alleviated. This is the twisted thinking of a codependent. If you relate to this, don't despair; you can be happy without feeling crushing guilt or sympathy. You may believe you are relieving someone else's pain, but in actuality you may be meeting their needs to stop your sympathy pains. You feel better when they're fixed, but this isn't something you can keep up forever without consequences of burnout.

Whether by psychology, biology, or spirituality, your recovery depends on peering into your psyche and making connections. We use the word *epiphany* in psychological and spiritual contexts. We feel their effects in our bodies where the memories take root and branch out into our learned behaviors, beliefs, impulses, and actions. Codependency, like addiction, is a lifelong quest for maintaining healing. Many codependent treatment centers use a twelve-step program model, but it doesn't work for everyone. I'll never forget when I went to my first Codependents Anonymous meeting— only one other person showed up, and the facilitator was nowhere to be found. I said to the other person, "I guess everyone's a no show because they're too busy cooking, cleaning, or doing things for other people."

I went home laughing, but I needed serious help, so I sought one-on-one counseling where we didn't work much on my current codependency; we worked on the roots. There were many intertwined, well-hidden roots, and it helped me to see how deeply they ran in my psyche. I didn't plant them there; many others did, and it took a professional to help me find them and discard them. I spent my childhood covering up abuse, taking a fall and rescuing many people in my family, and I was crushing under the weight of it as an adult. Being an extension of our family image of a healthy psychiatrist's offspring couldn't be further from the truth, but the seed germinated, grew, and took over my life. It felt normal and solid only because it had been established at such an early age, but it wasn't reality based; it was anxiety driven.

Look for the roots of your codependency. What childhood story do you have where you can correlate the past with the present? Do you think you were born this way, taught, spiritually influenced, or all three? If you like to journal, writing about it may help, or making a list of your roots under three main headings or more of your choosing may help expose the root. When you expose a root to the light, it withers, and in the case of codependency, that's a good thing.

Are You an Enabler?

Has anyone called you an "enabler"? If so, it is a misnomer. It bears repeating, you are not an enabler, you are *disabling* others from taking responsibility. Accepting the label of an enabler may cause you to feel more guilt and shame. It permits you to blame yourself for allowing someone else's illness to continue. We have used the term *codependent enabler* for many years, and it never felt true for me. How could I or anyone be held accountable for not holding someone else accountable? "Accountable" seems such a negative word and an "accountability partner" seems so punitive a concept. The billboards say "Drink Responsibly," not accountably. Holding others responsible begins with autonomy and a sense of personal agency. I have several responsibility partners in my life, and they are cherished. We listen to one another and guide one another lovingly and without judgment. They are all friends I grew up with, and we were on the front lines of one another's childhoods. We know about the roots and make sure to help one another prune any codependent branches that may try to pop up in our current lives, helping one another to be stable and able.

Is it enabling someone by not confronting them, intervening, or cajoling them about their afflictions? Addiction is a medical and progressive disease, and interventions happen all by themselves. Many clients who have endured interventions come to me feeling betrayed and humiliated and alienated from their families or loved ones. Holding someone responsible for their actions or inaction and not legally forcing them to receive medical care may allow them to come to the realization they need help. We don't criminalize diabetics if they eat sugar or don't take their insulin. In many states, including the one I live in, you can appeal to the court to put your family member in a drug or alcohol rehabilitation facility against their will, make them pay for it, and if they don't comply, they will be in criminal contempt of court, which will astronomically reduce their career and life choices.

Interventions may come from good intentions, but we all know where the road goes that's paved with them. Yes, there are extreme cases warranting some type of intervention, but if it is punitive in any way, guilt will become part of the experience for both parties. If an addict feels guilt, they want to feel better. The quickest way to feel better is to numb the feelings and use a substance again. This is why relapse is part of recovery, and it is for a codependent too. You may have to attempt to get your loved ones help many times and be disappointed or devastated at the outcomes. Decide to simply "be there" when they want your help, and you will be better able to assist them because they won't be resisting you.

Getting anyone to give up their substance of choice is a frustrating and nearly impossible task. If I told you that you could never do anything nice for anyone again because you were codependent, you would think I was crazy and rightfully so, as you're a natural-born or nurtured giver. You feel good when you give, and taking that away from you would cause you to want to avoid me. The same is true when you try to force someone to get help who doesn't want it; it drives them away, which is exactly the opposite of what you want to do.

Many codependents get very angry over the concept of stepping back a bit when they desire to devise ways to over-give or do things, such as force loved ones to stay sober and tell them they can never have a drink again. Clients who bring addicted family members in and beg me to make them get help are often surprised when I ask, "If I told you that you could never eat a carrot again, and you don't even like carrots, what would you do?"

They all say, "I'd start craving carrots and want one immediately."

Reactance theory is the name for this reverse psychology theory. No one likes being told what to do or how to do it. Free will is the privilege every human craves, and throughout history people have gone to their death to obtain and defend their rights for liberty. The human mind is powerful, and it develops strong desires for what it can't have. When you apply fear and scarcity, the "forbidden fruit factor" makes the desire more intense and impossible to resist. It also works conversely when you tell someone, "Go ahead and do whatever you want. I don't care anymore." Both of these ways of applying reactance can prove to be fallible. It's better to be truthful and not use tactics of manipulation, ultimatums, or pretending not to care because all of them are disingenuous and exacerbate the situation.

No matter what or how much you do to rescue someone against their will, you can only tread water with them for so long. They are not listening and getting them to listen to you is not your job—and it can exhaust you. Codependents don't listen very well either and I was one of the worst offenders. I learned it from my father.

I remember my father told me he was proud I went back to school to become a counselor, but he added, "I'm also sad for you because it is very difficult for people who work in mental health to get help themselves." He would know, as he was a psychiatrist who kept his issues hidden most of his life. His mother abandoned him, and his brother committed suicide in his twenties. He had seizures from a head injury he suffered in the Navy and offered a free group therapy for those who were also afflicted with epilepsy. The groups weren't codependent; they were kind and helped him heal too.

However, he worked from six in the morning to seven at night, and I assisted him with office and hospital duties many years in my youth. His accounts-receivable file was huge, and he didn't want to be bothered with money, but he needed it later in life. His heart attack and stroke made me rethink how I needed to help others in a responsible way, as I didn't want to follow in his footsteps of burnout and an early demise. The last thing he told me the day of his stroke was to take care of myself while caring for others because he had not, and he warned me how much like him I could be. He was wrong about no one being able to help you. He was stating his point of view about keeping his family secrets. I found plenty of help when I needed it, but I had to learn to ask for it, and it didn't happen overnight.

After my father's death, I had severe compassion fatigue from taking care of my mother who was morbidly obese and addicted to chocolate. I enlisted the mentorship of a wise physician who was an addiction specialist because I knew my codependency was becoming malignant. I was in an addictive cycle of wanting to feel good helping others, and I had gone overboard with no one to save me, which is often the isolated cry of a caregiver. I was the one who needed to be rescued from this cycle and relapse because I cared too much for those who didn't really care for me. My mother simply lacked the capacity to have empathy, and she was aware she cared more about things than people, often telling me this.

The addictions doctor helped me see patterns of codependent addictive qualities in my nature. I soaked in his expert advice on how to treat addicts in my practice and personal life, in addition to helping me understand what was driving me to "enable" others and disable myself. I'm so grateful that I went to an addictions doctor because his wisdom wasn't punitive or touchy-feely, but rather it was factual.

Dr. L. said, "Never call yourself an *enabler* again. It will call it in as a self-fulfilling prophecy."

He, like me, believed how you speak about yourself is from internal conditioning and is what you will become. We both believed that, through the power of meditation, the subconscious and conscious mind can communicate and ease many mental and physical illnesses. I was ill in body, mind, and spirit from caring for my parents while becoming a counselor. It's called double compassion fatigue when you're in a helping profession and have people at home who need you. You may have some form of compassion fatigue as well from being a caregiver.

Codependency is not a formal or diagnosable disorder, but it can cause burnout, which is a medical illness, and I had it. Burnout, in the International Classification of Diseases (ICD-10, 2020, code Z73.0) references the diagnosis as "problems related to life management difficulty." Can you relate to this diagnosis? If so, understand that burnout is serious and can ruin your immune system, making you forgetful, irritable, and accident prone. Codependents don't burn the candle at both ends; they give their candle away. Think of a memorial service where people touch one lit candle to another, and the light gets brighter as more people join together in this ceremony. If you are trying to be the one and only light without getting help or assistance from others, you will burn out, and no one benefits from your benevolence.

As Dr. L. said, "Enjoy your life!" Be there when others ask you for help or truly can't help themselves, such as the elderly or very young. Even when doing that, you must have respite times and live your life too, or you will be consumed.

They say in Alcoholics Anonymous, "You're only as sick as your secrets." Better put, you may become as sick as someone else's secrets if you are codependent. These secrets imposed on you are ones you must dispose of to become independent. You aren't responsible for anyone's sobriety, and you don't have to sacrifice yourself to keep your family and friends happy. You may love the feeling of being a "fixer," but it will cause you to become depleted.

Users, addicts, and abusers need a fix.

Codependents need to fix.

Attempting to fix others who do not want to be helped is self-avoidance. In doing so, you create an actual void of connection with your true self. Unless you are called to be a martyr, you probably aren't equipped to save everyone around you. Martyrs' lives were rarely lived well, and they also often ended horrifically or too soon. This can happen to a codependent. They neglect their health as another form of self-avoidance and can die earlier than those they care for as my father did.

You are not an enabler, and you no longer have to disable the people around you who can and must help themselves to be healthy. Now is a good time to do preliminary reconditioning and say three times, aloud and with elevated confidence each time, "I am not an enabler. I am not an enabler. I am not an enabler."

Why You Are Like This and What You Can Do About It

Many codependents often ask, "Why?" They want to know why they are like this. They want to know why others don't treat them as well as they treat others. They want to know why they can't find love like they love. It hurts to watch them get stuck in the asking, and at one time, I was one of them. I did a lot of asking why about others and not much introspection about why I allowed people to hurt me.

Then as we discussed, there are those who want to know why they can't make people get help as they vehemently believe they have the superpower to do it. The saddest cases I witness as a counselor are those in crisis after a loved one's death from addiction. They believe if they had done more, this person would have gotten sober. In the aftermath, one person wished she had given transfusions or vital organs to her dying relative and felt unbearable guilt for not being more preemptive. The grief and anxiety were mixed with fury at the doctors who should have allowed her to give part of her liver or a kidney so her loved one could have lived a little longer. This person got angry at me when I told her the doctors were acting according to an oath to do no harm.

Most codependents believe if you do something magnanimous and heroic for someone you love, they will miraculously appreciate you and change. But they will not change because they can't; they lack the capacity to desire help. As I mentioned, newer medications and cognitive behavioral techniques assist addicts in sobriety, but medical science does not have a pill for desiring sobriety, and they certainly don't have one for codependency either. Desire will be your greatest motivator, and you may have to hit rock bottom taking care of someone before you seek help. You can avoid rock bottom as a codependent, and I would love to tell you I did, but I didn't. My tolerance for bad behavior was very high, as Dr. S. and Dr. L. told me, but I didn't listen. I do now, and when I'm working harder than the person who wants help, I'm not beneficial to anyone.

When working with addicts, I now propose the question, "What if there were no mind-altering substances on the planet. What would you want to do with your life?" Many times, I would see fear in their eyes or tension in their body with a shocked expression on their face. I often heard the reply, "I can't imagine a world where I couldn't get high or drunk." The disease had overtaken them, and the prognosis for sobriety is extremely poor without the desire to do something else to replace the addiction.

I often see the same body language when I tell a codependent they're not able to make someone they love do whatever they think is best for them. They look stunned when I tell them they can't rationalize with anyone in the throes of addiction. This is also true of any narcissist or sociopath they have in their life. I have often called addiction "faux narcissism" because the addicted person doesn't understand they are truly an afflicted person, causing collateral damage to all their relationships. Their negativity is projected on those attempting to help them when they don't want it, and they blame others for their behavior, never taking ownership of their part of the equation. It is impossible to win an argument with them. They may even agree with you to get help and then renege time after time. In "agreeing," they are buying time to stop the immediate confrontation. Sadly, fixing these people is the codependent's "drug" of choice. The severity of the self-righteous indignation is indicative of their prognosis to recover from codependent compulsions.

If you want to know why you can't fix or change people, I only have one answer—I don't know. I do know from interviewing doctors and from extensive research that there are receptors in our brain that work with neurotransmitters. When a person craves a substance, the receptor is wide open, and the pleasure derived, though fleeting, is compelling. This is highly simplified, and we will look into it more in the neuroscience chapter. As a codependent, it's vitally important to know why your need to be needed or to rescue creates this same reward reactivity in your brain. You may be addicted to helping others who say they want to change but really don't.

Desire to change must come from within, and it doesn't work if it's externally imposed. You must realize you're speaking to a substance or a person who lacks empathy when you are trying to talk to or reason with an addict or a narcissist to get help. If someone is addicted to martinis, imagine you're talking to a giant bottle of vodka or gin because in essence, you are. If you're trying to reason with an abusive person, you're talking to an inflated ego that has no desire to hear your pain because they enjoy inflicting it to relieve theirs. The prefrontal lobe is offline; they're altered, and you're valiantly and frustratingly attempting to apply logic to a brain wherein it doesn't reside.

Codependents also want to know why people don't listen to them when what they are saying makes perfect sense. Sadly, codependents don't listen well when they hear why they are acting on instinct. It is simply because people have free will, and most of us need to learn things for ourselves, not because someone told us what was good for us. Codependents aren't any different, but you can be if this describes you—and it certainly did me. When you cease asking why, and start asking what you can do about this, you have crossed the threshold from illness to wellness and wholeness. Have you ever asked someone *why* they don't appreciate you for all that you do for them? If this is you, your seemingly unconditional love may be tied up in receiving gratitude from the other person. They may have a sense of entitlement and be unable to feel or express thanksgiving. This is giving to get something in return, and it seldom works. You can stop the cycle of giving and being unappreciated or dismissed, so begin asking yourself how much you desire to fix yourself first.

When you become conscious of your subconscious reactivity, you can change instincts that are propelled from past flawed conditioning. You can enjoy the state of being present in each moment of your everyday life. The past is irretrievable, and most of the future is out of your immediate control. When you accept this and don't resist it, you will learn to not lose sight of yourself. Authenticity will arise, and you will be of more value to those who really need your help, not those who take you for granted or frustrate you.

Who Am I?

Codependents often say, "I've done so much for other people, I don't know who I am anymore." Have you said that? If so, the answer is you're a wonderful, giving, and kind person who also needs people who are giving and kind to you. People who use others seldom ask who they are or what their purpose in life is, and they don't care. You're not defined by how much you do for others or for yourself. You exist, and your true sense of self and purpose will come as you begin seeking your truth and desires, and not under the guise of being good to everyone but yourself.

Be the journalist of your life story and use the *why* questions to lead you much further toward who you are and what you really want. Think about *who* and *what* made you feel you must do it all for everyone. Ask *where* your points of weakness are and use the answers as waypoints. Decide *when and how* you want to change, and this thoughtful, conscious compass will set you on a wonderful course to follow the direction of your desires to enjoy your life.

No one can do this work, this who-what-when-where-why-how work, for you. Resist the urge to ask for advice from anyone who taught you to be codependent or who hurt you. For some reason, they have a vested interest in making sure you remain codependent and controllable. Be fully conscious of this role they want you to play. You might feel conditioned to ask their opinions, but these are the people who made you what you are, and they won't be ecstatic, applaud, or support you to hear your desire to be free and independent.

They also know how to push your buttons, so don't make your buttons so available. Notice little things they do to keep you second-guessing yourself or your sanity. For example, if you tell them you want mint chocolate chip ice cream, do they bring home chocolate and blame it on you? If you tell them you have an important meeting or event coming up, do they create chaos around this time? Keep a small book or use the notes on your phone of any crazy-making behavior they display. This is often referred to as gaslighting and it is intentional. When you notice the intent, you can change your emotional reactivity to calm responses. The caveat is, when you do become more confidently and quietly confrontational, they may call you selfish. They don't want you to become anyone or do anything that makes you happy if it doesn't fit in their mold.

I can't tell you how many little things I gave up in order to make others happy, such as not scuba diving or flying because my ex was afraid. My ex loved riding horses, and I was afraid to do that but did anyway and took many a dangerous spill. I compartmentalized my feelings and repressed them to keep another person happy, even though it caused me to be in abject fear. He also was very jealous of anyone I knew in the past, and I wasn't aware at the time how narcissists want to isolate and alienate you from everyone and everything you love.

One day, I threw away all my diaries because my ex threatened to read and destroy them if I didn't. My teen years, college, theater, the KISS tour diaries, and all of my life was recorded in precious paragraphs in this assortment of road-weary books. The day I tossed them was near my thirtieth birthday, and I felt like a part of me had died. The severance with my prior emotional life and history felt indescribably unnerving and empty. I went back to the dumpster the next day to retrieve them, but it was empty too. Yes, I allowed it because I was conditioned to do as I was told without questioning or contradicting. I thought of a husband as an authority figure and not as an equal.

In order to keep the relationship with my husband, who was much like my family all rolled into one person, I lost myself and justified throwing the diaries away. I convinced myself I really shouldn't have kept diaries that had my high school and college romance thoughts in them. Compliance and not complaining are hallmarks of the codependent. In 2019, *O Magazine* published an article about this time in my life titled, "The Greatest Love of All." I recalled parts of the twenty years I had let someone else dictate what I wore, did, and portrayed. It was good to revisit how I allowed this to happen and how I got out of it. You can do the same.

You can repair what has been impaired and discover things from your codependent journey that may be the catalyst to catapult you out of giving your life away to those who use you for the betterment of themselves. Saying no to them isn't easy because the arguments they present are convincingly manipulated to make you feel like the selfish one. I hope this rings a very loud bell with you.

Like the horses my ex and I had, I was being trained to be more subservient than I wanted to be. Riding them, I used to think it was sad they had to be beasts of burdens. I quit riding when I went back to graduate school, using the excuse that I couldn't afford to be injured, but it was really because I could no longer live this incongruent life. I thought the horses should be able to run free with nothing on their backs or in their mouths that was meant to hurt and control them.

I was a songwriter in Nashville at the time, and many songs had my desire to be loved correctly filtered in the lyrics. I had a great songwriting partner to share this with. Having someone you can trust to talk to and support you who won't judge you is essential to your ability to leave a codependent relationship. It's crucial for you to develop friendships, no matter how much the controller in your life wants to isolate you.

The exit strategy took years and many mistakes, but I began by noticing little things. I had a decorative birdcage and I liked to keep the door open as a metaphor. Not long before I left, he began to shut the door of the cage. Every day I opened it, and every night he shut it. I said nothing, and neither did he, but it was an eerie game I was ready to quit. I wrote a song at that time titled "Bird in a Cage." The chorus lyrics were:

> *A bird in a cage may not be crying*
> *But she sings a sadder song*
> *And she longs for something more*
> *A bird in a cage, keeps her eye on the door.*

This was not about winning or losing but about salvaging my life, forging new friendships, and reconnecting with lost ones. After the divorce, you can be certain I got some scuba gear, flew to Hawaii with friends, got back in the water, and when I saw that first inquisitive and friendly sea turtle, I knew I was "home," back in my own skin and free to be me!

You can get back into your skin and be who you truly are by refusing to comply with people who don't have your best interests at heart or who won't allow you to pursue your goals, dreams, and adventures. I'm very content now and have learned to be true to my desires, no longer driven by a fear of being unloved or unwanted. This can be you, and though we are all works in progress, we are all meant to enjoy the lives we were given while giving to others. Constantly making sure everyone else's needs are met or thinking this is what your total life mission or purpose is keeps you choosing what is good for others instead of what is best for all, including yourself. You can choose to change your choices!

Codependent Conditioning and Reconditioning

Codependents often get diverted by some tool of repetitive manipulation from those who want something from them. This is conditioning. Beware of this in all your relationships because people who use others target codependents: they pick up on your desire to be loved, needed, and accepted, and they will do what it takes to unduly influence you to give them what they want. The best way to recognize conditioning is to make connections with your past and present and with the messages you may have received in your youth.

Ask yourself:

- Was more expected of you as a child than should have been?
- Was there repeated criticism or expectations for you above and beyond what should be asked of a child?
- Were you ever called ungrateful, greedy, or selfish?
- Were you told not to contradict a parent or caregiver, even if they were lying?
- Did you feel like the scapegoat child?
- Did you feel the need to be an audience to your parent(s)?
- Were you always told your room wasn't clean enough or you didn't do your chores right?
- Were you deprived of something because someone else in your family was more important?

- Did you feel like you weren't part of your family unit or not as important in any way?
- Were you the child of an addict, abuser, absent, or deceased parent?

All of the above, and anything you may wish to ask or add personally, are what conditioned you to your present state. If you were living in a constant state of fear of the breakup of the family unit when you were a child, you were being conditioned. It is terrifying for a child to be abandoned and unloved, and if you had the tendency to be codependent, adapting to hide your feelings or going to great lengths to be the family clown or little adult is a maladaptive, anxiety-driven behavior.

Codependency can also show up in a twisted manifestation of being a "co-narcissist" with a parent. Alan Rappoport, PhD, explains this codependent dynamic:

> Children of narcissists tend to feel overly responsible for other people. They tend to assume that others' needs are similar to those of their parents and feel compelled to meet those needs by responding in the required manner. They tend to be unaware of their own feelings, needs, and experience, and fade into the background in relationships . . . they may fear that they are inherently insensitive, selfish, defective, fearful, unloving, overly demanding, hard to satisfy, inhibited, and/or worthless. . . . They tend to have low self-esteem, work hard to please others, defer to others' opinions, focus on others' world views and are unaware of their own orientations, are often depressed or anxious, find it hard to know how they think and feel about a subject, doubt the validity of their own views and opinions (especially when these conflict with others' views), and take the blame for interpersonal problems. . . . Co-narcissists, however, are ready to accept blame and responsibility for problems, and are much more likely than narcissists to seek help because they often consider themselves to be the ones who need fixing. . . . As a result, they orient themselves around the other person in their relationships, lose a clear sense of themselves, and cannot express themselves easily nor participate fully in their lives.[1]

This was the story of my early life. I was the audience and entertainer to my family to keep them happy, laughing, and (I thought) loving. I was an anxious child, trying to read the needs of my mother, who was as impulsive as a teenager, my father, who was absent at his psychiatric practice, and my older brother, who alternated between kindness and intense, entitled rage. He could come uncorked at any moment. I looked up to him, hoping he would look out for me, but it wasn't a healthy relationship. I ended up covering for him rather than self-protecting. Conditioning was the culprit. I was being a co-narcissist, but when we are young, our frame of reference is tiny and tender, and we are easily malleable, unaware of the defects it can cause later in life.

You can unlearn what you were taught and recondition these false feelings imprinted in your psyche. You may experience withdrawal symptoms of anxiety when you decide to quit acting on these learned behaviors, but the clarity you will gain is worth the "detox" symptoms.

I used to call myself a "fetching child" because my mother's obesity made it laborious for her to walk, so I was always fetching something for her. Dad was a workaholic, so he was gone a lot. My brother didn't have to fetch things because he "was a boy" and "boys were more important." My mother often told me this, along with "Women are put on this earth to serve men." My father's conflicting message was "Act like a lady and think like a man! Never get married and be independent because men die, and men leave." Both extreme messages left me with the impression that I was to be left all alone to take care of myself, no matter which I chose.

What conditioning messages have you received and believed in the past that you would like to change now? Journaling them may help, and you will be guided to do so at the conclusion of this chapter. Children of alcoholics get the same message as they have to grow up and do more than their fair share all the time or cover for their parent. This creates a chasm of secretive shame they don't seem to be able to shake as adults. This also occurs in broken families through divorce or blending when children are expected to adapt far beyond what they can comprehend. In whatever way you were conditioned, you can oppose the imprinting and reinstate your genuine desires for a happy life. Think back on other repetitive messages in your childhood and challenge them. You can erase and replace codependent conditioning, and you can cross over from being bound to the past.

For example, you may have allowed someone in your family to tease you for so long that you have joined in with them with self-deprecating humor. You may allow people to tease you now, even though it hurts. You're actually telling them it's okay to laugh at you instead of with you. When you repress or deny the feelings teasing is causing you, you may become angry. You are not here for the amusement of others. There's a big difference between witticism and criticism, and people who are teased are called "targets" in bullying research. Stop laughing with teasers and challenge their remarks. You can also choose to be silent, and this will get their attention by your refusal to join them in hurting you.

If they say, "Can't you take a joke? You're so sensitive," you can quietly and confidently answer, "I love to joke if it's not at my expense or for your pleasure. I'm not here for your amusement. You're too insensitive."

When you attempt to recondition people who took part in conditioning your codependent mindset, don't expect them to rally to understand or apologize. It's not about changing them but about transforming yourself by speaking your truth. In doing so, you are taking your power back by reconditioning the abuser. Being mindful of how you feel about yourself when around other people will help you stay in touch with your authentic self. People-pleasing and approval-seeking behaviors will end when others see that your qualities are not flaws that qualify you to be the brunt of their jokes. Codependency is not a joke. It's a very serious matter. What you are reading is giving you food for thought and fuel for change. Reconditioning requires consciousness and self-compassionate motivation.

Think of how we rewind and record over something. It deletes the previous selection, never to be retrieved. The brain loves to default to what is deeply embedded from conditioning, but you can retrain your brain and record over prior messages that were put in there from a source other than your true self. "Record" new messages by affirmation, meditation, and making mantras or rhymes for yourself. Think of how lyrics of a catchy song can play in your head all day if you don't distract yourself and sing a new song. Pause, find the source of the original tape looping in your head, replace it, and you will soon be able to hit the fast-forward button of your life.

Early Trauma Bonds and Attachment Styles

In 1975, Edward Tronick and fellow researchers conducted the "Still-Face Experiment," and the results were astounding. Tronick filmed an affectionate mother with an infant.[2] The baby was engaged, happy, and trusting of the mother. Then the mother was asked to become expressionless and still her facial muscles and give no response to her infant. After a few minutes with the still-faced mother, the infant becomes agitated. He attempts to smile but the tension mounts as she shows no interaction. He then uses his innate grasping and clinging reflexes to reach for his mother. When all these attempts fail, the child first cries and screams, turns away after a minute or two, and then becomes expressionless and looks hopeless. From infancy, the subconscious memory stores this information, and it can negatively affect attachment styles and adult relationships without any awareness of why. This theory of needing to be loved and have connection with caregivers has been a cornerstone of much more research on developmental psychology.

Please don't try this experiment at home!

Children raised in traumatic environments are more susceptible to becoming codependent. They take responsibility for raising themselves or siblings. They become socially anxious or feel inferior, and this can be a lifelong battle. Trauma bonds form early and can become insidious intruders into your behaviors and how you allow others to treat you. Attachment disorders evolve, and it may take a good therapist to assist you to recover and form healthier bonds with yourself and others. Trauma bonds aren't easy to recognize; they're difficult to break, but it's not impossible. Recognition, like repetition, is a life-changing tool of seeing where the erosion of your true self began so you can make reparations at the foundation before moving forward.

Sexually, physically, or verbally abused children can be significantly and adversely affected by trauma bonds. Other types of neglect, abandonment, death of a parent, or other traumatic events contribute to codependency. Subconscious repression is the only defense a child has to keep a modicum of their safety. Remember the game with the daisy: picking petals and saying, "He/she loves me or loves me not." This is a child's version of a dangerous dynamic we will explore called "intermittent reinforcement." It is what pop psychology calls the love bombing and discarding cycle of a narcissist. Perpetrators manufacture attachment with a cycle of fear or rejection and reward of giving "love," and it causes physiologic volatility and helplessness. It is tolerated in adulthood because it was likely learned in childhood.

Traumatized children often develop physiological compulsions in their brains to make them think a relationship is healthy when it is not. When a caregiver is simultaneously an abuser, children become anxious and attempt to position themselves back to safety, but they are ill-equipped to do so as they are no match for a manipulative adult. They turn inward toward blaming themselves, take on false shame, and can feel unworthy of love because they have not received it properly. They can grow up to become fearfully attached or avoid getting too close in relationships. They may also become clingy and needy and will do anything to please their partner or friends to retain some semblance of safety.

Obedience is a hallmark of codependence, and it is also a symptom of perfectionism. Our memories become embedded from how our caregivers treat us, and we want to please them so we will be safe. In an unsafe household with cycles of feeling unloved, rejected, abused, or neglected, intermittent kindness can cause a child to anxiously attach to the very person who hurts them the most. It's similar to the Stockholm syndrome, which is better explained as a shock–hold impairment.

This may be unconsciously part of what you're suffering now as a codependent. Knowledge of how these persistent attachment styles may be showing up in your adult relationships is essential for recovery. If not, pain can be confused with love. Judging someone to be healthy for you when they are not is nearly impossible to do if you do not understand the results of early bonding and attachments.

Codependents apologize too much and get back into these relationships, thinking *they* are the problem. Narcissists never apologize. They may say, "I'm sorry you feel that way," but that's not an apology. It's another form of blame shifting and a potential trap. You could see this as someone who is "trying" to change, and you give them another chance.

Conversely, you may judge someone who is *really, really* good for you as not being good for you because genuine love is so unfamiliar. Your identity can become disturbed and attachment anxiety is temporarily relieved by attaching to someone like the caregiver you have unresolved issues with, and the result can be a lifelong repetitive string of codependent relationships.

Can you make this cycle stop? Yes!

Awareness of what is operating in your past and infiltrating your present can arrest these codependent attachments, and we will look into this throughout this journey. When you carry unmet needs into adulthood, you may have been in a series of reenacted relationships with "emotionally unavailable" partners. When trauma is experienced with repetitive layers, a person may become angry at themselves for allowing someone to violate them, and this kind of suffering is often done in agonizing silence. This emotional pain can cause severe physiologic reactivity, and healthy attachments are difficult to form.

Attachment styles evolve from our early beliefs about how we fit into our family system. The child with burgeoning, developing codependency may act out by trying to make everyone in the family unit happy. Some children can be very serious and act like little adults to garner praise while others may become the family clown in order to make everyone happy. These children may appear to be responsible or happy, but they are fearful and suffer from repressed anger. These are what the tears of the clown are made of and why many comedians come from dysfunctional families, suffering with depression and other mood disorders. A codependent child may not always be funny, but their pain is there. It is evident through valiant and frantic methods to remain attached, but a child isn't responsible for being good enough to be loved properly. Passive-aggressive behaviors or quiet rebellious acts may also indicate a controlling codependent type in the making too.

An assessment tool used in child psychology is to ask a child to draw a picture of their family.[3] One of my graduate school professors assigned us to do this in class as if we were children. I sketched my father, mother, and brother. The professor told us to note if we included ourselves in the portrait. I did not. He explained that if a child omits drawing himself or herself in a family picture, this is indicative of some sort of rejection or feeling like you are not as important as the rest of the family. I remember turning over my paper and realizing I had much work to do on myself before I could help anyone else. This is something you need to get a grip on as a codependent. You must help yourself before you can fully and freely give to anyone else. It is good to help others feel better, but if you are doing it to feel accepted, your attachment style may be worth looking into for clues.

John Bowlby[4] was a psychiatrist and early pioneer of defining attachment styles. There are four major types, and they relate well as to why codependents seek safety for others in order to be connected and protected.

- Anxious-Preoccupied
- Dismissive-Avoidant
- Avoidant-Fearful
- Secure

An **anxious-preoccupied** relational style is often how a codependent presents. They are more concerned with others than themselves. They may lack insight as to their motives, but they have a more negative view of themselves and attempt to connect with others by seeking approval and becoming despondent if they don't get it. They can become dependent on people to give them a sense of self-worth.

Other codependents appear to be autonomous and say, "I don't need anyone." They have **dismissive-avoidant** attachment styles. They push love away and have difficulty trusting others. They came from stoic, distant, or cold parenting. They may be the person who will do anything for anyone but doesn't allow others to get too close. They build walls and lack the ability to attain intimacy and vulnerability. They say things like "If I don't do it, it won't get done." In truth, they don't want to be obligated to anyone. It is a false sense of emotional regulation for safety. This form of codependence can cause debilitating loneliness, and they might hide their feelings. We punish people with solitary confinement, and codependents often suffer in a self-imposed prison of the mind and don't have anyone who they turn to for help. When they do come to me for professional help, they are usually exhausted or have suffered a consequence from their overdoing.

What I hear most is "I don't want to be a burden to anyone, and I don't want to become selfish or be told to change my loving and giving personality." They often defend their exhaustion by pointing out how they have been able to fix everything in the past and wonder where they went wrong in the situation that brought them to seek counsel. This faulty moral compass is misleading them, and they are reticent to accept it, just like I was in the beginning stages of recovery. Many times, they are embarrassed by their need for help and find it difficult to understand the accumulation of taking on too much for others without taking time for themselves. Many argue they don't want me to help them do more for themselves but ask how they can do more for others without getting burned out. Having been one of them, I sense the false shame, and let them know that when they are truly ready to understand that they can be of better service to others if they learn to self-care first, the door is always open. It's not shameful to desire connections of those you can trust; just be sure you do it in a healthy way.

Avoidant-fearful types are often former victims of sexual or physical abuse and may not be codependent in every sense but run the risk of reenacting adult relationships with people who are not emotionally available, narcissists, or at worst, abusers.

You may relate to one or all of these attachment styles, according to your relationships. This constellation of fear-driven learned behaviors can be transformed with understanding and tools of systematic reconditioning. You're not helpless to change. Learned helplessness, a term introduced by Martin Seligman, PhD, was a discovery in his conditioning experiments. He discovered that children who were neglected would cry, and if no one came, they weren't self-soothing, but rather they were giving up hope that anyone would come. The silence was despair. It can therefore be assumed codependency may begin in the crib.

Martin Seligman is also responsible for being a founding father of Positive Psychology, and his work in this field has helped prove that you can learn happiness! His authentic happiness theory[5] has resulted in remarkable improvement of authentically processing emotions and developing new skills, regardless of what you were taught in your youth. He focused on three major areas, beginning with processing the past with positive experiences to find "well-being and satisfaction," then to be aware of the present with finding "happiness and flow," and finally, looking to the future with "optimism and hope."

This is great news for codependency reconditioning seekers!

Adversity is not your destiny, and the day I realized this, the journey to wellness became a happier and more expedient one.

Let the Restoration Begin

You can consciously reframe your subconscious to work for you instead of against you. You can achieve restoration and happiness in all areas of your life. Restored people, things, and buildings are of much greater value because they stand for something that has surpassed merely surviving to thriving with a fresh and renewed purpose.

There's no one else in the world like you. You no longer have to keep on a path forced upon you; you can forge your own. The root word of restore is *rest*. Rest at each independent achievement marker you reach in this book. Let the lessons embed in your psyche and allow yourself the privilege to challenge past programming that has isolated you when you needed to be insulated.

Repetition established your codependent behaviors and repeated affirmations stir your beliefs up out of the past to new thoughts and behaviors. You can deny the past; it's right to reside in your life by knowing what you don't want. In doing so, you will discover what you do want. It's a good place to start for those who have been stuck in the angst of not knowing who they are or what they want. This is the beginning of the end of your codependency. You no longer have to call yourself one and can use the word itself as a visual tool:

CodepENDent

You are ending a phase of your life that has been too selfless, and the time has come to enjoy your life with meaning and happiness too. You can give what you want, where you want, and how you want, starting with knowing what you don't want.

Harness the energy transmitted by the power of your voice speaking to you, and it will transmute your life. This is the beginning of you listening to yourself. If you feel resistance, push past the pushback, release it, and be positive!

Revision Exercise

With your eyes closed, take three deep breaths in through your nose and out through your mouth, then briefly but vividly envision how what you just affirmed would look and feel like in the future. In detail, let your mind take you to the life of your dreams and include loving, reciprocal relationships. Before you open your eyes, take note of this feeling and commit it to your sense memory by noting where and how you feel the emotions in your body. When you open your eyes, calmly do the Life List below with your thoughts and feelings in that happy place.

Read the following affirmation slowly and deliberately. Relax into the statements by paying attention to the meaning of each word and how it makes you feel—emotionally, mentally, and physically.

AFFIRMATION: *I am transforming from being codependent to independent. I am a human being, not a human doing. I can do almost anything but I can't do everything for everyone. I am taking time, without guilt, to become who I really am and attain what I really want. I am releasing fears of abandonment and challenging my thoughts to recognize and neutralize the conditioning. I am reconditioning myself to achieve reciprocity and mutual respect in all my relationships. I desire to gain freedom from feeling abandoned to a healing life of abundance. I have taken the first steps in learning to give and live well.*

LIFE LIST

This two-column list you will write in a journal is for breaking the chains of not knowing who you are or what you want. It is an invocation and invitation from the depths of your psyche to enjoy a new life, no longer driven by the fear of abandonment. Write what you don't want in the left column. Write the opposite in the right column. Notice if you have included what you want for or from others and excluded yourself, such as "I don't want my best friend to live in that horrible situation she is in, and I do want to buy her the pretty house she wants so she has a safe place to go."

This list is about what *you* don't want and do want, and though it may feel selfish at first, try to express your deepest personal desires to yourself with limitless possibilities in mind.

You will be writing your personalized and progressive lists at the end of every chapter. When the time comes to ceremoniously release the negative left sides all you will have left is what is right for you! This is truly self-help and you will keep these powerful self-authored points for quick future reference. Here are two examples and your list at the end of each chapter should contain at least seven items.

What I Don't Want	What I Do Want
1. To be codependent	1. To be independent
2. To be used in one-sided relationships	2. Reciprocity in relationships
3.	3.
4.	4.
5.	5.
6.	6.
7.	7.
8.	8.

CHAPTER 2

Regaining and Maintaining Your Sense of Self

What is necessary to change a person is to change his awareness of himself.

—Abraham Maslow

How to Be True to You

You are your truest self when you feel at peace and are not looking to others for validation. Codependents seek validation by being as good as they possibly can be so they will feel worthy and good enough. But what is the definition of "good enough"? Have you sought validation by achievement because you didn't feel good enough? If so, it's okay. We all want to do our best and be accepted. However, needing and seeking constant reassurance is another sign of codependence. I've stood in clothing stores, asking total strangers to comment on how something looked on me. I wasn't fishing for compliments like a narcissist; I really can't tell if something flatters me or not because I was told what to wear by my mother and ex-husband for such a long time. Do you do anything like this? Do you buy a car because your neighbor has one? Do you ask salespeople what they think? Anything you do like this means you have lost a sense of what you really want, and you may not be able to make choices based on self-approval.

Seeking approval is why codependents often choose certain occupations or endeavors. Is there something you do to seek validation? If so, ask why and what you seek to gain from it. When you have goals to gain for yourself, that's great, but when you have points to prove to others, you may have lost sight of your true aspirations. If you need to tell everyone some wonderful thing you are working on to receive feedback or a pat on the back, step back. It's more self-actualized to go for what you want and tell people after you've done it. Your approval is all you need to succeed. When codependents tell too many people about their hopes and dreams, they run the risk of hearing a negative or invalidating remark, which makes them feel disapproved. This results in abandoning or discounting their goals, desires, and dreams. This repression stymies the dream as temporarily invalid, but later in life, it could be the cause of deep regret and anger. The anger may be directed at someone else, but it was really the codependent's choice. If this was you, as it was with several things in my life, give yourself an honest apology and keep moving forward. When you ease up on regret, you may find a new path to an old dream, and it may come alive in a new form.

Another symptom of codependency is apologizing too much or asking people if they are mad at you all the time. You are valid just as you are, and you don't have to prove your worth to anyone but yourself. Like a gemstone, you're unique. You have flaws to minimize and facets to enhance and shine. We all do. We all want approval and praise at some time in our lives. Television is full of award shows, and the red carpet is the ultimate approval-seeking venue. Sally Field's poignant and famous Academy of Motion Picture awards Oscar speech was "I can't deny the fact that right now you like me. You really, really like me!" Later in life, Sally Field had this to say: "It took me a long time not to judge myself through someone else's eyes." She found the secret to real success, and that is being happy with yourself.

There is a big difference between wanting to reach a goal for personal happiness or needing it to prove self-worth. Being brave enough to achieve things and get involved in a competition is not a bad thing to do because codependents often shy away from competition. They don't want anyone to lose, and they can feel guilty for winning. They often lose on purpose to not upset the other person, or they think if they let the other person win, they will be more likeable. This is often a sibling dynamic in a burgeoning codependent. They look up to their older sibling and want their approval so much they will lose a game or pretend to want to do what their sibling wants, hoping to be included. This may get carried into adult personal relationships and professional careers. The ideas of codependents often get stolen, and they don't receive credit. The film *Working Girl* was an excellent example of this. A woman comes up with an idea, her boss steals it and takes credit for it, and the working girl decides to become inauthentic to fix the situation, only making it worse. When the truth is out, and the confrontation is unavoidable, success becomes attainable.

If being noncompetitive or nonassertive is true of you, admitting it to yourself and vowing to toot your own horn is essential to well-being. It's okay to win or receive attention for something wonderful you've done. It's natural to want to be liked, loved, or recognized for a job well done or a great idea. If you're frustrated because you think others should do this for you or notice you and compliment you, realize most people aren't like you. Many people don't want to validate anyone but themselves. You can lose your identity if you wait around, expecting others to take note of your good deeds, great ideas, and achievements. If you have ever been betrayed by someone like this and didn't speak up for yourself, you know how bad this feels, but it isn't entirely the fault of the one who hurt you. You have the responsibility to stand up for yourself and let your talents be known.

Here are some ways subconscious self-betrayal may manifest:

- Morphing into a different person when you are around others you are seeking approval from, such as changing your speech or mannerisms
- Blending in everywhere but not feeling you fit anywhere, or you feel you are on the outside looking in
- Having compassion for others but little for yourself
- Downplaying your achievements or playing "dumb" to be nonthreatening or liked
- Choosing careers based on the extension of a family image or opinions of others
- Comparing yourself with others
- Competing in unhealthy ways, such as allowing your opponent to win or having covert competitive anxiety
- Wishing you were someone else
- Seeking excessive reassurance when making decisions
- Saying and doing things to be nice or agreeable because you don't believe in yourself

You may have allowed others to control you for so long, you really don't know what it feels like to be autonomous. Self-confidence means you can *confide* in yourself, and the best advice you will ever receive is from yourself. If you're an adult, you don't need permission to be who you are or make apologies. Many people come into my office and ask sheepishly if they can "steal" a mint, which are obviously there to take. They ask where they're supposed to sit or apologize for something, such as being a few minutes late. From the first visit, I think this may be a codependent person because I used to ask permission when it was obviously not required. Being in a good safe place to be guided back to themselves is how I help them to find their center and believe in themselves as worthy. When you get your internal compass directed back to your higher and actual self, anything is possible and highly probable.

Self-actualized people are not concerned with the opinions of others, and they stay true to themselves no matter who they're with or where they are. You don't have to feel like a chameleon anymore, constantly changing colors to suit your environment. Chameleons do this as a safety mechanism, but they are the most vulnerable while they are making the transition from one color to another. Being who you are will help you be confident and competent at saying no and yes honestly. If you feel like a chameleon sometimes and are trying to fit in, you also may feel unstable and inadvertently project this to others. You may feel like you can blend in everywhere but don't feel like you belong anywhere. Is this true of you? If so, be acutely aware of the danger of how vulnerable you are and the peril of losing yourself. Others notice something is amiss but aren't able to deduce what it is about you they don't like.

People are uncomfortable around chameleon-like people-pleasers because they are disingenuous and usually anxious. I was this way for years and occasionally slip back into this trap, but I get out quickly simply by becoming quiet and grounding myself back into my body. It reduces the fear of trying to read the feelings of others to know what to say or how to act, and I quickly become me again. This is done by pulling in your personal energy and focusing on how you feel and what you really want to say or do—and then say or do it.

Because of the highly empathetic nature of codependents, they don't know where their feelings begin and others' feelings end. They pick up energy transmissions of those around them and it can upset personal balance, literally and figuratively. Psychological splitting can occur, and what you feel may be what someone else is experiencing. If someone around you is sad or angry, you might feel that way and not understand why. About 20 percent of the population are born this way and without proper upbringing or learning how to protect yourself as an adult, you are at risk for codependency. It makes sense because if someone is suffering, you will feel it and want to alleviate it for yourself as much as for them.

Highly empathic people also feel the physical sensations of others so you must keep in touch with your body and emotions. You have to learn to protect yourself from the unwanted energy of others, and you do this by being self-aware in body, mind, and emotions. Feeling for people is one thing but feeling *with* them can be overwhelming. This is seldom a conscious exchange, and it is a complex, powerful force. Constantly recalculating to find your center will heighten your energy with ease. Meditation and grounding exercises (many included in this book) help as will understanding how codependency is not easy to detect as it takes on many forms and dysfunctions.

The Spectrum of Codependency

Codependency comprises a constellation of symptoms with extremes of behavior and individual variances according to people or situations. The "doormat" type is what most people commonly think of when they hear the term *codependent*. This extreme allows themselves to be walked on or used out of fear and conditioned compliance. They deny themselves whatever they think will *keep the peace* with others but give their peace and power away in the process. They appear depressed, anxious, shy, or unstable to the untrained eye.

Conversely, the controlling codependent is best personified by the statement, "I know what's good for you!" They appear bold and overly confident and can seem almost narcissistic unless you're able to detect the façade. They're always "busy" or busybodies, doing so much for others to keep up an image that portrays strength but have angry underpinnings behind closed doors. They often have a fake smile and could fool most people into believing them. They love to hear, "You must be a saint for putting up with (fill in the blank)."

Neither being totally selfless nor constantly selfish is good. Selfless is coming from a place that accepts less. Selfish is a self-absorbed need to impose your will on others to feel good about yourself. Both extremes are based on fear of rejection and abandonment and are intricately geared to retain unhealthy relationships. It's also possible to switch or vacillate in between the roles in this dynamic, depending on the situation or people.

Where do you fit in on the spectrum? Reflect on this and also make a mental note of how you may change roles with the different relationships in your life. Another way to discover where you may be out of balance is by evaluating the type of music and lyrics you listen to and pay particular attention to any favorite songs. Art imitates life, including songs of a codependent nature that center around the message of "I can't live without you" or "I live to love you and only you." I wrote plenty of them myself and looking back over them has changed my perspective. I was more of the doormat type and was often waylaid in my plans by seeking advice from the controlling type. Watch out for this in your family, friendships, and all relationships. Asking for professional help, which codependents find difficult to do, will help. It wasn't easy for me to ask for help at first, but working with a professional when I need it keeps me healthy so I can help others do the same.

People with codependency issues benefit from an empathic and nonjudgmental listener. Their experiences are validated, processed, and reframed, and their sense of their true self is reconditioned and restored.

A good therapist for a codependent will be someone who understands and helps the codependent become conscious of their extreme oscillation, or fluctuation, in engagement in activities. The extremes of this oscillation in feelings and activities may also create obstacles to forming a strong therapeutic relationship, and therapists may need to refer back to their training or consult with a peer to manage the emotional effects of this on the patient's self.[1]

The oscillation mentioned is a component of the spectrum and continuum of codependent manifestations. Real friends, like a good counselor, will listen empathetically and meet you where you are, without judgment, to help you find the best answer to arise out of the negative pull of codependency. They're also there to support your decisions and not chastise you if you make a mistake or don't take their advice. They don't say "I told you so" if you do make one. They help you find the wisdom in your decisions, good or bad, and you do the same for them.

Examining extremes is good to gain perspective to find the balance you need to apply, as you can potentially vacillate and oscillate in all of your relationships.

The Controlled Doormat/Victim Type

The doormat spectrum type might say, "I will do everything and anything to keep you happy." Sadly, when they do this for someone, it is often to emotionally unavailable people who lack the ability to recognize the width, depth, and breadth of your love. The people you are attempting to please are usually unhappy with themselves, they simply aren't in love with you, or they don't want to be in a relationship with you or anyone at the moment. No matter how many flowers you send or things you do, no one will love you if they don't feel for you what you feel for them. Not everyone likes all people, and statistically we only like or find commonality with about 10 percent of the people we meet. It is unhealthy to do what you are told when it goes against your belief system or has a controlling dynamic.

Sadly, and subconsciously, the doormat type tends to fall in love with a controller who takes deliberate pleasure in raising the bar of their happiness and watching you struggle to meet their demands. It's not that you're not good enough, it's that nothing is ever enough to please these manipulators. I was always seeking the approval of my parents and this is often how a codependent "falls" for a controller in adulthood. I'll never forget when one of my mother's best friends, Ann, approached me in my twenties and offered me free counseling because my mother had hurt her. She identified with me because her mother was similar to mine. Her only condition was that I didn't tell my parents. I honored the request and accepted the magnanimous gift. She became a great mentor and friend, and I shudder to think how life would have been had I declined her kind offer. She studied psychology and sought counsel with a psychologist named Dr. B. for her healing. I followed her example and went to him as well, thus discovering uplifting lessons in his enlightening sessions.

On my last session, Dr. B. asked, "What would it take to please your parents?" He quickly added, "Don't answer right away. Take time and really think before you answer."

When my answer came many minutes later, it was the *aha* and ha-ha needed to break the code of my codependency. I said, "If I bought them a mansion and parked ten Rolls-Royce cars in the front yard, each with a mink coat on the seat, the house would be the wrong style, the seats in the cars would be uncomfortable, and the coats would all be the wrong color. So, I guess the answer is nothing. Nothing will please them!"

He told me to never forget I said that, and I obviously haven't.

What would it take to please the people in your life? Did you realize you were seeking their approval and how this may be playing out in your attempts to do more, be more, or give more to make them happy? Take your time and think about this and take note or list anything bubbling up to the surface of your mind.

Though I got this message early in life, I didn't apply it well. I went on to reenact with unhealthy relationships and marriage. I also walked away from great relationships, which was confusing in hindsight. I was mistaking stability and love for boredom and not believing anyone could really love me. I had little to no affection as a child and didn't realize this could be transferred to other people in my life. Dr. B. should have told me more, but I can't blame him either. We can only learn so much at certain ages.

People-pleasing was the foundation of my doormat life. I helped many others live up to their potential while sacrificing mine. I did their homework, paid bills, took falls, covered up, and forgave anything they did to hurt me because I was taught it was the "right thing" to do. I received the intellectual knowledge from the psychologist but didn't apply the revelation. I sure do now, and I hope it's thought-provoking for you! New perspectives and thought awareness are instruments of change.

Thoughts are cognitions. *Recognition* (re-cognition) means to be aware of your thoughts. In doing so you can change any faulty ones or reinforce healthy ones. This will internally guide your subconscious to redirect your choices. You really are what you think. You have to recognize your part in allowing others to control you. You can't blame them or yourself, but when you take nonjudgmental responsibility, you immediately can reconnect with yourself. Learn not to be judge-*mental* with yourself. It will keep you stuck with a controller and create more false guilt. This "guilt" makes you think you can change how others treat you if you do whatever they want.

Have you ever thought, *If I love them enough, they will see how much I love and care for them and they'll appreciate me and change*? They won't, or they would have by now. If you keep feeding into a selfish person's desires, you are showing them they can treat you with disrespect and they don't have to change. However, they can change you for the worse. Challenging your thoughts about being a doormat will help you take the "welcome" sign off your heart and mind. You no longer will feel like something someone stands on to ring a doorbell.

Closet Controllers (The Nagger, Fixer, Rescuer, Intervening, or Unsolicited-Advice Type)

The other, less obvious spectrum of codependents believe, with good intentions, they know what is best for others. Remember, the road to hell is paved with good intentions, and the codependent and the person they are trying to fix will both suffer in this treacherous dynamic. Closet controllers are quick to give advice, even when no one asked for it, and slow to take any advice or correction from others.

This type of codependent appears confident and caring, but they are passively aggressive in their controlling style, and like the doormat, they're sacrificing themselves under the guise of being the guide and guardian for everyone else. They can act like know-it-alls and do-it-alls. They love it when people seek them out for advice, and they will gladly spew out or lecture you on what they would do if they were you. They are also quick to say, "Here's what to do," with little consideration of what you can handle. If you pulled back the covers of their secret life, you might find they need to take their own advice. They can become extremely angry if you don't take their advice, so beware of this type of friend too. They may use money, housing, acts of service, or ingratiating gifts as tools of covert control.

They also are the most resistant and reticent to believing they're codependent. I often hear them defending themselves and their actions, and typically, they only come for about three to four sessions. They ask me a lot of questions about my personal life or remark that I look tired or ask if I'm okay listening to everyone's problems all day. They are using their therapeutic time to find fault with me so they can justify not continuing therapy. When they go on the defense, their pain is evident by the way they struggle to accept they are self-harming by remaining codependent. At times, they may appear to become as offended as their narcissist counterparts and vehemently defend their position and moral code. That need is really a fear of abandonment.

If you choose to get professional help, your therapist must be someone who can help you listen to yourself with a compassionate ear. You may find you are resistant to a therapist's input at first as you may feel criticism concerning your genuine desire to be kind to those you are trying to rescue. You will learn in therapy and in this book, it is not criticism but a supportive call to treat yourself with the same respect and undying loyalty you give to others.

If you are a controlling-type codependent, your need to be needed may come across as an absolute need to be right, but it is actually pain cloaked in fearful resistance. This is a conditioned reactivity that takes time and compassion to help you heal at your own pace. A good therapist will not personalize any criticism or passive-aggressiveness you may express or direct toward them. You may have repressed your true feelings for so long that when you express them in a therapeutic setting, you find yourself venting for a few sessions before the reinventing can begin. You need to be fully heard before the discovery and recovery begins. Being compassionate toward yourself and your adamant stances will make therapy more effective. It's not about a short-term challenge but rather a long-term change. Patience pays great dividends when a therapist and codependent work in harmony.

In time, if you do choose to go to therapy, you will learn that needing to be right is highly overrated and you may discover the people you are trying to rescue may not be ready to accept help yet. This will be a therapeutic breakthrough for you. People learn by making their own mistakes, and allowing those you are rescuing to find their own way is a healthier approach to giving advice. We don't accumulate wisdom by doing things right—we mess up and learn what not to do next time. Assumptions are presumptuous and are condescending. No one likes to feel inferior, and it is far better to understand others' decisions than to convince them that you're right.

Many times, codependents are caring for others as a means to feel better themselves and they also avoid their problems this way. While studying counseling, our professors warned us about this kind of countertransference and that it is a fine line if someone's problems are close to things you have endured. Helping others requires constant self-monitoring, or else you may become more of a parent than a therapist.

Many adult children of alcoholics take on this subconscious "parenting" role. A parent has the right to monitor their child's welfare. However, in adult relationships, if you're counting beer cans, looking for bottle stashes, hidden pills, or any other form of well-intentioned surveillance to help someone "get better," you're wasting your life worrying and "parenting" someone who will resent you for it. Adult-to-adult relationships are the healthiest and happiest.

Codependent controlling features show up in behaviors such as

- Manipulating by using guilt, fear, obligation, or anger as tools of coercion
- Not being happy unless the people you care about are "fixed"
- Feeling anger if unsolicited advice isn't welcomed
- Forcing others to go to counseling or doctors when they are not ready
- Giving ultimatums, nagging, or staging interventions
- Frantically changing motivational tactics to get others to change

Controlling codependents fall under the guise of "being there" for someone, but it is just another form of the dysfunctional need to be needed. You are there, whether they want you to be or not. Amazingly, many codependents who manage to "get someone sober" end up leaving that person. When the goal of the "project" is met, the codependent no longer feels needed and finds new faults to fix. People are not projects. An example would be if your loved one achieved sobriety, then they began eating junk food. Nagging them to stop eating junk food would become your new fixation. You are not in touch with your intentions or your true self when you're a nagging or controlling type of codependent.

The reactance theory[2] you read about earlier is helpful for understanding this type. This is when someone feels they are losing their freedom and they resist the advice or help to further establish their autonomy even if they know what they are doing isn't good for them. If you "can't help yourself" from forcing others to get help, you may be reinforcing their desire to do the opposite of what you think they need to do. This "fixer" type of codependent rushes to help everyone in need while denying their issues. It is a subconscious attempt to avoid their own crisis or rock bottom. It's an admirable quality to assist others when necessary, but you may be subconsciously looking for people to fix.

If someone feels you're forcing them to give up a freedom to choose, the greater the perceived freedom lost, the higher the resistance and the distance they will keep from you. This inverse proportionate result is the polar opposite of what you want to achieve. Finding balance is essential. You can try to take over so much for others, but the rescuing can overtake you.

Stephen B. Karpman, MD, who is also a psychiatrist's child, delved deeply into transactional analysis, and one of his paradigms is a gold standard today. Known as Karpman's Drama Triangle, he described three personas involved in an exchange of rescuer, victim, and persecutor. Karpman states, "Each role covers a probable positive intention. I have observed the compassionate intention behind each role."[3]

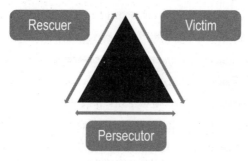

You may get drawn into other people's drama because some people need to be rescued immediately, and that is a good thing to do. However, if you notice a pattern of rescuing the same person or type of person for the same reason, you may be operating from a subconscious compulsion to avoid your own need for help. You can't recognize a pattern until there is one, but once you do, the clarity is restorative. The dark side of compassion can turn to an obsessive compulsion to rescue. When you rescue someone, you can become their victim, and then feelings of persecution and anger can become a vicious and pernicious cycle. This is why ultimatums and interventions are flawed and highly charged with humiliating negative energy under the guise of caring. There are occasions where an intervention may be warranted, but if you ask someone who has been on the receiving end of one, they will tell you they felt betrayed and ambushed.

Rescuing those who don't want it or need it may also revictimize the codependent. They get taken advantage of, then get resentful and feel unappreciated and sometimes devastated when someone doesn't follow through with their advice. Does this sound like someone you know? If it's you, it is possible to learn to rescue responsibly without self-sacrificing. Overdoing doesn't have to be your undoing. The phrase "No good deed goes unpunished" is an adage that well describes this unhealthy cycle of rescuing and revictimizing yourself. It doesn't mean you can't rescue those who really need it. You can give without giving out or becoming callous, pessimistic, or selfish, but it takes practice and noticing how you feel when you give— not how you perceive others feel when they receive from you. If you feel resentful, taken advantage of, or dismissed after you give to someone, check the motive of your ego. Did you rescue someone to receive appreciation or some sort of laudatory gesture? If so, you can learn to rescue without drowning in debt, fear, or other negative outcomes.

When I was a child, I grew up near a Coast Guard station. Every day they took the helicopter up for maneuvers. I loved to watch them drop the cable that tethered the rescue swimmer to the bright orange and white helicopter. Occasionally on the news, there would be an actual rescue, and it was enthralling and adrenaline producing. I was an adrenaline junkie as a child and didn't know it. It's far better than other "drugs" I could have used, but the danger to my brain was the same.

Going on house calls with my father made saving people seem like the most heroic of pursuits, and many times it was. I also wanted to be a rescue swimmer, but it wasn't something they let a girl do back then. However, I learned a thing or two through the years about rescue swimmers. They're very valuable, and if the person they're attempting to save frantically tries to drown them, the pilot sometimes has to make the horrific call to pull back the swimmer, forcing the other person to release the rescuer or wait until they are subdued enough to be rescued. Codependents hate to hear this in sessions, but when I explain that they are valuable to others who really need them, they begin to soften up to the idea. They realize how they may have rescued those who would destroy them and see that the result would be two incapacitated people.

You may feel resistance to the concept of not being able to rescue anyone again, but that is not the case. Assess your intentions and motives when you feel compelled to rescue someone, and ask yourself what the consequences might be if you do it. If there isn't a pattern of being used by someone, and this person is truly in need of assistance and is not just using you, then this isn't potentially hazardous; it is genuine kindness. However, if you relate to the drama triangle, it may be time to suspend rescuing certain people and work on helping yourself.

Many times, a loving family member can bail someone out of jail only to have them released to commit a larger crime. It's very sad to witness people who have gone through this traumatic experience. They don't want to give up on someone they love. It's very honorable, but sadly, it is not always possible. They have to learn for themselves, and you may also have to untether yourself from the chaos creators in your life. It may mean you have to let them suffer a consequence. At the very least, you need to take a break to recoup and regroup, and you may have to get back up in the "helicopter" and wait for them to want to be rescued.

So often those we repeatedly rescue cry and say, "I can't help the bad things I do. This is who I am!" When you attempt to help others who say they can't help what they're doing, believe them—they can't. Confusingly and equally as true, codependents can't help themselves when helping people. It's an easy way to see how self-destructive rescuing can be. Rescuing feels so right but can end up so wrong. If this describes you, it's time to stop bailing others out of their dramas, and it's time to begin your transformation to wholeness.

Balanced Self-Awareness

Have you ever said things like, "Look at all I do for you, and this is the thanks I get?" The doormat and controlling type both feel unappreciated on either end of the spectrum. Altruistic but frantic efforts on either end of the spectrum may result in greater self-loss. The disease to please causes intense anxiety. When fear is a driving force, decisions based on it seldom result in finding your true self, but you can find the balance of knowing how you desire to respond. Instead of asking others what they think you should do, or telling others what you think they should do, be still and listen to yourself. The best decisions you will ever make will be ones you, and you alone, think are best for you. You don't need to seek or give unsolicited advice when you have internal peace and self-awareness. Jealousy and mistrust will subside, and the fear of being abandoned or needing to be right will decrease.

I often do a role reversal by repeating a client's story back to them, asking them to suspend reality and be the therapist to me. I change a few minor details to assist them to actively listen as if their story was happening to someone else. They are better at solving problems for others than they are for themselves, and asking for their therapeutic advice and opinion immediately turns on their desire to rescue others or give advice. This works well with both types of codependent extremes and all in-betweens on the spectrum.

It never ceases to amaze me how many people remark that they never thought of solutions to their problems until they heard them in this healing context. They weren't paying attention to their pain, but they're able to hear it by listening to their story. They find their authentic self in giving advice to someone else. In the restatement of their advice, a light bulb goes on, and a huge chunk of codependency breaks away from their rock bottom. They no longer self-avoid and are able to solve their own problems through this vicarious technique.

Because codependents feel a disconnect within themselves, they ignore their internal cries for help but run when someone else needs them. This type of dissociative self-neglect is why many victims of rape don't report the crime, especially if it is date rape or a family member or friend. They take on the shame of their perpetrator and remain silent. When these victims come to my office, I assure them that I understand why they don't want to report it for themselves but ask, "Can you do it to protect the next victim?" They usually gain insight and find the courage to confront it and report it. Accessing and being understanding of their need to take care of someone else are often the catalysts for getting them to hold the perpetrator accountable, even if it has been years since the traumatic event occurred.

This role-play reversal is possible to do as a self-help exercise, and you're encouraged to give it a try. Record yourself talking about your problem and listen back to it. Your recorded voice is not the same as what you hear in your own head, so it is another effective tool of being your own therapist. Recording yourself talking on the phone with a person who triggers your codependency is highly effective as well. Listen to the pitch of your voice.

If it is higher or shaky, you're tense. If you're taking shorter breaths, stuttering, being interrupted, interrupting yourself, or sounding frustrated, you have an auditory example to help yourself. You will be able to convert your fear-filled speaking patterns into being able to converse with confidence.

Surrounding yourself with people who support and encourage you is vital. We're all works in progress and do well when we support one another in processing life events in observational, nonjudgmental ways. Somewhere between the extremes of doing nothing and taking a fall or collapsing by overdoing, there is balance. You can find it when you get in real relationships where you can be you, fear free.

It's not *what* you have in life but *who* you have in your life that matters most. If you have people who celebrate with you and for you and give you a boost, simply by being in their presence, you will be happier. These are the people who will tell you the truth if you need to hear it—in a diplomatic way that won't hurt your feelings. When you treat others this way in return, these synergistic and respectful relationships become simultaneously empowering and peaceful.

Bouncing ideas and desires off reciprocal friendships or partnerships increases confidence and reduces fear. Have you noticed when you're doing mundane things, such as showering, driving, mowing, or walking the dog, great ideas come to you? If you share them with others, do they shoot you down or build you up with encouragement or realistic optimism? If others are not supportive of you, it may be time to distance yourself from these people or realize you don't need to share your ideas with them. The only approval you need is from yourself, and many codependents give up on their dreams or ideas simply by sharing them with someone pessimistic. You no longer have to abandon your hopes and dreams once you release the need for support from those who won't or can't give it to you.

Your subconscious has been screaming at you, but until you distract your overanxious, overthinking brain to act on what you really want instead of what you think others want for you, you can't, quite literally, hear yourself think. The same is true when you are trying to fix other people. Suspend the overthinking and overdoing, and during this time of transition, allow yourself to be fully attached to your thoughts and feelings in the present moment. Accept yourself as you are without struggling to change. Wait for peaceful promptings to get you in a generous and glorious flow state. The Serenity Prayer embodies this concept and has been around for decades as a reminder for realization of and releasing the fear of things such as abandonment or loneliness.

> Grant me the serenity to accept the things
> I cannot change, courage to change the things I can,
> and wisdom to know the difference.
>
> —Reinhold Neibuhr

The fear of being left alone can be so horrifying that many codependents self-sacrifice their beliefs, moral compass, or principles within their love relationships. I surely did this, and when my ex had thyroid cancer, I felt so sorry for him that I got on my knees and prayed to God that I would stay if He would heal him, and I stayed a decade too long with an abusive narcissist. It was on his hospital bed the day after my prayer that my ex admitted he'd been lying for three years about destroying my recording contract with a major record label, for fear, as he said, "I would leave him if I got a record deal." He cried. He sobbed. He begged for forgiveness. I crumpled under the weight of feeling sympathy mixed with anger over the lies and deceit.

Sadly, I stayed because I made a promise to God. In my thinking, God would not want me to leave a man who finally confessed his misdeeds of taking away the *only* career I ever wanted or prepared to do. I thought cancer changed him, and he would finally stop mistreating me. I was wrong.

He was healed, but in the next ten years, his abuse increased. He destroyed another deal with another major label and a satellite radio company. I was losing pieces of me by keeping a promise and feared God would abandon me if I didn't keep it. I hope this illustrates how sinewy the narcissist and codependent are; they are intertwined by a fear of abandonment.

Do you see how jealousy is a manifestation of this fear as well? This is a component of how the connection becomes a toxic trauma bond. I gave up twenty years of my life to someone as a result of a faulty moral compass—not his, mine. The ugly, awful truth about me is that, I married someone else for less than five years, and he was worse than the first. The stories I relate will usually be about the first one, as the second isn't of value other than to help you to be aware, because somehow I managed to leave an abusive narcissist only to marry a sociopath. I jumped from the frying pan into a lava pit.

My tolerance levels for abuse had been contorted because I was told by Christian counselors that God could change the worst of offenders. I admit I wanted to believe it and that forgiveness would cause God to change them and help me. I overlooked the parts of faith requiring love, kindness, and joint heirship to wives. However, this thinking was a benefit solely for him and a detriment to me. I bought into the submissive role but no longer do that. I now trust my gut about recognizing bad behavior in relationships—and I don't ignore my feelings or pain. Pain is there to force us to attend to the source of it, and codependent angst is the same. Though forgiveness is admirable, forgetting what someone has done to you repeatedly is naïve and potentially hazardous.

I am free of allowing anyone to use a faith-based "argument" to make me subservient. It took years! No matter what your belief system, if the person you think you love is harming you repeatedly, they will not and probably cannot change. However, *you* can stir your style of faith to change by paying attention to your highest gut instincts, lowering your tolerance levels for mistreatment, and learning how to be true to yourself.

Seeking, Finding, and Becoming Your True Self

As a solution-focused therapist, I don't often ask the cliché question, "How does that make you feel?" I usually recognize how someone feels. I do ask how they felt as a child or during a life crisis, but the most important question to ask is "How do you want to feel?" This is the motivator and excavator of hidden desire. Digging deep into your emotions is like archeology. An actual archeological excavation takes time and tenderness to discover, extricate, and catalog precious items. You may be more fragile during this time of seeking and discovery. Tread lightly over the places in your heart and mind that have been covered over by time and neglect. First, to the best of your ability, separate yourself from those who do you the most harm. If you can't do it physically, try mentally by altering the way you respond to them.

Treat yourself with tenderness, and *don't* tell anyone toxic in your life you're working on becoming less codependent. I only told three people when I went back to graduate school at age forty-five, and no one in my family of origin knew until long after I earned my diploma. I didn't want to receive any negative opinions. Hurtful people want to keep you trapped in their ruined lives, and they often use offensive, berating, belittling, or demeaning tactics.

It also may be very important to keep a journal at this time to reflect on what you have learned or are inspired to change and ways that are authentic for you to begin the process of self-actualization. A journal is best kept in this context by venting what was or is going on in your life first. Once you vent the negativity, use your journal to reinvent the life you want by stating future goals and desires. This vent/reinvent format is highly motivating because it instills a future vision to challenge the past programming. Staying in touch with yourself in this way will help you connect with those who are healthy for you.

The power of one person in your life can make or break your codependency.

It may seem a trivial analogy, but the story of Cinderella is one of how an independent person can be transformed into a codependent one. Cinderella was born the daughter of a nobleman, and her mother was deceased. She and her father lived the privileged life until he remarried a woman with two mean daughters. When Cinderella's loving and protective father tragically passed away, her stepmother forced her to do all the heavy labor, and her stepsisters taunted and maligned her. Because of her childhood tragedy, this young, noble princess became a despondent adolescent who slept by the cinders. Her name was indicative of what she was conditioned to believe she would always be.

If you're thinking you don't have a fairy godmother to help you change pumpkins into carriages and finally marry the prince, that is true, but you do have your spirit. Cinderella had a royal spirit hidden inside her, and she daydreamed a lot. She envisioned herself at palace balls and in a better life. By changing her beliefs, she was redeemed from the cinders of servitude and became the princess she was born to be. Though this is a fairy tale, it's the same process for how codependents gain or lose their sense of self from early caregivers. One father passing away left Cinderella in fear and servitude. One prince passing by returned her to her original identity. What you think in your spirit when things look the worst matters most!

The Frenchman who wrote this fairy tale was Charles Perrault, an attorney turned author. He also wrote *Mother Goose*, *The Sleeping Beauty*, *Bluebeard*, and *Little Red Riding Hood*. He was far ahead of his time and wrote these tales to warn young women about the dangers of predatory men and wicked women:

> I say Wolf, for all wolves are not of the same sort; there is one kind with an amenable disposition—neither noisy, nor hateful, nor angry, but tame, obliging and gentle, following the young maids in the streets, even into their homes. Alas! Who does not know that these gentle wolves are of all such creatures the most dangerous![5]

This relates so closely to how a codependent is trapped by someone who acts kind but is not. If you have been the victim of a wolf in sheep's clothing, you can learn how to recognize predatory behavior. A predatory person uses many tools of deception. One tool is love bombing, which is when they inundate you with compliments, promise to love you forever, and keep you engaged with a barrage of texts, gifts, or words of undying affection. It feels real at first, but it is a setup to trap you in a trauma bond that feels like love but is actually a façade. When someone love bombs you, or they are extremely charming, engaging, or helpful, don't mistake this for the people-pleasing that you do. I'm not saying you have to become paranoid, but awareness and observation of character will help you not take everyone at face value. The masks of both predator and codependent have to come off for transparency and safety. Distancing yourself from predators will help you retain your power so you won't become more diffused or eclipsed from your higher self.

Curing Cognitive Dissonance

Cognitive dissonance is a psychological way to say a person is simultaneously holding on to two incongruent beliefs. It causes internal strife and dangerous compartmentalizing. Mental thoughts don't belong in compartments; they need to be integrated for healthy living. For example, a person who knows smoking is bad for their health and continues to do it anyway because it's helping them control their weight has cognitive dissonance. The internal conflict could be alleviated by seeking other options for weight control, but the truth is, they have chosen the path of least resistance for them.

In the context of codependency, justifications and rationalizations may be good *reasons* of how and why you are in toxic relationships, but they can become poor *excuses* for remaining stuck. An enlightened point of view is one that acknowledges the dissonance and diligently takes steps toward integrating the incongruency and finding ways to live with more authenticity. In doing so, you won't need to pretend or defend why you're in unhealthy relationships. You will look for ways to improve yourself so you can get out of them.

Craving the love of someone who lacks the capacity to feel is often a childhood dynamic reenacted in adulthood. Codependents often protest about leaving an unhealthy relationship by saying, "But I love him/her!" It is usually voiced with a painful whine, much like a child who has been refused a candy bar before dinner. This is not love; it is cognitive dissonance. This is an addictive denial stage, hooked by a fear of being separated from the familiar. You may be suffering from cognitive dissonance by staying in a toxic relationship. I have done it and had to learn to undo it, and you can too. The initial step forward is admitting it to yourself. Sometimes it even helps to list the incongruent beliefs in two columns. Writing it gets it out of your head with a visual aid.

A codependent can intellectually be aware that a relationship is impaired, yet they feel physiologically attached, hooked, and exhausted from repeated cycles of abuse, dissociation, and short recovery spurts, making them think things have finally changed for the best. The codependent may begin to mimic the narcissist partner's personality to keep the narcissist happy, like a co-narcissist child does with a parent. They do whatever it takes to keep the peace and, little by little, pieces of their self fall and fail.

I didn't want to go out to my husband's friend's house for Thanksgiving dinner because all they did was watch hours of calf-roping videos while I helped serve and clean up the dishes with the other subservient wife, and we didn't have much in common except that. My husband held a huge green velvet wing chair over my dog Peaches's head to make me go to their home. I begged him not to drop it on her. I got dressed, baked something, and went dissociated to his friend's house and was thankful Peaches was alive and well. The next day I wrote a song titled, "My Heart Is Sitting on Broken Glass." I had to have my cowriter friend Bobby E. Boyd help me finish it because it was too close to home for me. I was brave enough to tell him what happened. He later cowrote a huge hit, "Bless the Broken Road," and it reminded me so much of his friendship, mentorship, and becoming an unlikely ally.[4] He was there at the beginning of my journey from being codependent to independent and I appreciated it when he honored the request to write the Foreword to this book. Now you are on your own journey—find a friend or two who can help you move forward.

One trusted person can turn the tide of cognitive dissonance. Music also expedites the healing of dissonance by integrating your emotions, brain waves, and physical reactivity or numbness. Without music, I wouldn't have made it. You may judge me for staying with my abuser, but it is common for an abused woman to leave seven or eight times before she has the courage to do it permanently, and that was true for me. If you relate, I hope you find hope and the courage to reach out for help.

A codependent may become critical of themselves for staying, and this is another form of dissonance. They engage in the judgment calls of the narcissistic or abusive partner and join them in addictions and bad behaviors, or they isolate. Codependents often tell me they think they are becoming the narcissist, and the dissonance is externally and internally deceptive. You may tell yourself, "Things aren't *that* bad. They could be so much worse." They could be so much better too. Integrate that concept into your thinking, and things will change dramatically and expediently.

Distancing yourself from those reinforcing your self-splitting is essential for growth. Self-integrating restores congruency and enables you to be in healthy, respectful relationships.

The Fine Art of Finding Yourself and True Love, in That Order

"The Michelangelo Phenomenon" is a psychological term to describe a healthy process in which partners "sculpt" each other to their ideal images.[6] A person who is the most like you is more likely to like you or love you. The melding is symbiotic because the partners focus on shared similarities and don't criticize differences. Conflict and strife are reduced while kindness and intimacy are increased. This inverse proportion concept creates the kind of relationships you may have witnessed. These are the couples you've observed finishing each other's sentences without being offensive or interrupting. They intuit what their partner is thinking or feeling and have the other's best interest at heart. They can agree to disagree and allow each other to be their true selves. Trust is at the core of these compatible and communicative relationships, and they are often viewed as soulmates or twin flames in spiritual terms.

Conversely and sadly, in codependency, "The Pygmalion Effect" is more likely, and when you put it in rhyme, it is well described as "what feels charming may be harming."[7] Pygmalion was a Greek mythological sculptor who fell in love with one of his statues. It is as important to know what love isn't as what it is because rule-outs are as valuable as rule-ins when looking for great relationships. George Bernard Shaw wrote the play *Pygmalion*,[8] which was adapted into the musical *My Fair Lady*.[9] The linguist and narcissist, Professor Higgins, makes a wager he can transform an impoverished flower girl, Eliza Doolittle, into appearing as an aristocrat, teaching her to mimic his perfectionistic dialect and regal mannerisms. She works diligently and pulls it off flawlessly, and he pompously takes all the credit. He fell in love with his creation, but not the real person she was at her core. The dissonance of her double life made the girl angry at him and herself, but it also motivated her to run away from him, seeking solace and mentorship from the professor's mother, and the mother defended Eliza from her son.

Being born into poverty but pretending it wasn't part of your life story is another form of losing your true sense of self. It can create continued feelings of inferiority unless they are integrated with a current state of success. Even when you perform well outwardly, poverty can gnaw a hole in your self-esteem. Again, there's a way to be yourself without suffering from past programming. Finding where you feel valuable and at peace is your true nature, but don't mistake it for a comfort zone. That is a danger zone in disguise. Comfort zones are like great big recliners, difficult to get out of and bad for your health because they encourage watching television and being sedentary. You're watching other people live their lives from the comfort of your living room, and it's not living at all. It's much better to be a visionary to find your true voice and place on the planet.

In reviewing Eliza, she was able to find balance between the polarity of her impoverished former self and the manufactured faux-aristocrat one. When she found her true self, she found the love of her life and married someone in between the extremes. She genuinely fit in with someone who loved her just as she was and vice versa. She built her new life with a personal decision and not coercion. Shaw understood the richness of knowing yourself and loving someone like yourself and expressed that the possibilities are endless once we choose to act rather than react. That is exactly what Eliza Doolittle did, and you can.

From art and the scholars who apply it to psychology, you can learn much about resurrecting or constructing your authentic self. You may find you are watching things that are speaking to your subconscious to heal your cognitive dissonance.

We hear the term *self-actualized* from Abraham Maslow's Hierarchy of Needs[10] thrown around a lot, but not many people are sure what it means. The base of the pyramid contains what is needed for survival, and the pinnacle is becoming your best and highest self. No one reaches the summit with perfection, but the climb to reach it is crucial to your overall well-being and wholeness.

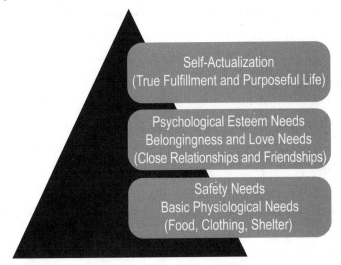

A large component of being self-actualized is not allowing others' opinions of you to sway how you feel about yourself. Self-actualized people seek solitude to reconnect with themselves and have peak experiences. They are happy with themselves. They enjoy life without compromise but are able to collaborate and be generous and kind. When they give, they don't give everything, and they are autonomous and spontaneous. They don't need praise to feel better, and they don't allow criticism to harm them. Controllers steer clear of the self-actualized.

In the beginning, a controller knows what to say, how to say it, and when to say it. They systematically and maliciously mold their target.

Their maladaptive identity issues are projected with a cunning precision when they find and groom a willing participant. They say things like Professor Higgins would say, such as "I made you what you are. You would be nothing without me. No one could love you but me." This produces fear and self-doubt in the target, whose sense of identity relies on the opinions of others. Self-compassionate intelligence can outsmart a conniving mind any day. You can learn what you don't want from people like this. Eliza did at the moment she felt dismissed as an object of affection instead of a living breathing human with feelings. She detached from the professor, and you can do the same with any controller in your life.

It's an unproven hypothesis, but my theory is that narcissists lack empathy for themselves too. They are unaware after years of controlling others that they are likely to end up lonely, isolated, and rejected, which is the exact opposite of what they wish to accomplish. By not thinking ahead about the consequences of mistreating others, they lose the best relationships and partnerships, and it's usually later in life when charm, charisma, or good looks are fading.

Controlling codependent types may end up the same way later in life from inflicting opinion and judgment. They say things like "I know what's best for you. I'm just trying to help you!" This is also producing self-doubt and forcing people to fit the projected image that may not be authentic. However, the narcissist means to be cruel while the codependent believes they are helping. Controllers are usually the most out-of-control people in their own lives, and those they are trying to control know it and avoid them.

I wish I had this revelation about controllers before I married. After we married, he got very controlling about my attire and education. He insisted I only wear Western-style clothing because that is what he wore. His imposed uniform was specific: I had to wear heavily starched cowboy-cut Wranglers, model number 13 MWZ, and 20X felt hats in winter. The summer hat had to be made of high-quality Panama straw with a meticulously squared-off front. Huge sterling silver belt buckles and cuff bracelets were required in excess to make him look prosperous, though he wasn't. I remember looking at a bracelet with a brand on it he devised and felt like a cow being branded. The wardrobe restrictions grew wearisome, and I felt like a caricature, as I wasn't born to this look. I was raised in a beach community that was a commercial fishing village and wore bathing suits and boat shoes. The Western style wasn't me at all; it was him. I thought I was keeping the peace and being a good wife by wearing what made him happy, but I really was falling to pieces inside and out.

He went nuts if I talked about going home to scuba dive. I went from bathing suits to cowboy boots to keep the peace. He was a record producer, and I was a wannabe singer at the time. I did what he said because I thought he was helping me become successful, much like Professor Higgins, but I felt disingenuous like Eliza Doolittle. The cognitive dissonance was telling me that's what it took to make it in Nashville. Boots and hats were in style at the time, and this is how I rationalized and compartmentalized it. I wish I had known about cognitive dissonance then because every aspect of my being personified it.

Our home looked like a Texas steak house, and I never felt comfortable there. I despise animal abuse, and he had buffalo and deer heads mounted everywhere. I told my close friends I felt like I was living in a Sam Peckinpah movie. I longed for a decluttered, modern, organic-style Zen home. This sanctuary of authenticity seemed unattainable, but I am living that way now.

Back then I had not heard of the Pygmalion Effect, though I had seen *My Fair Lady*. I earned a Bachelor of Fine Arts in Theatre, and Lerner and Lowe were my songwriting heroes. You'd think I'd make the connection, but codependency is an invisible slave driver. I also read *Pygmalion* and loved Shaw. Again, you'd think I'd have noticed my husband was a version of Henry Higgins and I was Eliza. I didn't because it was a reversed version of the process. My husband was grooming me to act like a country cowgirl instead of allowing me to be my intellectual "geeky" self. I watched every word I said because I would be severely reprimanded like a child if I discussed intellectual subjects or expressed any of my eclectic interests with others.

I didn't understand this because he told me he went to college, but it wasn't true. We were married over fifteen years before one of his family members spilled the beans that he had never graduated from high school because he assaulted a teacher. He assaulted many people in his life, and I was unaware of it until later in our marriage. Being one of his victims also made me feel ashamed as I didn't want to be perceived as one. Many abused spouses, like abused children, take on the shame of their perpetrators because they're told they brought it on themselves and they are ashamed of their victim status.

When I would go to preachers for counsel, I often heard some version of "stay, obey, and pray for him." That's the way it was back then, but now I take responsibility for staying too long. When I went to secular therapists, the light bulb turned on, but not until graduate school did these revelations fully kick in to motivate me to take action.

A song I wrote titled "It's All Your Fault (but I Only Had Me to Blame)" was a pivotal point in finding myself and letting my abuser's influence go. You might relate to the first verse and chorus lyrics:

> I've been putting out fires you started
> I was so tired and brokenhearted
> I never had the strength to leave you and I always believed you would change
> But the truth is, I knew the truth
> I had all the red flags and plenty of proof—
> I knew what you were like when I fell in love
> There's a reason they call it falling

Now I'm ready to rise above it; my heart hears a higher calling

I was too strong for too long at the point of going insane

And I always thought it was all your fault...and it was all your fault

But I only have me to blame.

(Mary Joye © 2010)

It was his fault for constantly controlling me and undermining every attempt I made to be personally successful and financially independent, but I only had me to blame for staying, trying, and hoping he would change. I allowed him to hurt me because of my severe codependence. I can blame role modeling, but at some point, I had to be me, no matter what the consequence. I formed an exit strategy in the last three years of our twenty-year marriage. It's never too late to learn self-pity is a trap and blaming others does nothing but prevent self-actualization. Blaming yourself is also a trap, and the way out is to forgive the most difficult person to forgive: yourself.

Forgiving yourself for allowing someone to use or abuse you is one of the most significant components of codependent recovery. If you continue to blame or shame yourself with feelings of guilt, you will make decisions based on unworthiness. You are worthy of receiving and giving, both guilt free!

Recalibrating the Mind and Brain from Lack to True Prosperity

Is there something imposed on you externally that is eroding your true self? If you don't resemble who you want to be, you can incrementally work on being yourself and no one else to regain your dignity and humanity.

Dissonance will dissipate the more you evolve with self-honesty and integrity. Forgiving yourself will help you move on more quickly, and you will no longer be attracted to those who aren't like you when it comes to love. Use your amazing problem-solving skills to learn self-reliance, which, like most learning, is done by trial and error. Continue to think about an ideal life in as much detail as possible and take at least one step toward it every day. You may not receive everything you want, but you won't get anything if you do nothing. Experiment!

Think of the quantum unified field of connection and limitless possibilities. Daydreaming about personal desires is encouraging for codependents and unfamiliar to them. They dream for others and not themselves, but it's amazing when you think about what you want. It may feel selfish to think lavish thoughts but realize that if you have resources in abundance, you will be better able to give fully and freely of them to those in need without lacking anything you need. Notice how your abundant thoughts make you feel physically, mentally, and emotionally. There's no harm in grandiosity when you're imagining with childlike enthusiasm. The mindful focus will get you on track to stay true to yourself, but there's more to it than that. Visualizing and taking action initiates amazing synchronicities. When you imagine your ideal life, your brain, like a GPS, recalculates your path to achieve it or find something better for you.

Heading toward your dreams is not a straight-line path, and detours are not the end of the road. They are places to turn around and move toward a desired destination. Rearview mirrors are small and solely for a reference or backing up safely. Windshields are huge for a reason. Quit looking back and keep your eyes on where you're going in your vision and *revision* of your independent future.

Meditation for Integration of
Your Subconscious and Conscious Self

One of the most expedient ways to achieve knowing your true self is through quiet contemplation and meditation. You can become your more resilient self with meditation practice. Resilience implies a give-and-take and coming back to a true shape. Like a rubber band when stretched, if you don't come back to your true self, you will snap. You can avoid the snap by shaping your thoughts quietly and confidently, and this will install heightened resilience in your brain. Ten to twenty minutes of meditation once or twice a day can rejuvenate your sense of self and improve every aspect of what prosperity is in the truest sense of the word. If you are more prosperous, you can be more generous with your time, talents, and finances.

Guided meditations break old patterns by creatively visualizing new ones. Imagining scenes of your desired and happiest life is an excellent way to know what you want and who you want to become.

Revision Exercise 1

1. Put on calm meditation music. Close your eyes after you have read the exercise.
2. See yourself standing in front of yourself.
3. How do you feel? With compassion and kindness, tell yourself anything that you would like to change to become your personal best. Don't be critical. Be comforting, encouraging, and kind. Pause and take three deep breaths.
4. Imagine you have become your ideal self. In detail, notice where you are, what you are wearing, how you are feeling, and so on. Energize the image by feeling the emotions and allowing more details to unfold. Spend at least five full minutes a day doing this, and you can change the image as many times as you like. It's all about you!
5. Take three deep breaths and open your eyes. Build on these images and increase the time you spend on them, and you will be amazed at how you'll be led to synchronicities and manifestations.

Revision Exercise 2

Make a playlist of uplifting songs about coming to know yourself. Intersperse them with songs about perfect, healthy, real love, not the fairy-tale kind but the kind that lives long after happily ever after. If you have time, watch movies that inspire you. Music is powerful. Cognitive dissonance symptoms are significantly reduced by listening to your favorite music. Peaceful, fluid music with meditation creates an atmosphere of greater self-awareness. Sound waves of different frequencies are healing.

Music, meditations, visualizations, and affirmations spoken out loud help you hear and feel the inflection rise in your voice. Doing this seals the message with an auditory boost. It directs your higher self. When you discover the right meditation practice, you will feel how you become attuned to your true self. Allow your higher self to lead you to knowing who you really are and how you want to evolve and resolve your codependency. When I rediscovered meditation, the cognitive dissonance disappeared, and self-actualization became easier as I incorporated calming music into the practice. I do it every day, and if for some reason I can't find the time, anxiety creeps in, reminding me to make the time, even if it's just five minutes of stillness or walking in nature.

Meditation is inspiration from within your soul. Allow what transpires from within you to inspire you! You won't be imagining a happy life for long. You will take action to live it.

AFFIRMATION: *I am pushing past the past. I am not resistant. I am resilient. By repetition of positive meditations and affirmations, I am redirecting the story of my life. I am not a doormat or a controller. I release codependent, anxious thinking with positive self-affirming persistence. I am able to regain and maintain my true self. As I meditate on who I want to be, I am inspired to transform into my ideal life.*

LIFE LIST

Write down any remaining resistance you might feel to releasing your codependent traits on the left side of the list below. Then write the opposite on the right side. Add to the example.

Who I don't want to be	Who I do want to be
1. I don't want to be a doormat or controller.	1. I do want to be self-actualized and independent.
2.	2.
3.	3.
4.	4.
5.	5.
6.	6.
7.	7.
8.	8.

The Neuroscience of Codependency

Everything having to do with human training
and education has to be re-examined in
light of neuroplasticity.

—Norman Doidge

Learning about neuroscience was an enormous turning point in my codependent recovery. I no longer wondered why I said yes to things I didn't want to do and deprived myself of things I did want. The nature-versus-nurture debate has been argued for decades, but now we are learning through imaging and research conclusions that there is an interconnectedness in how we are born, how we were raised, and what happened to us in life. It may sound complex in the context of codependency, but Barbara Oakley and others refer to it in research as "pathological altruism." When I heard the term, it caused a visceral reaction. Could it be possible that being codependent and altruistic is biologically driven and can become pathological? Apparently it is, and Oakley's research reveals:

> Empathic modeling gives rise to one of the mechanisms that promotes altruism: because other people's sensations are simulated inside an observer's brain, normal observers experience distress at witnessing the distress of others; they experience pain at witnessing the pain of others. Thus, normal observers are motivated to reduce pain and distress in others to minimize discomfort generated by simulations of that pain in their own brains.[1]

Our brains seek safety. Humans have an innate negativity bias that acts as a safety governor. Though we are curious by nature, the bias helps us explore novelty with caution. Through a myriad of experiences, we learn what is safe and what is not. Memory is needed to store the negative information. Over time, even if we live in a relatively safe environment, some of us hang on to negativity more than others. We focus on what we think will keep us safe and in status quo instead of what will really make us happy and motivate us to pursue it.

The pleasure centers that make us feel selflessly altruistic can actually be emotional cues to stop the pain of others so we don't have to endure witnessing it. Motivation to help others isn't merely an emotional or psychological reaction—it is chemical and critical for you to understand. As you have probably learned from experience, you can do more harm than good to some people you've helped and vice versa. If this is true of you, pause and take a moment to reflect how this happened and what sparked your motivations to give. Deep feelings of sympathy can lead you to believe it's your job to relieve suffering for everyone or everything that touches you, but this is impossible to do. Think back and take note of the times this has happened in your life. An example would be if you gave someone money to pay their rent, and they used it to buy drugs and then called you again for the rent money and you gave it to them again. It's pathological to "help" someone and harm them or yourself in the process.

The good news is that with awareness of your motives, you can understand how to break these patterns in your brain and access and activate the pleasure center by overriding the negativity bias and challenging the false messages with positive, motivational thoughts that push you to take action. The reaction of the past becomes neutral unless really needed. It comforts my clients to know codependency has biological components. It is more rewarding for them to understand they can change because they have neuroplasticity, which means they can retrain their brain. It gives them tremendous hope. Although I am not a neuroscientist, my final internship was with a neuropsychologist named Dr. G. who taught me to self-care while caring for others. I am forever grateful to him.

There is not an immense amount of research studies on codependency because it is not a formal disorder, and there isn't a pill to fix it. Pharmaceutical companies pay for many studies, so what's in it for them? Corporations aren't codependent at all, or they would go out of business. However, many are socially conscious, and this isn't pathological but logical. Everyone benefits as social and fiscal responsibilities enhance and elevate society as a whole. Unless you have the resources of a major corporation or are extremely wealthy, you may not be able to take care of everyone you feel a sense of urgency to assist. Biochemical reactivity is part of codependent behavior, and your altruism could be making you sick. If you feel tense or ill every time you see a number on your caller ID and you know they only contact you when they want something, this is a physiological reaction and could be pathological if you're meeting their every need to relieve your anxiety.

Roger Vilardarga and Steven C. Hayes developed these key concepts of biological connections:

- Codependency is an inability to tolerate a perceived negative effect of others that leads to a dysfunctional empathic response.
- Codependency likely shares roots with *pathological altruism*.

- There are evolutionary, genetic, and neurobiological components to the expression and propagation to codependent behaviors.[1]

You can be too good for your own good. "Pathological" means ill or diseased. Codependents become ill or dis-eased when someone taps into their guilt and empathy. Empathy is necessary to keep society safe and is the basis of healthy interactions, but when it goes awry, the brain takes over to relieve pain and suffering. You can willingly give while graciously receiving. Brain imaging in neuroscience is making exponential advances, but there is so much more to learn. In research, neuroscientists can see brain activity in real time with positive emission topography (PET) scans. If you pay attention to your own reactive exhaustion of how you feel when you "help" and it hurts, you are your own case study in which something other than compassion is driving you.

Developmental Aspects of Codependency

The brain develops early in the womb, beginning with the neural plate. The neurons you have from birth remain with you through life. Newborns have instincts and reflexes to receive love and nurturing, which are fundamental for safety through social interaction. We're born with the ability to grasp and cling for security, and when we cry, we're expecting to receive immediate attention. Most of us don't remember what happens in the crib, but our brains store the memory, and it can cause changes in the way we experience the world as feeling safe or not. As discussed earlier, Dr. Edward Tronick's "still-faced mother" experiments prove this innate need for safety and frantic efforts to regain it if lost begin at infancy and continue throughout the life span.

We learn by mirroring our caregivers. If your caregivers were cold and unaffectionate, anxiety and fear of abandonment can affect you through life. Conversely, when a parent and baby bond properly, oxytocin, the trust hormone, is released, and the child grows up feeling safe. Brain activity in the first two years of life is mostly in delta waves and is a lower frequency. Theta waves become active until about age six, and the imagination is superior at this time. It is what enables a child to put a red towel around their shoulders and not just think they are Superman but believe they are Superman. These are the same waves activated during meditation. The guided imagery exercises in this book are geared to help you improve neuroplasticity and thereby reduce codependency.

Brains develop in sequence, so it's vital for a child to receive proper love, attention, and affection when and how they need it. If you want to learn more, Erik Erikson, Abraham Maslow, Carl Jung, Sigmund Freud, and John Bowlby were some pioneers in this field. They concur that what happens to a child from birth to six or seven years of age is crucial for holistic development. You are born into this world to immediately engage and bond with your caregivers and are meant to love and be loved and enjoy wholeness and universal interconnectedness. Babies cry without worrying about the needs of others, and it is the first sound they make. Infants are fully focused on getting their needs met and are helpless. However, if an infant develops in an environment where basic needs aren't met, they can become clingy, needy, extremely upset, or ill if rejected in adult relationships. It is when a child detaches from their family in adolescence that they may begin reenactment, which is a subconscious compulsion to gain mastery over the past. Many codependents swore they would never marry someone like an offending parent, yet they have, only to figure it out much later.

Codependency is an overactive empathic reaction that is dysfunctional and can stem from infancy, creating a propensity to be attracted to those who will mimic early trauma bonds. Once the faulty bonding is created, it tends to repeat through reenactment of childhood roles, carrying unpacked emotional baggage into adulthood. When we develop, memory centers and other parts of the brain establish imprinting. The hippocampus, amygdala (the fight/flight/frozen drive), and the entire limbic system work together with other parts of our brains to form our consciousness. If we bury or suppress wounds from childhood, we may have circuitry that is crossed in our brain. It can damage the synapses in our hypothalamus and adrenal system, and thus our ability to cope with stress. This is simplistic, but if childhood was trauma-genic, the brain not only seeks safety and solace but has difficulty recognizing it when it does appear. Fear-based suspicions can arise or doubt of the relationship can ruin it with constant questioning and jealousy. Self-fulfilling prophecies can occur, such as when you accuse someone of cheating who has been faithful for decades, and they become exhausted by it, give up, and seek someone else to love. It is imperative to recognize when your brain is telling you the truth or not.

We biologically need to receive dopamine, oxytocin, vasopressin, serotonin, and other happy hormones and peptides needed for proper attachment and safety. The same attachment hormones that made us fall in love go awry when abandoned. If we were abandoned as children, we may subconsciously fear it so much as an adult that it destroys the ability to trust. If the people who are supposed to care for you frighten you, abuse you, or neglect you, you begin to simultaneously compartmentalize or split the person as someone you need to take care of you and someone who may harm you. There is no sense of security for this child, and it can wreak havoc in adult relationships. It is imperative to make connections between the past and the present to see if you are compartmentalizing your current relationships in a similar way. An example of this in adulthood would be to think that your spouse is a good provider, so you can overlook or tolerate neglectful, controlling, or abusive outbursts, and then you make the connection that this is how your father treated your family.

A professional can help you safely relive programmed reactivity and make connections from the past and present to facilitate a better future. There is direct correlation with codependency and trauma and seeking professional help may be essential at some time in your life. Make certain it is someone who understands the complexity of codependency. Trauma can cause hippocampus shrinkage, and this is part of your limbic system and memory forming. We learn when we get burned, but it may be a false lesson based on reactivity from the past. We need to release and form higher truths and responses to be healthier. A therapist who knows about the nature of codependency can help nurture you to retrieve memories and process them in a safe environment.

Mirror Neurons and the Codependent

Though it would be wonderful to have a positive emission topography (PET) scan to see the real-time activity in your own brain, there's another way to "watch what you say" through mirror neurons. Reaction shots in films are an easy way to understand this principle. The person talking in the film is not necessarily the one on camera. The reaction of the listening actor shows the audience how to feel. Method actors use sense/emotion memory exercises to apply them to their portrayed character. They act from the "inside out." They are feeling real emotions from a time in their own lives, translating into the character and mirroring the emotions to the audience.

My undergraduate degree in theater used many of the same exercises adapted into psychology, such as the trust circle. A person shuts their eyes, falls backward, and trusts they'll be safely caught and placed back in a standing position. This aids in building healthy trust and teamwork. One of the more difficult action exercises is when actors sit twelve inches apart from one another, face-to-face. While keeping the facial expression as still as possible, the instructor calls out an emotion and only inward feelings through eye contact are used to convey it. The eyes are truly the window to the soul. If the actor breaks concentration or laughs, it's considered a failure. This teaches actors to pay attention to the other person and to how they can feel and convey emotions with no body movement or verbal expression.

This mirror neuron exercise applies to the codependent through their ability to notice pain or need in another, even when the body language might not be there. It's fine for actors to do this while collaborating character interactions in a play, but if you do this in real life, the subtle intricacies of attending to the cues of others could cause a great deal of identity disturbance.

Mirror neuron responses can also cross certain species. If you're skeptical about how this applies to codependency, try this experiment. If you have a dog, whimper and look sad. Within seconds, your dog will attempt to comfort you. When you stop whimpering and relax, the dog relaxes too. Auditory distress signals and mirror neurons cause innate responses. Emotional support dogs assist the anxious person by buffering incoming neural input. This is a healthy, interdependent exchange. They both get the reward of connection and affection.

This is also the dynamic of the healthiest kinds of reciprocal human relationships. Mutual supportiveness is a skill you can learn. It doesn't mean being someone's scaffolding for you to hold up while they work on reconstructing their lives. It means relating in a reciprocal way while remaining able to apply compassion to yourself.

Empathic Responses

People who are born highly empathetic have more capacity to sense the needs of others through mirror neurons and other complex brain interactions. The greater someone experiences empathy, the more they will receive pleasure in helping others. Empathy resides in the most evolved part of our brain, which primarily is the prefrontal cortex. Reading mirror neurons is best done through others with whom we have commonality, as there is an implied foundation of mutual understanding and consideration. This creates healthy bonds and safe, shared circuitry interactions. If you're codependent, you might misread someone and become entangled by projecting how you would feel and what you would want someone to do for you. This also can cause unintentional harm to relationships.

We are all egocentric to some extent for survival. We interpret one another from our own filters of experiences and levels of understanding. If your life has been vastly different from someone you are talking to or in a relationship with, you may have vast miscommunications due to an inability to empathize from their point of view. Your emotions and empathic reactivity may be misleading you. Be aware when you share because the mirror neurons you're projecting may be what attracts unhealthy people to you. You may also misread someone's intentions by looking at them through your subjective filter. In doing so, you could become involved with them on a potentially harmful level. Restating the meaning of what you think you heard is highly effective to reduce miscommunication, and it is a therapeutic tool. This is why in many conversations we say, "Let me get this straight." It is a sentence that precedes what you think the other person is saying. In a healthy conversation, the exchange is helpful to consciously verify the subconscious mirror neuron input.

Why Giving Feels So Good

When we give, feel-good chemicals, such as dopamine, serotonin, oxytocin, and endorphins, elevate. Generosity is more than a learned trait; it's essential for us to survive as a species. When we collectively give and watch out for one another, we have protection and provision. This was important in the tribal communities of early man. Working together toward the goal of keeping others safe was a survival tool of the community. It still is today, but community support is not as crucial as it once was. Most of us live in smaller units now, and families or close relationships may be what you define as your "tribe." If you are the only one who seems to be taking on the lion's share of responsibility, you may be feeling the effects of your pathological giving. Many codependents are reticent to believe they may be over-giving to increase feeling good to reduce anxiety. I was one of them, so I know how reluctant you may be to accept that you are harming yourself when you over-give to others. Generosity is a good thing, right? If it results in reciprocal altruism, yes, it is. If the motive behind the generous acts is fear, image, forced culturally, guilt-based, or coerced by others; no, it's not.

To a codependent person, this brain/body/mind awareness may save you thousands of dollars, hours, and other resources. Give-and-take is good, but not if you're doing all the giving and someone else is doing all the taking. Subconscious brain rewards may induce your innate generosity. If we are healthy, our brains are wired for generosity, and they activate the same reward circuits as when we eat or have sex. When we give, we feel better, even when we may feel coerced to do so, simply because we do what makes us feel good, cheerful, and purposeful.

Giving is good but check in with your intentions before you write a check or volunteer time or resources. Altruism is a wonderful thing, essential to the well-being of society, but it is important you're not giving out of unsustainable resources. People tend to give more to close family members or friends than strangers, so it's vital for your well-being to beware of anyone close to you who asks for too much too often or only contacts you when they need something. If you're lonely, you're more at risk for caving into them to retain the relationship.

Why Not Giving Feels So Awful

It may seem like a ridiculous question at an airport when they ask if someone packed your bag for you, but it makes perfect sense in codependency. Has anyone packed emotional baggage for you? Who was it, and how can you lighten the load if you're carrying it today? We relate guilt and empathy in brain and neural responses, and it makes sense. If you're sitting in a park, about to take a bite out of a sandwich and see someone sorting through rubbish to find a morsel to eat, you'll feel empathy and give them your meal. That is empathic kindness, not an act of codependence. However, if you do this every day, it could take a toll on your ability to keep up with the demands of the less fortunate. Kindness is expansive and meaningful. Involvement with others who band together with you to meet needs in your community may be something you have to consider if you're giving too much out of false guilt or sympathy.

If you are giving from guilt, this could be catastrophic and eventually could put you in codependent crisis. Guilt is good in the sense it can keep us accountable for misdeeds, but too much emphasis on the dark side can make us over-responsible and feel false guilt. Guilt is a necessary primitive brain response founded on the fear of being shunned and abandoned, left to fend for ourselves.

A random sample from my private practice exemplifies this. Severely codependent clients have become challenging when asked if their over-giving might be guilt based. They sometimes get resistant and angry, at times accusing me of asking them to be selfish. I can self-disclose enough to be of benefit and tell them I have suffered consequences of losing homes, job, and security. Many times this helps, but in some cases it makes clients believe I have become jaded or selfish. I understand, but if they lack insight, they may be headed for ruin and continue to overextend themselves. It's not my job to change their thinking, just to present options. I tell them there's no judgment if they give and get hurt and want to come back to process it further. False guilt needs to be examined in the context of your codependency because it will cause as much suffering as rejection or abandonment. Ask yourself if you're basing decisions on sympathy and not your ability to meet the need. You don't need to know the answer right away, but introspection may help you to be generous within your means.

Revealing and Healing Codependent Physiological Reactivity

Neuropsychologist Donald Hebb said, "Neurons that fire together, wire together."[2] The Hebbian Theory is well related to "neuroplasticity." If you were born thinking a certain way, science used to believe you couldn't change it, but now we know you can. If you change perspectives, beliefs, and thoughts, your brain will change. Thoughts and behaviors can be modified, and you'll no longer be controlled by fearful reactivity.

Understanding how your emotions work on the autonomic nervous system (ANS) of fight/flight/freeze reactions also expedites recovery. The parasympathetic nervous system contains the vagus nerve that is partially responsible for facial expression and cueing mirror neurons. It is the system that makes you say things like, "It takes my breath away." Have you ever noticed your breathing becomes shallower around difficult people? If not, pay attention to your breath. Breathwork is a fundamental tool of meditation and mindfulness practices, and with it, you can calm the vagus nerve that travels from your brain stem to your face, throat, heart, lungs, and all your vital organs.

This nerve kicks off in physiologic reactivity exchanges and gives us our proverbial "gut feelings." Codependents often ignore gut feelings as they get caught up in paying attention to the feelings of others. They may have skewed or faulty *interoception* from traumatic family or relationship conditioning. Traumatized or codependent people may be so detached from their physical sensations, it is difficult to see triggers ahead of time and emotionally self-regulate. Body awareness quickly reconnects the person to their emotional responses. Knowledge of the concept of how interoception creates physiological reactivity and what to do about it is crucial for emotional regulation and recovery.[3] Codependent interoception may be self-deception. Pay attention to your body and any tension you feel. This is interoception at work within you. You can reconnect with how you really feel so you can regulate your emotions. Without mindful self-awareness, a codependent may think they are picking up correct signals from others, but those signals could be far from valid or potentially dangerous.

I developed a vagus nerve calming exercise for my clients. It relieves codependent reactivity and improves self-awareness. We take in much information visually, so closing your eyes reduces neural input and reactivity. Muscle relaxation enables a person to state intention with authentic responses. Calming, unrhythmic music is good to use with the exercise. It achieves better connections for brain waves so you can be more in tune with yourself. It will also keep you attuned to the needs of others without disregarding your own.

Revision Exercise

Vagus Nerve Relaxation and Codependent Self-Awareness

1. Close your eyes. Sit in a comfortable position with the soles of your feet pressed gently but firmly into the floor.
2. Become fully present. Feel the chair around your body. If thoughts of the past or future come into mind, observe them, then release them.
3. Take three deep, cleansing breaths; in through your mouth and out through your nose.
4. Place the palms of your hands gently over your eyes.
5. When you feel calmer, with gentle but methodical pressure, run your fingertips symmetrically from across your forehead, stop at your temples, and gently massage them in a circular motion. Take a deep breath in through your nose and out through your mouth.
6. Continue with pressure from your fingertips down past your ears and up along your brain stem. Massage the hollows where your neck and head meet

and gently massage there. Take a deep breath in through your nose and out through your mouth.

7. Run your fingertips down to your jawline and stop. Take a deep breath in through your nose and out through your mouth.

8. Using opposing hands, place your left hand on your right shoulder and pull the tension away and down toward your clavicle. Then, with the opposing hand do the same. Take a deep breath in through your nose and out through your mouth.

9. Gently caress your throat with your hands crossed as if to protect it, feeling the warmth from your hands relaxing it. Take a deep breath in through your nose and out through your mouth.

10. Cross your hands over your heart with slightly more pressure. Take a deep breath in through your nose and out through your mouth.

11. Cross your hands over your solar plexus with light pressure. Take a deep breath in through your nose and out through your mouth.

12. Place your hands together with your palms up and relaxed in your lap. Notice residual tension and release it. See it going into the floor where you are pressing the soles of your feet. Doing this barefoot will be more grounding. When you feel centered in your body, gently open your eyes.

With practice, this calms tension when you are tempted to go into "programmed" codependent reactivity. You don't have to "obey" your subconscious anymore. You can regulate your feelings. When you recognize physiological responses, you can neutralize them, and you won't be as vulnerable.

1. Pay attention to your physiological tension.
2. Shift to your authentic, confident intention.
3. Seek, then speak your truth.

Other mindfulness and meditation practices also enhance recovery.

The University of Wisconsin neuroscientist Richard Davidson, PhD, conducted instrumental testing studies with the Dalai Lama on meditation and how it enhances the brain and body. When we become still and centered in the continued practice of meditation, negative emotions dissipate and positive ones elevate. The mind/body connection helps us holistically heal on many levels.[4]

Understanding how to harness the power of your brain through meditation and affirmations will help you to remain true to yourself and authentic with others. Meditation is like a vacation from the constant worrying of the codependent brain. If you worry about the same thing over and over, you already know how to meditate but to the negative. Positive focus and nonjudgmental observation will recharge you in amazing and unexpected synchronicities. Meditation on positive thoughts may take time to change your brain, but many people find it better than medication. It reduces blood pressure and vagus nerve reactivity and keeps brain waves in communication to assist with authentic and calm responsiveness.

AFFIRMATION: *Education is liberation. I am no longer reactive but proactive. I am conscious of past programming. I have neuroplasticity and can change how my brain responds. I am no longer controlled by reactive impulses. I am able to emotionally regulate my feeling of empathy and respond with authenticity without depleting or harming myself or others.*

LIFE LIST

On the left column write physiological codependent reactivity. On the right, write how you would like to be proactive. Add as many traits as possible that you would like to change from negative ones on the left side to their opposite on the right side.

How I physiologically react	How I can respond authentically
1. I am tongue-tied during conversations.	1. I can be at ease while verbally expressing myself.
2.	2.
3.	3.
4.	4.
5.	5.
6.	6.
7.	7.
8.	8.
9.	9.
10.	10.

CHAPTER 4

Family Secrets
and Inner Child Healing

In every adult there lurks a child—an eternal child,
something that is always becoming, is never completed,
and calls for unceasing care, attention, and education.
That is the part of the personality which wants
to develop and become whole.

—Carl Jung

Keeping family secrets is highly overrated. Your family is not Las Vegas. What happens in your family doesn't have to stay there. It also doesn't have to play out in multigenerational reenactment. It's surprising to see how many behaviors, like physical attributes, run through the generations. These aren't handed down through the generations intentionally or psychologically. Many behavioral traits are those formed of a biological propensity. Good, bad, or neutral, you're an amalgamation of your ancestors and influenced by your environment. You don't have to be a dismissed, abused, or neglected child to become codependent, though it is often the case. Simply being obedient to keeping family secrets can cause a sense of shame and a need to cover up for someone.

Has anyone taught you to keep family secrets? If so, what are they, who are you protecting, and more important, what was the reason given to you to protect this person(s)? You may want to journal this or make a list of those you are protecting and for what reason. Secrets keep family peace at great expense to you. If you're keeping a secret for someone who violated you as a child, this is far more insidious than keeping secrets to uphold a family image. This is taking a fall for criminal behavior.

Victims of these family crimes often feel subconsciously ashamed or guilty as if they had some part in it. You did not, except for compliance to coercion. You probably lacked the understanding or the vocabulary to say no or to tell if this happened to you as a child. Often when children do tell, they are met with denial, dismissal, and anger, which all add up to severe emotional rejection and can cause symptoms of post-traumatic stress disorder. Taking on the perpetrator's shame is one of the strongest forces holding a former victim hostage to severe codependency. It is an internal battle of feeling entitled to justice versus feelings of worthlessness. The cognitive dissonance can create major disturbances in adult relationships, but the good news is it can be healed.

Those who abuse children choose the compliant, quiet, pleasing, or fearful ones. They stay away from the defiant ones who will tell or rebel. Every person who abuses children makes them feel guilty or responsible for it. The innocent child becomes a vault of secrets. Horrifically, an abused child hears statements such as, "No one will understand our special love, so we have to keep it a secret or you'll get in trouble." Note anything said to you like this, and you may need to find professional help to process it if it is infiltrating your present quality of life.

Small children crave attention to feel safe and aren't aware of inappropriate touching or neglect unless forewarned by a truly loving parent or caregiver. Without support, a child can be conditioned to keep quiet and live according to false "rules" as an adult, such as

- Don't air your dirty linen.
- Don't disgrace the family.
- Take these secrets to the grave.
- Keep family skeletons in the closet.
- Blood is thicker than water.
- Children should be seen and not heard.
- Respect your elders.

Dirty linen should be thrown away. Skeletons in closets should only be in healthcare schools. Blood may be thicker than water, but it won't quench your thirst. Children need to be seen and heard, or they become emotionally mute, unable to express themselves as adults. Respecting your elders is a lovely concept, but if they harmed or neglected you, you won't understand what respect necessitates. Development of self-respect may also become stunted or nonexistent. These messages are falsely shaming, and by perpetuating the secretiveness, you're protecting perpetrators. This can also be seen as a form of self-betrayal. Facing facts and opening up to someone you trust with the truth will set you free.

Breaking Codependent Role Modeling

You may not have been abused, but you may have been told to keep family secrets anyway. Children of alcoholics and addicts are often asked to cover for the offending parent, particularly if that parent is the financial provider. A false sense of over-responsibility and anxiety develops, and a deprivation of a normal childhood occurs. What rules or roles did your family impose on you? Without judging yourself, look back, find origins, make the connections, and see if any of your childhood was put on hold because of family secrets.

When I was thirteen, I told an eighteen-year-old close family friend a family secret. I also told a PhD psychologist who was a friend of my father's. The latter should have called child protective services, but professional courtesy for a psychiatrist's family overrode the law in those days. They both told my mother, hoping she would confront this person. My sexual abuser was the family "golden" person. I felt like silence was golden for everyone but me. I was told our family would fall apart and we'd lose our home if I ever spoke of this again. I was coerced to say I lied to keep the status quo. I did, and it was emotionally numbing. I remember feeling unprotected and violated and sold-out for a house and a lifestyle I didn't get to enjoy with equality. It was the beginning of believing I didn't matter as much as other people.

Not until many years later did I confront those who allowed this to happen. When I was met with more anger, I said, "I will gladly pay for lie detector tests from a professional of your choice, and I will pass and you won't." It felt so bad to have to defend myself in this way, but I was never lambasted again. I also wasn't called "crazy" or treated like I was making it up to explain why I married an abusive man or was distanced from this relative. All of it broke my heart and nearly my spirit. Confrontation is frightening, but sometimes it is the only way to stop the self-doubt and shame imposed on you for telling your truth.

Long before I found the courage to confront, I sought relief by connecting with friends who also had difficult childhoods. We still support one another today, and though we didn't know it in adolescence, we were forging a safer and saner "familyship" as we call it. These precious people remain best friends today. We refer to our childhoods as catalysts and catapults that flung us outward and upward. My friend, Michael, who coined the term *familyship* explained how we were expected to enhance our parents' image, and this was such a perfect metaphor.

Michael said, "We were the hood ornaments on the vehicle of our narcissistic parents' lives."

Laughing about it prevents us from crying or whining, as it doesn't allow what drove us in the past to stagnate in our present psyche. Old friends who "knew you when" can be your best allies. Who are yours? Connect with them if possible as soon as possible. Put this book down and do it right now if you feel inclined.

Wonderful memories you make with great friends can overwrite your prior history. A lifelong friend can keep you aware of both potential triggers and residual codependent secrecy or false shame. You can guide one another to triumphs, and you won't dwell in the past or be anxiously attached to foundational dysfunction. The camaraderie of those with similar childhoods is group therapy in its purest form. Staying pure of heart requires you to tap into every component of your emotional intelligence, and having great friends who believe you will relieve you in reciprocal relationships. They will help you discard the heaviness of the past, and they will stop along the way to help you deal with anything too weighty for you to carry.

Leslie, my dearest friend, and her husband, Bill, took me in to live at their house when I was going through my divorce. For the first time in my life, I felt like I was part of a family complete with children and grandchildren. I never felt judged and was always encouraged. Leslie got me back on track with school, and I wouldn't be a therapist without her belief in me when I had little faith in myself. With this kind of friend, you reach and teach others to find the impetus to move forward, onward, and upward.

A quote that has been inspirational to me for many years was from Albert Einstein, who said, "You can't solve a problem with the same consciousness that created it." I don't focus on hurting the people who hurt me or how to get them back for it. I focus on solutions when the past triggers or infiltrates my present-day living. It reduces conditioning and stimulates new perspectives, helping me make authentic, quality decisions and revisions.

Think about all the major and minor facets of your family role. Were you:

- The scapegoat?
- The sensitive one?
- The clown?
- The "crazy" one?
- The problem child?
- The good one?
- The little adult?
- All of the above?
- Another one? Add your own if you like.

Codependent maladaptive personas manifest in a myriad of inauthentic ways. Recognize any way you have worn some sort of mask or caricature to disguise your fear of being judged, abandoned, or misunderstood. Think about how this may hold you back from living a fulfilled life. Remove the masks and any reminders of them as they are no longer serving you. Purging the past will keep your past from merging with your present and future. Anything that pulls you back in time to a childhood trauma or maladaptive role of subservience or acquiescence needs to go.

Looking through mementos one day, I found a second-grade report card. My teacher related her concern that I was a burgeoning perfectionist. She wrote, "Mary's work is satisfactory in every area. The only word of caution is that she does her work as carefully as possible every day so that no careless habits will be formed...She is dependable and always willing to help with extra jobs."

My father, a psychiatrist, wrote, "Mary lulls us into a false sense of serenity...and we must remember she is a small child."

I was seven! How could you not notice I was a small child? What this teacher didn't know was that my father was teaching me cursive writing and how to play chess, and this was pushing me too far. At a time in my life when I should have been hearing lullabies, I was accused of being manipulative and "lulling" my parents intentionally. I took this report card to my former supervisor, Dr. G., and he read it and handed it back to me with a sigh, waiting for me to divulge my feelings, which were mixed.

I smiled and sheepishly asked, "Thus beginneth my codependency?"

Dr. G., who knew my father, replied, "Your codependency began long before this report card."

I asked if I should throw it away, and he quickly said, "No, you might need this someday."

I am sharing this with you so you can see if you have any codependent souvenirs that need to be processed with a professional or with a trusted family member or friend. You may have been pushed beyond your capacity as a child, and the good side of this is, you become accomplishment driven and can get things done. The dark side is someday you get so tired from pushing yourself, you don't know how to relax or to enjoy being a child or an adult. Over-responsibility takes root, and perfectionism burns out as procrastination sets in and little gets done for fear of not being good enough. Is anything from your past operating in your life like this? It's important to make these life-changing connections so you know what to change and how to change it. You may not have been able to recognize this in your youth, but you can now. The caveat is not to allow it to make you bitter but to use it to make you feel better.

If you have been keeping family secrets because it's the "right thing to do," reflect and expand more on your list of who told you why you had to keep secrets. What did they say to twist the truth and make you believe protecting a perpetrator would be in your best interest? Usually, their reason is self-serving and all about keeping up an image or financial gain. If your closet of secrets is overstuffed and you have no more room, they come tumbling out in every area of your life. I had to keep many secrets and witness many traumatic events as a child and was told it was all so we could keep a roof over our head so Dad could keep working and providing for us. I felt shame for things I didn't do and had no control over. This caused me to feel different from others and damaged in some way, but as a child I didn't have the words to express those feelings.

These are the trauma responses that can keep us trapped if we don't let them air out in the light of day when we are adults. If family secrets have turned to shame in your life and you feel like the trauma separates you from "normal" people, it's time to heal so you no longer have to live out trauma in cycles of emotional flooding and numbing. I'll repeat the message: you can't help others in a beneficial way until you get help for yourself. This is counterintuitive in many cultures, but it's true. I had to receive help before I could give it to others. Many of us are taught helping others helps us, and it does. As a child you were drafted into a family, and like a military member, you're just taking orders and are expected to complete a successful mission for the good of all, no questions asked. These family secret missions can take a toll on your ability to communicate your truth. You may find later in life, as many first responders do, that you're reenacting some family crisis through your work. You'll burn out if you don't take time to positively process the swirling emotions of how to rescue wisely and with the least collateral damage to your psyche.

My father later apologized for things I endured as a child when he was recovering from a heart attack. My mother did not. I was over forty when this occurred, but better late than never. I accepted the apology and appreciated the validation. My father's recognition, approval, and apology changed my sense of self-worth immediately. Hopefully there has been someone to validate and alleviate any shame and unworthiness silently imposed on you. It is rare when you get an apology or validation from those who formed your codependence. Sometimes they have to get their hearts broken to do it, but if you're fortunate enough to have this occur, accept the apologies and validation with graciousness and forgiveness, no matter how or when it comes. It will set you free.

You can rewrite roles imposed on you. Begin with changing your codependent beliefs. One of the quickest ways to accomplish this is to gather the information your childhood has taught you. There is wisdom in here, and it is teaching you something. No matter how horrific it was, it taught you something good, and like smelting gold, the value may come through intense conditions. This is the heart of positive psychology—to process things in an enlightening way.

There are probably also some happy times in your early life. If there were, remember those events as it helps in all forms of trauma recovery. For example, my parents would take me out of school to go to doctors' conventions in amazing places. I had wonderful multicultural exchanges, and it taught me how to be open-minded and, most important, to see how people are more alike at the core than they appear externally. I discovered the oneness of humanity when I didn't possess the words to express it. My mother taught me about the arts, music, and culture, and my father taught me about human behavior and a strong work ethic.

What is the greatest positive lesson your childhood taught you? Think about this in a nonjudgmental way. In the question, don't ask how you learned something good from horrible things, simply state what the good thing was. It will take some of the pressure off the negative past, and it will expand your mind to have perspective and not be caught in the stagnation of self-pity. Gratitude changes everything! Thankfulness and negative emotions don't coexist well in the body, mind, or spirit. Recalling anything good that happened alongside the trauma teaches your brain to be less hypervigilant and more balanced. Among the rubble of trauma lies treasure if you patiently dig for it.

There is also something I call "Positive Rebellion" (PR). In PR, you learn from your early caregivers what *not* to do. You rebel by doing the opposite of what you are told. You no longer have to be the family scapegoat or secret keeper. Many children from adverse conditions go on to become the most tenacious and successful. We all love redemptive stories, and yours can be the same. When you take action to change, your brain engages, your emotions catch up with you later, and what you want manifests when you act with positive rebellion. Positive processing begins with a choice to detach from the anchor of the past and set sail for the future, fully and freely.

A much more famous psychiatrist's daughter, who also was raised to keep family secrets, was Anna Freud. She wrote, "I was always looking outside myself for strength and confidence, but it comes from within. It is there all the time." She later wrote she was glad she didn't have children. Her father was a cocaine addict and thought everything was about sex. Her mother was cold and distant, and maybe she was intuitive about DNA.

Epigenetics is a new frontier, and to simplify, DNA has much to say about our innate behaviors, but fear not. Research has shown we can alter DNA with what we say, think, eat, who we associate with, and how we feel about ourselves. It isn't easy or immediate, but it is possible. Believe it, and your life and reality will change from the inside out, and your negative family history won't be repeated. We study history in the macrocosm because it repeats itself. We gain wisdom from wars and tragic events. It is the same in your family microcosm, and you can chart a new course for your life, free from reenacting family bondages. You only have to extract and take with you what is good and leave the rest behind so you do not vilify or sanctify anyone or yourself. This is what someone with borderline personality disorder does, and it is an emotional roller coaster to have this disorder or to live with someone who does. A healthy person can integrate and accept others, holistically, for who and what they are. Your caregivers often had poor role modeling themselves, and though this does not excuse them, it helps you realize they may lack the capacity to love anyone, including themselves. Being factual about their flaws will help you not take what they say or do personally. What a narcissist says to you is almost always how they secretly feel about themselves.

They project their self-loathing onto a willing participant and that is usually a codependent, but you don't have to be the one they use for a self-loathing proxy. Taking your power back will enable you to see them in the light of their painful overcompensations. It will give you a point of compassion for them without playing the role of the companion for their misery. This new compassionate, but distant, vantage point will free you to move onward, unencumbered by the desires of others not aligned with yours.

Using Your Past as a Compass Toward Your Future

I've interspersed generalized pieces of my life story, and I hope you will pause to reflect and journal about how your story affected you throughout your life. However, writing or talking too much to too many people about tiny details of your traumatic past clogs your mind and forms deeper negative neural pathways. If you feel yourself flashing back with emotional flooding, stop journaling and do something that keeps you present.

Sadly, we can flash back when something happens out of our control to return us to our childhoods, and many clients have this occur at funerals, family reunions, or by external reminders or triggers. Do your best to process any of these triggers as expediently as possible with a close, trusted friend or therapist if you feel stuck.

Because of the untimely and horrific circumstances of the death and burial of my only brother, I was forced to reveal most of my family secrets, under penalty of perjury, to the state of Texas. I'm glad Texas is such a big state because our family had a huge number of secrets, and it was a relief to put them on paper and get them out of my head and heart. Like other codependents, I said I was fine when I wasn't, and it became more difficult to listen to the trauma of others when having to deal with this event. Ten months after my brother passed, I took a break from counseling others to heal myself. I didn't want to burden my friends anymore, but I did have (and still do have) my life partner Tommy and our two rescue dogs. We drove to Sedona, Arizona, and stayed for a month. One of my favorite reset places, natural beauty abounds there, and it nurtures a trauma-weary soul.

Sedona is a great place to hike in solitude unless you go off the trail, which I did when hiking at Courthouse Rock. The trails in Sedona are red dirt, marked by red rocks surrounded by red mountains. With no cell signal or water, I took off my shoes and attempted to ground and become mindful and reposition my bearings. My training was useless in my own acute stress. Lost and scared in this sacred place, I cried so hard my nose bled. My immediate thought was I didn't want to die alone in a desert like my brother. I couldn't carry his pain and mine anymore. I covered up a lot for him so he could have a good life. Sedona used to be the bottom of the ocean in ancient times, and tasting the salt from my tears and the air triggered a survival response. I had been suffocating on rock bottom for too long. I looked up and prayed, "Please, God, may this be over now? I just want this to be over." I calmed myself in cathartic resignation, and the fear subsided.

Within seconds, I heard an unsteady *clop, clop…clop, clop* of horse hooves. An experienced horsewoman appeared. She looked like an angel but didn't act like one. When I told her I was lost, she said, "Follow the horse manure." She used a more graphic word than manure, but I needed to hear it. I got back to my car right before the darkness descended and had a revelation about her seemingly harsh words. What an inspiring metaphor! I revised the story of my life in that very moment and had an epiphany. Horse manure is what makes great fertilizer. The end of my brother's privately tormented life was over, and it gave me the courage to live mine out in the open. I got some grief counseling and never sat in my counseling chair the same way again. It was the beginning of knowing I mattered! I thought everyone else mattered but me until that moment. I reconnected to myself through nature and spiritual nurturing, and my personal growth was exponential after this. I also began a journal that became the basis of writing again.

If you need to heal, find a safe and sacred place and write about what you are learning and hearing in nature. It's strange to me how *scared* and *sacred* are so closely related. It is also the same with the words *journal* and *journey*. Be the journalist of your life and make connections in your writing that inspire you to move forward. Pay close attention to every word you write. The best way to do this is to read it long after you wrote it. Look for personal epiphanies you may not have recognized when your pen was on the paper. Reading your own words out loud can be very therapeutic. One subtle nuance or inflection of your voice can expand on the original feelings or meanings of the text when you wrote it. Pay attention to the little things in your life that point you away from your family secrets and into the light of your truth. Then you can make rewrites and revisions that will get you back on the trail of your life, no longer stuck in the past and fearful of the future.

Your story doesn't have to stunt your life or take you off course anymore. You can tear up the old outline of your life and write a new one. Asking for help doesn't make you weak; it makes you stronger, human, and more humane. Seek wisdom from those who have victoriously come out on the other side of where you are now.

Harness the life-changing power of taking responsibility for speaking your truth as you feel it and know it. Through the power of healing your inner child with restorative visualization from accessing your higher adult self, you'll no longer be bound to fear of abandonment or keeping up images for others that erode you. As you revise and rewrite the scripts of your past and present, you will no longer be lost, and you will find and enjoy the flow of improvisational living in your future.

Changing the Dialogue

Your internal and external dialogue is a great place to begin. Speak your truth when you're ready to tell someone you trust, but first journal it to yourself. When you voice or write your childhood stories, you're allowing and inviting in your higher and wiser self. As you know now, codependents ask for permission, apologize, or minimize much. You don't need permission to get help if you need it. Family conditioning writes a script of codependent catchphrases such as

- "Are you mad at me?"
- "Did I say something wrong?"
- "What did I do wrong?"
- "I can't do anything right."
- "I'm the only one who can do anything around here!"
- "If I don't do it, it won't get done."

Catch your catchphrases. Release them and write independent statements:

- "I can't do everything for everyone."
- "I'm taking a day to recoup and regroup."
- "I wish I could help you with your problem, but I don't have the energy at this moment."
- "I'm not afraid of being alone."

Language is a picture of your life in spoken word. Creatively imagine yourself feeling more independent, and you will not say fear-based statements. You will no longer be afraid of abandonment when you seek abundant and reciprocal relationships. This first had to begin with you in the very early stages of your childhood. Even if you believe you had the perfect childhood, something in it taught you to be codependent or over-responsible or you wouldn't be reading this.

Inner Child Healing

When you were a child, you may have had to dissociate to deal with the dysfunction. You can re-associate with your inner child from a place of adult self-compassion. Be gentle as you process and heal your inner child and seek professional help if this work is too intense. Going it alone may not be the best choice as flashbacks are possible. You decide when you are ready or if you need to seek professional help. If you can't afford help, then work slowly, and when you feel incremental positive changes instead of negative emotional reactivity or flashbacks, you're ready to move forward.

Be mindful as you go back in time by remaining grounded in the present. If you feel a trauma trigger or experience over-reactivity, open your eyes during this exercise and describe an actual object you see in close proximity. This mindfulness exercise will keep you present if you feel a flashback or emotional flooding. Trust your instincts and pay attention to sensations in your body in this revelatory healing.

Meditation communicates through creative brain waves and returns you to these childlike states of ease of belief. Think of this as being your own imaginary playmate. You can change the role and rules of your early life here and integrate the past in a way that detaches you from the subconscious reactivity of it. You will be able to talk about emotional things in your past without flashbacks or dissociation, and you'll stay present, not looking too far behind with sadness or too far ahead with fear.

Children go between fantasy and reality with ease and through imagination and meditation. With this exercise you can re-parent your child self from the bondage of the past. Your brain is like a computer. You can remove any virus placed there by changing the data entered. This is more than a rebirth; it's a reboot.

William James was the first person to introduce the concept of neuroplasticity, and he suggested making our nervous systems our allies rather than our enemies. This exercise is one you may return to many times in your life to increase neuroplasticity. Recognizing how you were parented to become codependent is information you can use for liberation from the past. Inner child healing takes time, but it moves you away from what you were made to be toward what you were meant to be.

Revision Exercise

Turn on calming meditation music. Create a sacred place of serenity and comfort. (Close your eyes after you have read how to do the exercise.)

1. Take three deep breaths, in through your nose and out through your mouth. Imagine you are inhaling light and exhaling any toxic or negative darkness into the surrounding nature to purify it. Think of your slow and steady inhalations and exhalations as the same breathing process required for life-sustaining photosynthesis.

2. Resume natural breathing, and if it becomes shallow or too fast, return to observing it and resetting your emotions before moving forward.

3. Calm the vagus nerve as you learned in the lesson before. Pay particular attention to relaxing your vocal cords and any tension there. (We all learned some form of the lesson, children should be seen and not heard, and the vagus nerve is huge in your throat. This is why we have a lump in our throat when fighting back tears.) Release this tension or massage your throat lightly, and it will reduce the internal fighting in finding your true voice.

4. Press the soles of your feet gently into the floor and wait until you feel your body grounded and centered.

5. Imagine yourself as a child or adolescent when you felt oppressed, misunderstood, or traumatized. What age bubbles up for you?

6. With an awareness of all physical senses, see yourself as this child. Where are you? Who are you with? What are you doing or seeing? What is being done to you? What physical sensations do you feel in your body? What emotions are you feeling? If the scene is traumatic, work slowly or open your eyes.

7. Observe your feelings without judging yourself. Release the feelings and relax any tension by bringing your adult self into the scene. How do you want to rescue yourself? (Example: If you're crying because a parent turned out the lights and you're afraid of the dark, envision your adult self turning on the lights, and comfort your child self by holding them and reading a funny story.)

8. What do you want to say and to whom? See yourself saying and doing those things to any perpetrator or person who caused you to feel frightened or over-responsible as a child.

9. Remove your child self from the scene.

10. Impart wisdom from your adult self to your child and speak to him or her softly and kindly. Make it something simple, powerful, positive, and life-affirming about their future. Give any warnings and follow up with praise and words of wisdom.

11. Allow your child self to receive this healing from your adult self. Stay in this state for five to ten minutes.

12. Let all tension subside. Then gently and slowly become cognizant and fully present, here and now. See the visualized scene dissolving into a healing light with a soothing inner softness and outwardly protective glow.

13. Tenderly pull your child self into your higher adult self, shielded and integrated with light and love.

14. Take three deep breaths in through your nose and out through your mouth, and when you are ready, gently open your eyes.

AFFIRMATION: *I am fully integrated with my higher adult self. My inner child is safe and protected forever. I am not the keeper of my family secrets anymore, and they have no power over my present life. I release dark secrets to the light through trusted people and my Creator, or through my spiritual or scientific belief path. I am walking away from the dysfunction of my family tree, and I am not a branch of it anymore. I am making new roots. I am no longer a helpless child. I am*

*a loving and loved adult. I am rewriting the story of my life through
reversion of the past and re-visioning of my future. DNA no longer
has the final say. My family's history is not my destiny. I am finding
purposeful, meaningful, and inspirational metaphors and miracles
in the mundane. I am living guided, guarded, and protected. This is
my happy beginning of living and loving independently, freely, and
joyfully.*

LIFE LIST

In the left column, write any codependent roles you played as a child that
continue today. In the right column, write independent roles you wish for
your future such as in the first example below.

Maladaptive Roles	Independent Roles I Desire
1. An insecurely attached adult	1. A securely attached adult
2.	2.
3.	3.
4.	4.
5.	5.
6.	6.
7.	7.
8.	8.
9.	9.

CHAPTER 5

Higher, Happier, and Healthier Relationships

Become the one you are waiting for.

—Anonymous

You can enjoy finding wonderful relationships when you dare to make the one you have with yourself the most important. You have been brave for others, and it is time to put your courage to work for yourself. Dreams of soulmates, best friends, and wonderful relationships of all kinds can come true when you enter into being your own soulmate and best friend by making the relationship with yourself a priority. Your higher self is the one who knows what's best for you, and as a codependent, you know what is best for others. You already operate at a high calling to help others reach their potential and achieve their desires. When you apply the wisdom you have for others to yourself and act on it, you will draw to you those who will reciprocate and make your life happier and more complete, purposeful, powerful, and rewarding.

Early in my music career, a seventh attempt to find an excellent voice coach worked. Though many people in my life doubted my ability to sing, I was tenacious and compelled to believe in myself. I did and still do think in melody, rhythm, and rhyme; though I wasn't a great musician or the best vocalist in the world, I could play well enough to compose. I could naturally write songs in my head and needed to sing to record them and pitch them to producers and artists.

Yes, it was a lofty dream, but it was also about proving myself to my mother who wrote in one of her infamous "I love you, but..." letters, "You're beautiful and smart, *but*...a songbird you'll never be." I had about twenty letters like this, and she sent them to my friends too. Thank God for the friends who told me she did this because some people believed her, and she did this to my brother too. It's most likely my mother had borderline personality disorder, though my father told me she had obsessive-compulsive personality disorder. It didn't matter what the label was; it hurt deeply and was always done in retaliation if I didn't do something she or my brother wanted.

I learned to do something amazing that broke the chains of these letters. I read them and then set out to prove them wrong. The positive rebellion you've learned about is the "I'll show you spirit," and it saves every codependent from self-doubt. Somewhere in your life is someone who will negate the messages of those who want to keep you down. Don't give up looking.

I met my seventh voice teacher Ernest Nichols through KISS tour acquaintances, and he became the man who would show my mom and every voice teacher before him that, not only could I sing, but I could also perform. Ernest, whose name means honest, introduced me to more than my voice. He tapped into my spirit after he immediately recognized my fear of rejection.

"You're so tense and sing way too high," he said kindly. "You're speaking

voice is soft, and you're an alto. Your vocal cords are so strained from singing like a soprano. Whoever said you were a soprano was wrong. You also
look like a deer in the headlights when you sing, and you are probably your
own worst critic." He swiftly encouraged me by saying, "We can fix this!"

He placed a mirror on top of his concert grand and told me to sing
into it, explaining that if I could sing to myself, I could sing to anyone else.
He played elegantly while I continued to sing timidly. His compassionate
mentoring crumbled the fear as he taught me to smile while singing. He
guided my posture, breathing, and projection, and if he noticed tension,
he pointed to my reflection in the mirror. Little by little, he guided me to
watch myself, and it silenced my inner critic as I sang out with confidence
after a few months' time. My true voice emerged, with feeling and fullness,
and it became effortless.

One day he explained his method, "To connect with an audience, you
must connect to yourself first and be confident. If you believe what you're
singing about, the audience will believe it."

This "self-mirror neuron" exercise repaired years of criticism. I didn't
get onstage wondering if people liked me or my songs anymore. I believed
them, and the audience received them. I wasn't singing *at* people anymore:
I was sharing music *with* people. It was my spirit connecting to theirs,
interdependently. Gene Simmons from KISS noticed my singing while I
was ironing his red satin cape in the dressing room and arranged a demo
session for me. He was not an easy man to work for but having four rock
stars as bosses was a piece of cake after being raised in my family. Gene
praised me in a way no one else ever did, and I appreciated it.

I was a makeup and wardrobe assistant for them from 1979 to 1982,
and it was a learning experience of a lifetime. It is important to note that I
had begun meditating at this time, and when they did occasionally become
demanding or get tense before a show, the ability I had to remain calm
served them and myself well. My first day on the job, Gene was screaming

at me about why I wasn't upset about his new costume that came in pieces when it arrived on the road. I quietly and politely told him if he stopped yelling, I could have it ready by showtime, and I did. If you don't believe in the power of meditation, I can't stress enough how it reduces stress, particularly for codependent "fixers." Many people assume I must have been a wild child working for KISS, but it was quite the opposite. Imagine how levelheaded you had to be to meet the demands of four rock stars for three years. This was the perfect starter job for my codependent nature because I had been conditioned to meet the high-stress demands of going on traumatic house calls with my father or going shopping for my extremely picky mother. Caring for the demands and needs of four celebrities was a piece of cake compared to my family dynamic, but it wasn't authentically where I belonged. Through the teaching of Ernest Nichols and Gene's help, I was able to make my way to Nashville with an open door, but I had paid my dues and then some.

Being a singer/songwriter was something I envisioned much earlier in life. The power of creative visualization is strong, and I didn't even know it had a name back then. If only someone had told me this could apply to relationships as well. I had no role modeling of interdependent relationships in my youth, but I was learning, and I had to lean into my true nature to do this.

It is never too early or too late to begin imagining the perfect partner and friends for you. Stop thinking about my story and consider your story in the past. Make a connection between how codependency is serving you well and how it is harming you. It is wonderful to be able to be selfless if your work requires compartmentalization. Compartmentalization sometimes has a bad reputation, but it is an ideal temporary tool of emotional self-regulation. However, it can't be done consistently without pausing occasionally to process what was put aside in the mind.

If your ability to meet the needs of others serves you well in your profession, it isn't codependence but rather your gift making a way for you to have *provision*. Pro-vision is something you need to see for yourself.

So many codependents do so much work for free, discounted, or above and beyond what they should be doing. You were born to be helpful, but you need to have others help you. Great relationships work this way too, and up until now you have most likely been attracted or responded to those who "need" you. This isn't love, and it isn't being liked for who you are but rather for what you can do for others. Sharing your true essence with equanimity is essential to higher, happier, and healthier relationships.

Breaking Abusive and Toxic Attractions

To reiterate so you won't forget about the importance of mirror neurons, you really do attract what you reflect. If you project a desperate need to be loved, predatory people can see this in your body language and hear it in your vocal inflection. Fear tenses the vocal cords and can cause you to sound like a scared child. It is what Ernest Nichols taught me to extricate from my voice. When you speak with a lower tone and don't talk about any fear, loneliness, or despondency you may feel, you will protect yourself with the confidence you project. Much has been written and produced about the codependent/narcissist dynamic. These resources are excellent at telling you how narcissists operate but offer little advice for the codependent, except going "no contact."

Burning bridges is not always wise or possible. If you have a narcissistic parent, spouse, boss, family member, co-parenting ex, or child, no contact isn't practical or sometimes not even advisable. They can be very vindictive and destructive behind your back. You have to extricate yourself from these tangled and often triangulated relationships. Recognizing is neutralizing. Three guidelines to handling a narcissist are

1. Don't argue. They will find a way to win.
2. Don't ask questions. The answer will always be some version of "It's your fault."
3. Don't react; respond calmly and gently. Make clear, brief, and powerful statements or say nothing at all.

For example: don't ask "Why are you so mean to me?" to a narcissist. The answer will always be some version of "It's your fault."

Instead, say, "I won't tolerate you being mean." This is a statement, and after you make it, walk away. No matter how much they badger or try to push your buttons, simply don't respond or react, and there will be no buttons to push. They can't keep playing this game if you quit and walk away. Not reacting to gaslighting or crazy-making behavior will help you take your power back and leave them without theirs. This is not manipulation; it is self-preservation. It will cause anxiety at first, but if you have ever been "loved" by a narcissist, their pattern is threefold:

1. Love bombing or attempts to trauma bond you with imprinting, calling, texting, checking up on you, gift giving, sending photos of you with them, and other over-the-top displays of affection
2. Gaslighting (crazy-making behavior)
3. Leave you or hurt you (the discard)

If you have ever broken up with a narcissist you "loved," this is also a threefold pattern:

1. Break up
2. Love bombing from them
3. You take them back, and they hurt you again

Because codependents usually have high levels of trust that match their ability to empathize, they often rationalize staying in relationships with toxic partners, spouses, and friends. Narcissistic and sociopathic people tend to trust no one while codependents err on the side of overtrusting users and abusers. Trust is best when it develops and isn't instantly bestowed. It's okay to have reservations while engaging in new relationships. This is healthy, but to a codependent, it can feel like suspicion and is not as natural a trait as it is for their dark counterparts. In extreme delusional beliefs, a battered or abused codependent can vehemently defend their abuser, and this frustrates the legal system and causes societal judgment. "Why don't

they just leave?" is the public outcry. Statistically, it takes an abus
seven to eight times to leave successfully.

They are stuck in the hook of intermittent reinforcement thinking the
"nice one" is the real one. Nothing could be further from the truth. The
one who hurts you is the real one. I can't count how many clients express
self-righteous indignation when they hear this. They want to believe the
nice one is the real one and refer to Dr. Jekyll and Mr. Hyde. I explain Dr.
Jekyll is the false persona that Mr. Hyde is hiding behind. The conversation
usually goes like this:

"You mean to say this person *never* loved me? I don't believe you! They
were so nice at first, and then they changed. I may even have had something
to do with that." This reference guide will help you see the discorded
dynamic of toxic relationships and the symptoms of abuse or trauma.

I kindly say, "This person is incapable of loving anyone, including
themselves. They were nice to trap you, and when they did, they didn't
change; they became their genuine, dark self."

Narcissist	Codependent
1. Likes to be in direct control of their anxiety by getting others to comply.	1. Likes to indirectly control their anxiety by meeting desires or demands.
2. Has false confidence.	2. Lacks real confidence.
3. Uses or hurts people to make themselves feel better.	3. Helps people or rescues them to make themselves feel better.
4. Subconsciously loathes themselves.	4. Subconsciously loves themselves.
5. Lacks genuine empathy or feelings of guilt and remorse.	5. Has overactive empathy, false guilt, and remorse.
6. Loves to play the victim for attention.	6. Rescues victims to feel good.
7. Is grandiose and feels like they are special and superior.	7. Likes being around those who seem special in order to not feel inferior or invisible.
8. Desires to be served and admired.	8. Desires to be of service and admired.

Narcissist	Codependent
9. Takes responsibility for nothing and blames others.	9. Over-responsible for self and others and blames themselves.
10. Never apologizes.	10. Over-apologizes.
11. Uses flattery, false compliments, and ingratiating gift giving to get people to do what they want.	11. Over-complimentary and over-gives to get people to like them and stay in relationships through generosity.
12. Wants people to please them.	12. Are people-pleasers.
13. Has shallow emotions and uses intermittent reinforcement of giving and withdrawing affection and attention to create a trauma bond with anxiety.	13. Has deep emotions, is empathic and loyal, gives of themselves to retain all relationships, unhealthy or not. Does anything to please others to stop the anxiety.
14. Is not loyal to anyone.	14. Is loyal to a fault.
15. Refuses to be alone and uses people for fuel. Replaces people easily.	15. Hates to be alone. Mourns lost relationships.
16. Creates chaos and drama to keep people orbiting around them like an entourage.	16. Loves to rescue and fix drama of others to stay connected and may become an entourage member.
17. Sets you up to get upset and then is calm when you do.	17. Falls for gaslighting and doubts themselves or feels crazy.
18. It's all about them.	18. It's never about them.
19. Is insensitive and arrogant and feels entitled to everything from everyone.	19. Is overly sensitive and compliant, and feels anxiously obligated to everyone.
20. Is subconsciously driven by fear of abandonment.	20. Is consciously driven by fear of abandonment.

Understanding personality disorders will help you get away and become healthy by seeing the crazy-making patterns. You can't recognize a pattern unless you have one, but when you do realize and take responsibility for your part in the pattern, it will stir a desire to leave. You will no longer place the abuser's interests before your own or doubt yourself. Conversely,

When an abuser recognizes any of your self-negating codependent traits, they will move toward you. They often covertly create a chaotic situation for you and then rescue you from it. For example, a sociopathic person may let the air out of your tire when you aren't looking and then notice it and rescue you by changing your tire for you. It is to gain your trust and is a well-choreographed tool to get you to dance to their tune.

It was a scary day when I asked a self-proclaimed "ladies' man" how he chose his targets. He was a voracious hunter and only enjoyed seeking out rare animal prey. He had them mounted; it was a house of horrors, and if you are animal lover, you would be ill seeing them. I was studying to become a counselor and he was unaware of his transparency. I asked him how he chose his victims.

I asked, "Do some women have V-I-C-T-I-M written on their foreheads?"

"Yes, they do," he answered. "I listen to them and know what to say to get them in bed. It's like chumming up deer with corn. You don't have to do much. You just wait until a deer comes along, and then you shoot it. I ask them about their relationships, express sympathy, and they get close and feel safe with me. I know what to say. When I'm done with one, I move on to the next or keep a few in sight all the time." Yes, this is a true story! He was bragging about bagging women and using them and losing them. It's a good thing he didn't have a conscience, or I wouldn't be able to share this chilling account with you.

Exit Strategies

Predators count on your maladaptive trait of self-deception that altruistically believes they seem to "know you better than you do." They actually do, and if there is anyone in your life like this who may seem too good to be true, they most likely are. This is not to make you paranoid but aware of their pathology that feeds off your feelings of altruism. However, you can be vigilant by being more realistic instead of altruistic.

Abusers are negative and faultfinding, and cause you to doubt and second-guess yourself. Your natural instinct is to fight back, but this can cause more codependent feelings of false or phantom guilt. It feels real, but it isn't. You have unwittingly but willingly joined them in their internal misery by their deception and your faulty interoception. You could have circumvented by not engaging in a battle meant to drag you down to their level of negativity. It is when you fight back and become like them that they have you in a trap of revictimization.

The "crab in a bucket" theory is why controllers don't want you to be well. In the real world, if a bucket of crabs is caught, and one gets near the top to escape, the others pull it down. This shows how the phrase, "If I can't have you, nobody can," is so dangerous.

You get out of the trap by developing an exit strategy.

Many of my clients feel self-contempt at the term and resist by saying they will feel they are using the person. You are not using the person; you're preparing for an exit, and it takes time, money, resources, and a plan. This person has been using you emotionally, mentally, and physically. Safety is paramount when you do decide on an exit strategy. You may have to appear to be falsely compliant for a while, but it will keep you safe. When you don't fight back, you take their power away by disengaging. Unless you are in eminent physical danger, it is best to remain calm when an abuser picks a fight with you, and they will. If you don't explode, they will implode upon themselves. With no one to fight with, they seek the closest chaos they can find, and this is often with themselves. As a snake backed into a corner who bites itself, so is the abuser when there is no one available as a victim for them to strike.

Narcissists and sociopaths set you up to get you upset, and they know exactly what they're doing, though they may not know why. They present lose–lose situations. An example would be if a narcissist bought you a black dress and a red dress and asked you to go out that night. If you wore the red one, he would ask why you didn't wear the black one. How can you wear two dresses at once? Lose–lose scenarios are gaslighting tools.

You can read people like a book to help them, and they can read others like a book to hurt them. You can protect yourself by not being such an open book, and this works by allowing relationships to evolve with time and verification of the other's intent. It's a delicate and devious dance around the heart of a codependent so attuned to feeling sorry for someone. You need to get to know who someone else is before you let them know who you are. Proceed with optimistic caution, not fearful paranoia.

The most covert and dangerous of all narcissists are those who play the victim. Codependents fear being alone and hate it, but a narcissist can't and won't be alone. They are always seeking someone to be their source of self-assurance because at the core, they have none themselves. They medicate themselves with people and demand immediate attention. They aren't happy until someone else is miserable. If you have ever been in a fight with one, notice how they talk over you, get you to scream, and then say you sound crazy for screaming. At the very moment you have snapped, they get calm because they got what they wanted and that is to know you love them enough to fight for the "relationship." This is not a relationship but a battleground. Lay down your weapons, walk away, and stay far away.

The most extreme case of being trapped by an abuser is in battered woman syndrome, a legal defense term for when a victim becomes so trapped by an abuser, they turn and become the homicidal one. Get help quickly if this is you, no matter what it takes. Online counseling is an option, and you can even do it by e-mail or phone. Love yourself enough not to become like them. Don't return accusation for accusation or question for question, criticize, or raise your voice. When you remain silent, they will "hear" you better, as silence speaks volumes. You have them under your control when you respond with calmness and not exhausting retaliation.

I hope if you are in one of these relationships, as many codependents are, you will find a way to make an exit strategy.

Limiting contact is the most highly effective way to live with a narcissist when you can't go no contact. I developed a simple formula for my clients.

Less Exposure = More Composure

If you do have to burn the bridge with a narcissist or sociopath, have reverence for the severance. Do it kindly, with as little cruelty as possible, and it will reduce their desire for vengeance. Don't become like the person who hurt you, as vindictiveness is a fleeting pleasure that briefly lights up the reward center in your brain. Waiting for vindication or looking for the love of your life may be delayed gratification, but it is much more empowering and peaceful. Become the one you want to attract, not the one you wish to repel.

If you're codependent, you know how it feels to go from delighted to discarded. It is devastating, and for a codependent, it can be repetitive. I've had many a narcissist come into my office and ask me how to get their partner back so they could dump them at a future date in retaliation. They get angry when I question their dark motives. Several have said, "I'm paying you to do what I say," and I remind them it's my duty to do no harm to anyone, and I refuse to help them in this way.

Do your own research case study and trace the traps you may have fallen into from someone like this. What trapped you in the past from a selfish person or narcissist, and how did they do it? Has this been a pattern for you? If so, how? Think how you can change it by being with someone who is empathetic like you.

Rethinking the Opposites-Attract Model

Instant attraction is most often how a codependent enters toxic relationships. It may seem a preposterous proposal, but codependents and narcissists are not polar opposites, though they have dissimilar relational styles. Many loving, generous, forgiving people partner with selfish, emotionally unavailable, controlling people. They appear as opposites, but at the core is the same reenacted fear of abandonment or being alone driving the force of attraction. We use the term *magnetism* to describe how we seem to be pulled toward those we're attracted to even when we know it may be someone wrong for us. Magnetism is more complex with the codependent/narcissist attraction's unhealthy dynamic.

In the physical world, magnets of like polarity repel each other. If you attempt to put them together, they repel each other with a strong force, making it impossible to bond. Magnets of polar opposites attract swiftly and with a fervent force. However, this relationship metaphor can fool you. Opposites do attract, but you're not a magnet; you're human. When placed side by side, magnets neither attract nor repel but coexist in parallel peace and not forces of polarity. This is a metaphor for how healthy relationships work, and it's a good one for you to recognize with instant attraction or repulsion, as you may be mistaken.

In human relationships, qualities attracting us in the beginning may become repulsive over time. Humans tend to fall in love with a person different from them, then try to change them. This is human nature because the more alike we are, the more stable the bond. It's healthy if you can agree to disagree without pushing someone to be more like you, or you like them. This is collaborative and complementary, not compromising.

However, when a codependent and a narcissist try to change each other, it can become a disaster. The spectrum of codependency is important because if you are the doormat type, you will lose yourself in doing what the other person wants. If you're the fixer or controller type, you'll lose yourself in making your partner do what you want. The worst scenario is you may not recognize the greatest love of your life because they are standing right next you, peacefully but powerfully.

To simplify, the attraction is there because

1. Codependents project a lack of genuine confidence. They have a fear of being alone and have boundless empathy.
2. Narcissists project false, overcompensated confidence. They have a fear of being alone and have little to no empathy, even for themselves, because they fail to think ahead of the losses they will face when they lose relationships due to their dysfunction.
3. The lack of attraction to someone who is best for you may feel like a boring neutral that lacks excitement.

A codependent's lack of confidence often leads to long-term relationships with those who lack empathy, but the realization comes in hindsight. The same is true of a narcissist. As they age or hurt other people, they become less attractive and able to pull off being charming. They hurt others so often they're unable to retain friendships or loving relationships. They suffer consequences of their own bad behavior, and sadly go to the very end of their lonely lives believing everyone else has a problem, not them. Neutrality through stability and fidelity is healthy. People are emotionally available when they can express vulnerability without fear because they are being supported, essential for long-term happiness.

Look back over your relationships with people who turned out to be the opposite of what you thought at first. Notice how any magnetism in the attraction may have been twisted, or how you may have wanted or were led to believe you had common ground. Did you overlook or forgo inklings or gut feelings of losing your authenticity to gain connectivity? Was it a fear-based relationship, drawn together from subconscious invisible forces? Was it love at first sight, then you got blindsided? Journaling any revelations can keep you focused on spending more time with those who you know are best for you. Love at first sight is a wonderful feeling if your early life was healthy. However, it could be reenactment of taking your breath away and then pulling on your heartstrings. This can be quite literal through physiological vagus nerve reactivity. What you think you feel may be mistaken by subconscious mixed signals.

The plot of all romantic comedies runs on this premise of love at first sight being wrong. Usually two people meet and don't like each other at first. Most often they're engaged or involved with someone else. Then a series of events happen and they find themselves pushed into a situation where they fall in love, have conflict, resolve it, and live happily ever after. These modern fairy tales are how art imitates life, and these are actually healthy relationships. They show how deceptive instant attraction or repulsion may be. Older fairy tales are just as damaging. The princess is abandoned to live in the wilderness or alone in a tower, waiting helplessly to be rescued, and the first person who comes along to do that is the one she falls in love with marries, and they live happily ever after.

If you have been instantly attracted to someone who hurt you, think back about it and how it felt. Who was this person, and can you see how they subconsciously reminded you of someone in your past? Did they somehow rescue you or you them? What did you learn from any instant attractions you had? I used to be ashamed to say it, but I have done this more than once, and each time, it taught me a little more about myself and how to avoid pitfalls of instant attraction.

Gain clarity by paying attention to what instantly attracts you, such as a "type." Years ago, I found a movie actor to be instantly attractive, but I knew what I'm teaching you now. I thought to myself, *I bet he's mean.* A few months later, he was arrested for assaulting a paparazzo.

You can break this conditioned cycle. It isn't easy, but it's simple. You're wasting time if you try to change a selfish person. Changing your response to them is best. If you find yourself instantly attracted, slow down and become observant of your feelings and why they are there. Are they love bombing you? Do they have a pattern of using and losing people? The only way you will know is if you allow time to reveal their true nature as you remain true to you.

You can live without this person, though it may not feel that way today. No one wants to be ostracized, but you don't have to put up with maltreatment to stay connected. Yes, you can live with them too if you practice self-care and expect little from them, but is this living or loving well? Only you have that answer. The opposite of love is not hatred; it's indifference. Some day when you least expect it, don't be surprised if you find yourself calmly and systematically developing an exit strategy.

Whether you go or stay in unhealthy relationships, you need to be independent mentally, physically, emotionally, and financially. It may require education or a certification. Whatever adds value to your life will empower you. Say very little to the narcissist about your future desires, or they will sabotage you in some way; you will hear negative pushback or criticism.

It's an exaggeration, but if you put one hundred people in a room and one of them was a narcissist and the other a codependent, then you turned out the light, it wouldn't take long for the two to find each other in the dark. It is in the dark parts of our unresolved issues or relationship trauma that these relationships take root. Like a weed, they grow too fast and wither too soon. They are built on cracked foundations and operate from brokenness, never to flourish, but you can blossom when you detach from them.

The Value of Wholeness and How to Achieve It

Codependents often say, "I'm not attracted to the nice ones! They bore me." They mistake stability for boredom. Here is some emotional math.

1 broken person + 1 broken person = 2 broken people

This dynamic is a bunch of interminging damaged pieces with jagged edges.

1 independent person + 1 independent person = 2 happy interdependent people

This is wholeness and happiness.

We all have some broken or damaged pieces in our lives, but they are not who we are; they are merely things that happened to us. They don't have to define you; they can refine you. Take some time to heal yourself before becoming involved with someone else. Codependency is costly, and self-care is a preventive medicine against a future broken heart. This is improper English, but you can't *not* afford to take the time to pick up the broken pieces of your heart before moving on with another. The narcissist in your life will repeat the same unhealthy pattern, but you won't if you allow the sanctuary of solitude to restore your fortitude. You can and will love greatly if you take care to become the one you want to attract patiently. What is broken can be more than restored; it can be renewed.

I've collected Venetian glass since I was a child. My grandmother gave me my first piece, and I cherished it. When I went through a divorce, my ex-husband bragged how he carefully packed this glass for me. Though suspect, I thought maybe there was a glimmer of compassion in him. Nope! He was trying to break my spirit more. He threw the glass in the box without one piece of bubble wrap between them. The mover apologized profusely when he opened the box and also said, "That's the meanest man I ever met, and you seem like a nice lady." If a big, brawny mover noticed a narcissist/codependent dance, hopefully you will see if it is operating in your life too. Seeing the broken pieces of treasured glass assisted me visually to see leaving him wasn't merely the right thing to do, it was the only thing to do. It isn't pretty to leave a narcissist, but it is a beautiful thing to accomplish.

I hung onto the shattered pieces for years, thinking that maybe an artist could make something beautiful out of them, but the box bothered me every time I saw it. One day, I marched it to a dumpster and surrendered the pieces. The clanging pieces of glass falling into the abyss were so loud and agitating, but the silence to follow gave me peace.

But wait. It gets better!

A few years later, friends asked me to meet for a cruise that began in Venice, Italy. I was conditioned to be afraid to go, but at that moment I was afraid *not* to go. The island of Murano is where they make Venetian glass! I got a blue heart vase with gold flecks and more pieces. It was a happy ending and a new beginning. I thank God and my friends because without them, my heart would not have healed, and I could never orchestrate this kind of vindication. Living well is the best revenge!

The Vital Importance of Healthy Friendships

You can repair your shattered life by being with people who support you. They are out there; you can find them and they're looking for you too. One of the most important questions I ask clients is if they have close friends. Real friends make great therapists. They look out for each other and check in on each other. The most successful people in life spend time with those who lift them up and encourage them.

Real friends don't judge, reprimand, or command. They don't conspire against you or backbite. They celebrate your successes and don't berate your failures. They inspire you and have your back, and you have theirs. They are happy when you do well and comfort you when you don't, and you do the same. They listen to you and you to them. They are not trying to fix you or make you a project. Layers of empathy and simpatico run deeply between you. The bonds are strong and flow with mutual respect, and these are the same qualities the love of your life will have.

Codependents often end up in one-sided friendships and relationships. Note any that you have and work on developing more reciprocity, since well-developed friendships aren't perfect, but they are some of the purest forms of love. Good ones all have some facet of your personality or common interest. They may not all like one another, either, since they are parts of you. You may have one friend you share deep secrets with and another you shop with, and this is healthy. Find these friends by recognizing how you want to share your life with others. Cultivate them and keep them, and you'll be renewed by them.

Good relationships complement one another with no agenda, and if there is conflict, you mutually and respectfully work to resolve it. You really can diplomatically disagree without trying to change the other person's opinion through understanding and listening to a viewpoint other than your own. You're allowed to do the same. These are also people who are secure enough to pay compliments to one another. Keep a good vibe to your tribe! You only need one to three close friends to be healthy.

You also need acquaintances. A deep pool of acquaintances may become the well of lasting friendships. There are also people in our lives who are there for reasons and seasons. Staying in contact with these precious people is important too. These are the pick-up-where-you-left-off friends. Independent people don't fear "losing" friends, they allow others to come and go; when paths cross again, it's the stuff that makes for hugs and happy reunions.

Friends and acquaintances are a network that works. They also are a safety net. Connectivity creates sanctuary, and everyone needs this to be happy and healthy. Everyone needs these connections, and more important, it is wanting what's best for you that keeps you from settling for less. Choosing what is best over what is good takes trial and error and begins with being able to trust yourself to know the difference.

Transforming Fear into Trust

Saying "I need" implies lack and is fear based. Saying "I want" implies desire and contentment.

Feel how these sentences resonate.

I *need* a husband/wife. I *need* a person to be with me.

I *want* a loving husband/wife. I *want* to share my life with the perfect person for me.

The first is fear filled, but the latter is fulfilled. Healthy connections are not desperate; they are confident. They are happier and higher ones. But who can you trust?

If you trust no one, you probably don't trust yourself. You may balk at that, but secure people trust themselves. When you emit a guarded or timid vibe, you don't trust people, and others sense something amiss and may not feel they can trust you. It's those pesky mirror neurons again. People-pleasing is another disingenuous self-betrayal that conveys a lack of trust. Many codependents are this way, and I certainly was. My mirror neurons and perhaps yours can emanate desperation by people-pleasing or trying to be excessively affable. Being overly effusive or agreeable also turns people away. Being confident and gut honest about how you can portray your genuine personality will attract trustworthy people to you.

Many asked after my divorce if I was going to ever trust a man again. It was a resounding, "Yes!" But I added, "There are many trustworthy men in the world. What I don't trust yet is my ability to choose a man." It was a pivotal revelation and one of taking responsibility without placing blame. I was the common denominator of these relationships. Being honest with yourself is the best way to bring someone honest to you.

I'll never forget reading in a textbook that codependents stay in unhealthy relationships to avoid loneliness. I rewrote the sentence on the margin to say, "I will endure loneliness temporarily to avoid unhealthy relationships permanently." Knowing what I didn't *want* to attract helped me to stop needing it. Rearranging a few words completely transforms the semantics into a newer, happier, and healthier meaning. Around the time of this revelation, I wrote a song that was the opposite of my marriage. It was challenging the pain of needing someone to validate me. I was stating, with words and music, what I *wanted* as if it was already mine.

Just Because You'd Never Ask Me To

I'd lay down my life, surrender my soul

Let go and let you take control

Just because you'd never ask me to.

I'd gather up everything that I bought,

Give it to you without a second thought

Just because you'd never ask me to.

You love me just for who I am

You would never try to change me to fit in your plans

That's why I'd do anything and everything for you

Just because you'd never ask me to.

I'd silence my heart and its deepest desires

Go one step down to help you go one higher

Just because you'd never ask me to.

I'd give up my hope, forget all my dreams

I'd forsake everything I believe

Just because you'd never ask me to.

You always try to give more than you take,

Never ask me to bend so far, my spirit breaks.

When I recorded this song as a duet, I felt a shift and things changed direction. It was like a force greater than myself took over when I quit talking about what I didn't have and began concentrating on what I wanted. It wasn't overnight, but it has been a miraculous journey, and it is ever-evolving with love and kindness. I learned from writing this song that if you shift from lamenting to stating things as though they have already happened, you are calling in what you want, and it arrives in unexpected but wonderful ways. There is a force in our brain, and to those of you who believe in your spirit, that guides your decisions to higher relationships.

When you focus on what you really want through concentration, you attract it. Concentration is a word that means undiluted and pure, but it also means the ability to focus our thinking. It is not so dissimilar a concept, as you can't dilute thinking about what you want by meeting the desires of other people. Love may truly be all we need, but it has to come from the purest of sources.

Finding the Love of Your Life, Beginning with You

We hear so much about self-love these days, and it's a difficult concept for a codependent to grasp. There is almost an aversion to thinking or saying, "I love myself." It sounds like the very thing you are trying to avoid, which is narcissism. Remember, narcissists secretly loathe themselves and have to make others feel as badly as they do about themselves. I hope this opened a window for you to let the fresh air in concerning the term *self-love*. When codependents can't grasp this as an important ideal, I ask them how it feels to hear the terms:

- Self-respect
- Self-compassion
- Self-confidence
- Self-care

The last one gets them in the gut. Systematically, they find that the mercy, honor, and kindness they bestow on others is something they have the right to receive as well. If you are looking for the love of your life or plan to someday, it is your own soul you need to delve into before connecting with another. Think in terms of *self-like* as a great diving board for springing into action to find love from within.

Your soulmate will be someone who likes you, is like you, and allows you to be you: *all* of you. As you become emotionally available to yourself, you'll find an emotionally available person, or you'll keep looking until you do. You won't have to settle down with someone, you can settle up! This isn't about romantic excitement. Romantic excitement feels great, but infatuation isn't sustainable. There's a reason we call it *falling* in love. You can *rise* in love. Genuine love doesn't sweep you off your feet; it is balanced.

You *rise* as an individual and support each other as a couple. Compatibility makes for great companionship. It may be someone who has been codependent like you, and that's not a bad thing. You will always look out for each other's best interest and protect each other lovingly and happily. You won't enervate each other; you'll both be energized and grounded. Safety and security preside over these relationships, and you reside in pure and peaceful contentment. If something has content, it is substantial. It is also sustainable. More so, you must believe it is attainable. You begin by being content with yourself and finding those who love you and like you as you are.

> You fall in love with somebody who fits within what I call your "love map," an unconscious list of traits that you build in childhood as you grow up. And I also think that you gravitate to certain people, actually, with somewhat complementary brain systems.[1]
>
> —Helen Fisher

Helen Fisher is an anthropologist whose research has been the foundation of the algorithms for dating websites. She used technology in her quest to understand all forms of love with functional magnetic resonance imaging, which looks at blood flow and brain activity. Interesting to note is that it is a machine working on magnetization. Her extensive research helped many people to understand how to find the best love for them. Her work is eye-opening and heart healing, and millions of people seeking love are encouraged by it. However, Fisher herself admits that no test or research can explain or create a spark that ignites the flame of finding the perfect person for you. Whether you're in a relationship or not, you can change your codependency, and in doing so, you will find more happiness.

If you are in a relationship, you can make it better by loving yourself. When you become loving and caring toward yourself, the person you are with will change. If they become critical or controlling, ignore it. You may or may not stay in this relationship, but you will always be with you, so make the relationship with yourself the best it can be and see what transpires.

If you are not in a relationship, the same applies. Love who you are at this moment without judging, and you will soon be setting out to be who you want to attract. Honor your future desires. In times of quiet contemplation, daydream about how you want to love and be loved. The energy you put toward loving the image of what true togetherness looks like will cause your feelings and beliefs to unfold.

If you're beginning a new relationship, don't talk about past ones. Just don't. It's tempting, but it will bring you down and will bring the vibration of the relationship down too. Start over with a fresh slate like you've never been hurt. It will raise the vibration of your very first meeting from fear to self-confidence and worthiness. As you project this to others, they will see, feel, and hear your self-respect and will project it back to you. As Albert Einstein once said, "Everything in life is vibration."

Harmonious Love

Harmony is an unexplainable but wonderful experience in music and relationships. When voices or instruments blend musically, they simultaneously resonate and vibrate from a single source note to create a pleasant-sounding chord. Harmonious love also strikes a chord. Discordant relationships are when personalities clash. We also say we are "in sync" or "in tune" when describing relationships. These musical terms are not a coincidence: they are excellent metaphors for human relationships and how we are in tune with one another or on the same wavelength. In some new thought circles, the word *universe* means "one song" (uni-verse), but there are many other definitions too. For codependent recovery it's important to stay true to your vibrations and stay true to your wavelength and the universal need for acceptance and healthy interdependence.

Our bodies give off energy in vibrational waves too. If it sounds far-fetched, get in any busy high-rise elevator and observe how you feel as a person enters or exits the elevator. The vibration changes. This relates to codependency because we don't pay much attention to how we feel around others. Notice the vibrations of total strangers and how they affect you. It can open up a world of conversations, and a few kind words may be the beginning of a beautiful relationship.

What we say is as important as how we say it to others and to ourselves. Talking to yourself is perfectly normal but be sure you are saying good things when you do it. Sound waves never stop traveling. When you speak affirmations, your words carry out in waves that travel through time and space. In this tangible and scientific way, see your words moving through time and space as signals to the universe that you are ready for harmonious, interdependent relationships. Like my voice coach, be your own coach to find yourself and then to connect with others who resonate with you.

Fear operates at a low vibration or frequency. Think of the theme song from *Jaws* and other horror movies. Happy songs have a higher vibration, and this is why music is the universal language. We can tell if a song is happy or sad no matter what language it's in, and the language of the heart is no different. It needs to be heard, like the birds in the trees calling to one another to let them know they are not alone. It's important to speak to yourself to note sensations in your body. This is what you project in three of your five senses. Brain waves respond to sound waves, and if you don't believe it, the songs you listened to in high school cause significant emotional responses because puberty is the most exciting time in your life.

Certain frequencies of sound waves affect our physiologic responses, and this is why visualization, affirmations, and meditation combined enhance and accelerate radical change. Our brains are chemical but also electrical. The brain is our greatest resource for transforming our lives. When positive sensations engage, they fire and wire together in our brain to heal it. This is why music therapy has been getting so much attention because now we have imaging to back up what our emotions have told us from the beginning of time: music heals.

It may be better to see a simplified diagram. There are differing opinions on these waves and what they do, but this may help you see in a composite form what happens in your brain. That being said, neuroscience imaging is discovering more than the electrical brain waves listed. (One hertz, or Hz, is one cycle per second.)

- Beta Waves—15 to 40 Hz: A strongly engaged and focused mind
- Alpha Waves—9 to 14 Hz: A person at rest, meditating, relaxed, present, and mindful
- Theta Waves—5 to 8 Hz: Daydreaming, imagining, visualization, intuition, and learning
- Delta Waves—1.5 to 4 Hz: Sleep, healing, regeneration, and empathy[2]

Delta is the *resting* state, which codependent people seldom do well. Their minds are always spinning at night with things they "have to" get done. You have to get a balance between exercise and rest, or you won't be able to do anything well. Restoration begins with getting rest! Gamma waves (38 to 42 hertz) are a more recent discovery, and sometimes are a mystery. They show up in imaging related to altruism, love, and peak spiritual experiences.

It's important to know about brain waves in codependent recovery because the more empathic you are, the more you're reacting to energy emitted from others, usually while ignoring how you feel. Seeking solitude to connect your subconscious mind with your conscious choices is essential for recovery. When you're stressed, have you ever said, "I can't hear myself think!" You really can't. This is what a person with compassion fatigue or someone who needs rest may feel like. Listen to any phrases like this that you say. With awareness, concentration, and meditation, you can form new neural pathways and have harmonious, happier, higher, and healthier relationships.

Yes, things may have happened that make you feel bad about yourself, but you are here, and this is a new moment. Be present and stay focused. Be brave enough to be as kind to yourself as you are to others. There really is power in the here and now. You aren't damaged beyond repair unless you think you are. What you once thought of as damaged can be processed as places to work on to restore and gain wellness. Restored or repurposed items or homes are of far greater value than new ones. You can attract people who can love you as you love them in higher, happier, and healthier ways because you are leaving the codependent self behind. There is and will be more evolving to do, but love will come as you want it to be by simply being you.

Holding a space and place for yourself and others simultaneously creates harmonious and loving relationships. Being content with whom and what you are right now and taking steps toward your future will help you to find love more easily. We're all works in progress, not meant to be stagnant. If you want to move higher and be happier, you have to do something novel to break the rituals of the past. You can even write your own affirmations and guide yourself in creative visualizations and meditations.

Revision Exercise

Move slowly and gently with this exercise and be self-compassionate. It's okay to laugh too, as you are rewiring yourself with your own mirror neurons.

1. With soft music on, look into a mirror and make sure that there is some light shining in your eyes, preferably natural light.
2. Notice every detail about your eye color and any specks of gold, and peer into

them as if looking into your soul. (You're doing just that.)

3. Think of something you love about yourself or compliment something you like about one or more of your qualities.

4. Softly tell your image what you love about yourself.

5. Wait until you experience some sort of loving response, such as tears or a pervasive peace, come over you. Embrace this feeling. This is how you are meant to think of yourself and others—with kindness. Say "I love you" or "I respect you" to yourself, or whatever is comfortable and soothing. Believe it.

Continue speaking kindly and listen lovingly to your voice as you say the following or read your own. Your brain waves will thank you for it!

AFFIRMATION: *"I am attracting higher, healthier, and happier connections, beginning with myself. I simultaneously hold a space and place for others and myself with equanimity. I disconnect from people who cause me to feel badly. In doing so, I am inviting real friends, true relationships, and the love of my life to appear. I am opening up my mind, body, and spirit to harmonious, reciprocal relationships of all kinds and at higher levels. I am worthy of true love. I am attuned to myself and others and elevate into the fulfilled person I am meant to be. I am becoming who I want to attract."*

LIFE LIST

Below is the most important list in this book. There is far more to it than what appears. Don't read ahead. Write ten bullet points of what you don't want to attract. Then write ten bullet points of your *ideal mate*. Don't overthink it. Shallow or deep, these are the qualities, internally or externally, that you want in your ideal mate.

What I don't want in a mate	The ideal mate
1. LIAR	1. TRUSTWORTHY
2. THEIF	2. EVIRONMENTALIST
3. FAT	3. ACTIVE
4. INACTIVE	4. FUN DRINKER
5. ANGRY	5. FIT
6. HATERED	6. LOVES MOM
7. LITTERBUG	7. GOLFS
8. WASTEFUL	8. TRAVE LOVE
9. ANTI SOCIAL	9. ADVENTUROUS
10. ALCOHOLIC	10. FUNNY

Read your ideal mate list back to yourself, out loud. This is someone you know very well. I hope you immediately realized it is you. This is proof that you love yourself! Add more to this list as time goes by, and what you write will rewrite how and who you love.

I do this with clients who say they hate themselves or have a broken heart and feel unlovable or unworthy. Loving yourself isn't an esoteric or abstract concept. It's possible here and now. Your list is you! You're already the one you want to attract.

Congratulations!

You already learned narcissists secretly hate themselves but now you know codependents secretly love themselves! You do love you, and though there's more to learn and discern, be patient and gentle with yourself. You're realizing your true value and becoming stronger and more able to be authentic and to receive and give love wisely, fully, wholly, and harmoniously.

CHAPTER 6

You Are Valuable!

Many people overvalue what they are not
and undervalue what they are.

—Malcolm Forbes

Valuing Yourself

C odependents sometimes feel less valuable than others and treat themselves accordingly. This overtly shows up in people-pleasing and over-giving behaviors to compensate and makes them vulnerable to time stealers, chaos creators, and financial abusers. We've all heard that *love* of money is the root of all evil. However, some codependents hate how money has been used to control them, or they may use it covertly to control others. Was money ever used to control you, or did you use it as a way to keep people attached to you? Did you feel any helplessness or resentment concerning financial aspects in your early or adult relationships?

**Financial independence is one of the last things
a person considers in codependent recovery.
However, it's often the only thing holding them
hostage to unhealthy relationships.**

Financial lack is the main reason domestic violence victims stay with their aggressors. Widows, those who are grieving, or those who are in divorce recovery are easy prey for a user or abuser because of their extreme vulnerability. The user is like a buzzard flying over broken hearts. It's imperative you guard your heart and mind when you are going through any major life event so you won't become a target. A good person will be truly helpful with no agenda if they are sincere, but a user will act sincere and extract time, love, or money from you. Financial con-artistry is the easiest trait to recognize if you educate yourself and learn to extricate yourself.

Becoming financially independent gives options to create exit strategies or the ability to enter your best life going forward. Many codependents say, "I've stayed because I had no place to go." This is a sad truth, but if they had money, they could go anywhere, anytime they wanted. Attaining financial independence and improving value through education, networking, or finding ways to use your talents prosperously will propel you upward. If you are in one of these relationships, get help if you need it. I was many years ago, and I assure you that you can get out and get on with a wonderful life as soon as you make the decision to be financially independent. Being self-sufficient is liberating and gives you choices.

Financial abuse can come about by a codependent's compulsion to over-give. This is where clients push back the most in therapy. They rebel against the belief they may be giving to relieve their own anxiety or guilt. They don't want to stop giving and become anxious when it's suggested they suspend over-giving while in recovery. Motive is everything when it comes to giving anything. You have to seek the reasons you are giving to others, particularly if it is depriving you in any way. As a natural-born giver, it makes sense if you see something you think someone would love, and you want to give it to them. I love to do this and have not stopped by any means, but I make sure it is within my means. It's fine to give, but if you overdo it, you may be motivated by people-pleasing or a desire to be liked. A friend pointed out to me that her family liked me without bringing them anything, and my generosity was appreciated but not necessary. It lifted a burden and relieved anxious giving.

It's also good to know many people feel obligated to return a favor or gift to you. Someone else told me he felt guilty when people gave to him because he hated to shop and despised feeling obligated to reciprocate. I didn't realize I was making him anxious or to feel pressure, which is the last thing any codependent wants to do to someone. This was a real friend to tell me this, and he noticed I was an over-giver to many others who didn't appreciate or reciprocate the kindness. Gifts were my way of showing affection and attention and helped me to be happier. A study on prosocial spending and happiness was performed with adolescents and the finding was that those who were more generous were happier. However, the money they gave away was given to them by the researchers. They had to receive to give and could keep it or give it away by choice. Those who kept it felt ashamed, and it released cortisol, a stress hormone. Being charitable or generous relieved negativity reactivity for this sample of students.[1]

I looked at my bank statements and was shocked at how much I spent on others compared to myself. It was time to go through over-giving withdrawals. The symptoms were phantom guilt and feeling stingy, but balance was necessary in my checkbook and my life. Checking motives before writing a check is something I diligently practice, and I enjoy the balance of generosity and the cycle of reciprocal giving and receiving. It is a financially comfortable and capable reality.

The Balance Sheet of Self-Valuation

There are two extremes of codependent financial abuse. One extreme is codependents with money or a heart bigger than their wallet who fund everyone else's needs or desires. The other is usually trapped in unhealthy relationships because they don't have enough money to leave. Codependents believe if they give enough, or do enough, the people they do it for will love them more and treat them with more respect. They actually respect you less and only come around when they need you or to butter you up occasionally so when they do need you, it won't be so obvious. Balance requires awareness of patterns in others and self-awareness of your reactions to them. There is a test to determine whether or not someone is using you. If someone asks you to do something that you would never ask anyone else to do, don't do it. Just because you don't use people, doesn't mean they won't use you.

"Dee" was constantly bailing roommates out of jail, cosigning loans, and paying everyone's rent. She was the quintessential "good girl." Her dream was to transfer to a major city where her company had a branch but said she couldn't afford it. We did the math and discovered the thousands she spent on roommates would have more than paid for relocation.

She cried, "I don't feel heard! My friends would do this for me! They promised to pay me back." They never did.

She was deceiving herself about what love was. She lacked insight on how damaged she was becoming by these "friends." In her divorce, she signed over everything she was legally entitled to from her ex-husband because she didn't want to be perceived as greedy. Her parents had conditioned her to believe she was "selfish" and "greedy." She was the opposite of these things. She was subconsciously motivated to over-give from a need to feel loved. Love is not a commodity to be traded; it is priceless. She sacrificed her happiness and became extremely depressed, not understanding why other people didn't understand her and help her.

I assured her that I understood her. I had been her at one time in my youth and had done the same thing in divorce. Some codependents, like Dee and me, have lost homes, cars, careers, and cash by thinking it was better to give than to receive. I knew how to help Dee, but she was resistant to hearing that she could follow her dreams by detaching from her nightmarish "friends," and sadly, she was so resistant, it may take many more years before she hears her own cries for help. She had a high tolerance for sociopathic friends because one of her parents had been incarcerated, and this was "normal" for her. They projected their greed onto her. By bailing her friends out of jail, she was subconsciously attempting to feel better about not being able to bail her parents out of their situation, which had left her feeling abandoned.

We refer to sociopathic people as "reptilian" or cold-blooded. The reptilian part of the human brain seeks instant gratification without empathy or regard for others. Selfish people use people; that's what they do. Again, ask if you would go to someone to bail you out of something you did wrong. You probably wouldn't. Note anything else you do to financially benefit others to your detriment. Your need to rescue may be drowning you in debt. Charity cases you support might make you one yourself.

Users have complex ways of increasing guilt while decreasing your assets. They use sympathy to coerce you with chaotic, sad stories. They may not ask you for anything, but you find yourself compelled to give or lend to them. They never take responsibility when they can't return the favor or money, and layers of resentment and contempt build. The person who owes you stays away from you unless they need you again, but this cycle can stop. Your money trail may lead you to see where your heartstrings are being tugged. Ask yourself:

- Does this person only call when they want something?
- Do I feel guilty or have emotional reactivity until I give to them?

- Do they thank me or show appreciation?
- Does this happen repeatedly with the same person or people?
- Do I feel used?

One friend told me, "It makes me sick to my stomach when certain names come up on my phone. I know they want something, and I'm not the family ATM." However, he continues to send them money and gifts. He's a good man but is also a fear-filled person, and feeling false guilt for his success, he gives from his finances. As he ages, he could see the well run dry if he continues to draw from it in his later years.

Don't ignore physical symptoms like getting sick when you see a name on your caller ID. Your pounding heart or shaking hands may be telling you something through your vagus nerve. If you feel anxious, coerced, or obligated, this is not healthy giving. To find balance, you may have to temporarily suspend giving and set better boundaries.

The Gratitude Sandwich Script for Saying No

It's nearly impossible for a codependent to just say no, but I devised a way for myself, and others love how it works for them too. I call it the gratitude sandwich. If someone asks me to do something or give something beyond my ability, I calm my vagus nerve.

Then I say, "Thank you for thinking I am able to do this for you, but I am overextended right now and have to decline. I couldn't do my best for you and thank you for understanding."

The implied but never spoken "no" is sandwiched between expressions of gratitude, which will relieve guilt for you and convey a kind way to say no to others.

Codependents can't easily accept the concept of "No is a complete sentence." It is too jolting when coming out of years of conditioning. The gratitude sandwich is a great way to segue from saying yes to everything to being authentic in saying no. The beauty of it is that it's true and you never have to actually say the word *no*. You have been overloaded, and you won't do a good job if you're resentful or overstressed.

Notice I didn't say, "I hope you understand," but rather, "Thank you for understanding." This has more power, is less apologetic, and is very diplomatic. End the discussion as politely as possible and don't allow anyone to hound or manipulate you. Users are very adept at telling you what you need to hear to make it sound as if giving to them was your idea. The word *conman* came from "confidence man." They gain your confidence, often by giving ingratiating gifts to you first. They may systematically set you up with flattery and sympathy. They know how to manipulate your soft heart to get your hard-earned money.

There is an adage, "No good deed goes unpunished." Become conscious of your motives, intentions, and expectations. If you expect praise, accolades, attention, or affection, you may be giving to get. Have others referred to you as a person who will give the shirt off your back, bend over backward to help, or give your last penny? If so, you may become shirtless, exhausted, penniless, or worse. Sincerely ask yourself why you do this. If the answer is "It makes me feel better," then notice how your finances look afterward. If you still have plenty, that's great. If you are left without something you really need or want, be aware of your emotional impulses. Get honest with yourself and see what is influencing you.

Undue Influence and True Affluence

You may be a current target or backup plan for someone's financial future and not know it. *Undue influence* is most often used as a legal term, but it is an emotional and stealthy process. It can be explained as the use or abuse of power or close relationship over another person to coerce, extort, frighten, pressure, or otherwise compromise their free-will decision making. It is the worst deceit, and it is often seen in elder abuse cases. The exchange of money for "friendship" or "love" is unconscionable. Those who are wealthy or have desirable assets are most at risk. Codependents are more vulnerable and are easier prey in situations like putting someone in your will, giving them money, or doing things that are not in your own best interest. The other person may be nice when they are trying to extract what they want from you, but will then turn on you after they get it. Don't sign anything until you know all the facts. Seek legal counsel before acting on someone's request that could potentially harm you or your heirs. I help victims of this in private practice and know many people personally who have suffered some form of isolation and control.

Beware of loneliness and who you let in your innermost circle as there may be hidden financial agendas.

Those who have little affluence are also targets for undue influence. Anyone who has been a "trophy" spouse will tell you the pedestal they were on was lonely and could be destroyed by the person who put them there. They were used to provide an image, and a trophy spouse is a conquest, though they are miserable. True affluence is being loved and feeling secure for who you are as a whole person, not solely based on financial assets or physical attributes. You won't be used by others seeking validation or admiration.

Personal Value Is Much More Than Money

There is a type of over-giver who is solely or mostly a money codependent. They feel strongly about being financially responsible for everyone in their circle of family or friends. They feel if something goes wrong, they have played a part in it, and they fix family problems by doing things like paying for the mistakes of others. Like Dee, their extreme generosity is taken advantage of by many people who purport to love them, and they are usually unaware of how they are being influenced and feel guilty about having so much, even though they worked hard to get what they have.

I was guilty of being "extremely generous" in order to feel better about myself. I didn't know that was the motivation at the time, but it was. One Christmas, I made seventeen key-lime pies, eight pans of lasagna, and thirty-six jars of jalapeno jelly for friends. Many of them were "orders" friends asked me to make. I was so proud they appreciated my cooking. My friend Leslie told me this wasn't necessary to do for everyone, and she helped me to rein in my giving after noticing how I was literally spending a great deal of time and money. She mentioned it was more important to make happy memories than to give beyond my means. Her honesty helped me see the light, quit rattling the pots and pans, and gave me time to reevaluate my motives.

Remember, there's a high price for low self-esteem. Many of you have come from a background like I did where you learned, "Don't go anywhere empty-handed." I still adhere to this tradition, but now I don't empty my bank account to do it. Does your gift giving have childhood messages of not feeling good enough unless you do more than enough? Does anyone admire a talent or skill you have and ask you to do things for them? How does it make you feel? Proud? Exhausted? Both? Think about how your finances can be used for you to seek codependent recovery or to enjoy your life, using your money wisely and happily, and write about it in your journal.

In ancient times, money was referred to as *talents*. Talents take time to develop. Time is precious, and you can't buy a second of it back. If someone could sell time, they would become the richest person on Earth. However, you can use your resources to move forward, or you may need an advocate to intervene for you. My music publisher called people who recorded our songs and didn't pay royalties. Songwriters need these agents as we are not generally good at asking people to pay us for what we love to do. The publisher always began the conversation by thanking them for liking the songs and then he asked what they did for a living. For example, if they would say, "I'm an accountant," he would ask, "Would you do my taxes for free?" They would say, "No!" He would then say his songwriters didn't write for free either.

It's okay to give a benefit performance or give art away, and entertainers love giving in this way. The camaraderie of rallying around a cause is wonderful and spontaneous, but it can't be continuous. You can't always sing for someone else's supper; you need to eat too. Adding value to your life by any method can help you to live better and give more purposefully. It may mean going back to school or finding a job. I returned to school at age forty-five and had to take out a student loan. You may have to suffer in the short term for a lifetime of happiness. Don't feel guilty about this as you may need money to reinvent yourself or for the inevitable rainy days we all have. Now I give from authenticity, not fear, obligation, or guilt. I am of more benefit to others when I have financial peace myself.

Divesting from the Past and Investing in Your Future

When I was eight, I was adamant about feeding the homeless in one particular shelter. My mother said if I wanted to do it, I had to use my money. Her father had set up an investment account for me, and Mom took me to the big blue bank and withdrew it all. We used it to make meals for the poor, and it felt wonderful. Before you find nobility in this, pause. How much does an eight-year-old know about money? Nothing! Though my family helped me do this later, that initial jolt set the tone for money codependency. I vividly remember the cold terrazzo floor and scary bank teller. I felt that if I wanted to help people, like Dee, I had to give it all because my mother said so. My grandfather's kindness may have accumulated into millions by now as he started it when I was born. I will never know why my mother did this, and when I asked about it, she denied remembering it. It wasn't a good message to give an eight-year-old.

I have given all I had to many people in my life with nothing to show for it, including talents, time, and finances. Reenactment was the culprit, but responsibility was the catalyst for change.

What is your first codependent money memory? Does it relate to you today? Do you feel fear or lack? Explore it, expose it, and write about it to see how your history may be what you are experiencing now. See if there were any money "mantras" you heard as a child. Telling children, "Put that back! We can't afford it!" creates money anxiety and feelings of unworthiness. Children don't understand money or have the vocabulary for it. It was years before I understood how psychological self-worth played a role in creating financial freedom.

Money and emotions are inextricably woven together. Money issues and debt are the number one reason that couples divorce. The stock market has a "Fear and Greed" index and uses emotional terms such as market "volatility," "collapse," and a "stable" economy. The number one reason we seek employment is for security, and yet, hardly any job posts the wage or salary, and few people ask about it during job interviews. This is very true of a codependent. The most successful people in life have no fear about discussing finances, and though it may seem arrogant to some, it is really self-confidence and self-care. The wealthy are more able to give to those in need than those impoverished or in debt.

Codependents often give to greedy and ungrateful people. Divest from these people and invest in yourself. By doing so, you'll be able to give free from fear. Learning about finances and how your emotions may be tied to them in codependent or healthy ways are vital for emotional stability. As a giver, you need to understand how your handling of money is directly reflected in how you are investing in yourself while you give to others.

Money Mentors for
Financial Responsibility

My first money mentor was Gene Simmons. He balanced generosity and frugality and was and is a brilliant businessman. I asked Gene how he handled money, and he said, "Money is simple. Money in. Money out. Keep it balanced. If you live a little below your means and invest, you'll never go broke." Applying this later in life was one of many ways I gained self-worth after I exited an abusive marriage. My ex would spend twice what we had and could rack up debt like a teenager with carte blanche privileges to my credit card as his credit was bad.

He took a copy of our deed, whited my name out, and recopied it as if he was the sole owner of our home and didn't tell me. He borrowed fifty thousand dollars from a farmer's bank in Tennessee, and they didn't bother to drive to the county clerk to get the real deed. Then he filed bankruptcy on the bank and the Internal Revenue Service, also not telling me. When the bank called and asked me to come in and sign the loan, I was shocked and refused, and I had to sell my beautiful farm to pay the tax debt.

When I signed the sale papers to pay the IRS, I was sobbing, and he was smiling. I asked him how he could be so sinister, and his reply was bone-chilling: "Now you have no place to go!" I silently vowed to use my master's degree and do whatever it took to find a way to get away. I couldn't bear this or the accumulation of other financial malfeasances. The sale of that farm was my codependent rock bottom. I sought more help and advice, and the kindest of all was the woman from the title company. She called the day after the sale of the farm. She saw my pain and said many women had lost their homes to men like this, but unlike me, they didn't have enough equity and still owed the IRS. I will never forget her kind words, "Darlin', you've lost your home, but you are debt free and free to leave this man. Other women aren't so fortunate. They lose their homes and still owe the IRS."

Kindness and mentoring can come from the oddest, but best, places. If strangers notice your despair, you certainly should. I was financially tormented in many ways, but my mother overspent while my father worked himself to death. I was so glad my IRS attorney told me to leave my husband as well, and though it took a few years and other mistakes along the way, I have financial peace and, more important, prosperity of spirit.

I often direct clients to educate themselves by following financial professionals' advice. I encourage them to choose the person who resonates with them. Most of the professionals say to stay out of debt for financial freedom. The number one reason couples split is because of money issues. Financial infidelity can be more detrimental to your future than you might realize. Think of how many people you know that stay in toxic relationships for financial reasons.

An indirect money mentor for those trapped in abusive or codependent relationships is the film, *What's Love Got to Do with It?* Tina Turner left her abusive husband, Ike, with less than forty cents in her pocket. She moved in with her former background singer who taught her how to meditate. She rebuilt her life by using her talents anywhere she could find work. She pursued her happiness by divesting from the past and investing in her future through her talents. Tina moved with her wonderful new husband to Switzerland: a country known for neutrality and peace. Her meditation music is another talent she used to help others.

You don't have to stop helping other people; you need to know how to do it and retain your well-being too. It's okay to give yourself permission to enjoy your life. Take a moment to journal revelations about value and money mentoring that you have received. Are you applying it or denying it? If you don't have a mentor, find one. Financial security and peace are essential to personal freedom.

The Synergy of Philanthropy

When you divest yourself from users and losers and invest in self-worth, the change will yield miraculous returns. You can give in new ways too. Finding organizations and contributing to causes you believe in are ways of investing in others with passion and purpose. When you change your thoughts about a constant, simultaneous flow of receiving and giving instead of only giving, you can change your life for the better. You can enjoy your resources and join with others in philanthropic endeavors. Socialization and money also go hand in hand, and it's so much more than a handout that may be potentially hazardous.

"Claudia" came to me brokenhearted after so many people had taken advantage of her. She was very resistant to suspend helping others for a while. The next week she came to see me, she admitted she put herself in peril by picking up a person who was homeless. She bought this person a cell phone, was stalked, and they nearly stole her car. Claudia related she grew up in poverty and felt guilty every time she noticed someone suffering. She couldn't discern dangerous people from safe ones, as she grew up where danger was the norm. It was proposed that whenever she felt compelled to give, to do so through organizations equipped to supply phones, food, and other necessities. She was relieved she didn't have to stop giving but could do so in a way that provided safety. We worked to help her understand her false guilt and compulsion to give when she was in need herself.

Many Claudias have come through my door, and I know what it feels like to be one. They all love understanding that philanthropy isn't codependency. It is joining forces and resources with others of like mind for causes you believe in, and together you become synergistic agents of change. When your financial life is balanced, you can enjoy centered and grounded healthy living and giving.

Revision Exercise

Visualization for Elevation of Your Value

1. See someone asking you to give something you don't want to give but you know you will feel guilty or fearful if you don't.
2. Visualize yourself challenging them to find creative ways to help themselves. If this isn't possible, see yourself refusing, then immediately see them figuring out another way. (Hint: selfish people always have a backup plan. It doesn't have to be you anymore.)
3. Now visualize doing something you enjoy, living and doing what you want to do with your life. Envision being in a community of like-minded people energized with helping others in synergistic ways. Feel the peace? This is true affluence.

AFFIRMATION: *I pay attention to how I feel when spending money, time, or talents. I value myself. I magnify my generosity through the synergy of philanthropy. I can live and give well with authentic intentions. I divest myself of those who influence me with fear. I invest in my true worth with faith.*

LIFE LIST

On the left, write how you need to *divest* from one-sided giving. Note the messages you received during childhood under each one. On the right side, note practical ways to *invest* in yourself. Write messages of adult value as in the example that follows.

Divest	Invest
1. Over-giving to others	1. Getting an investment account
2. Fear of rejection	2. Being loved for who I am, not what I have
3.	3.
4.	4.
5.	5.
6.	6.
7.	7.
8.	8.
9.	9.
10.	10.

CHAPTER 7

Nurturing Your Unique Spiritual Nature

Scientists are pinpointing the brain regions
that become active when one feels fusion with a
higher power, such as God. Perhaps this
brain region is also involved in love.

—Helen Fisher

The Power of Your Spiritual Life

You are well aware by now of the scientific proof that your brain is wired for love and acceptance, and this can emanate from many sources. Even if you don't believe in God or a higher power, there is a force of nature spurring you on to love and be loved. Spirituality is a sticky subject to some, so with great respect to everyone, we will take a gentle but powerful journey to explore another origin of codependency and another way to heal it. You may feel trepidation questioning your beliefs as it is instilled in many of us not to do this. However, exploring how your beliefs may be infiltrating codependent behaviors may shed some light. Spiritual connections contain valuable information, and only you can decide what to do with any revelations. Even if you're an atheist or a person of science, you have some kind of moral code or compass. This chapter is not about changing your beliefs, as they are sacred to you.

It is to see if and how your beliefs may have contributed to codependency and what may guide you out of them. Cognitive shifting and spiritual lifting may occur if you ask your spirit to connect to something greater than yourself, and if you are uncomfortable with it, you can modify this chapter to fit in your mold. No two people believe exactly the same thing, though they may not dare voice it. This could particularly be true with codependency. If you feel vague underpinnings of unworthiness, perhaps doctrine or cultural principles or beliefs are the root. Many beliefs have a system of "paying" or making restitution for misdeeds. When we make mistakes, we want to fix them immediately. Guilt is there for a reason, and when we make amends, there is a sense of freedom. However, feelings of false guilt or imposed shame hold us captive, and many codependents laboriously attempt to run on the toxic fumes of these impostors.

Codependents can go too far in the struggle to compensate or eradicate guilt. When is enough, enough? How much or how long do you have to keep paying for your perceived mistakes or misdeeds? Self-punishing or ruminating thoughts, such as *I'm a bad person,* are unworthiness in which shame thrives and independence dies. You are enslaved by beliefs if you make decisions based on feelings of inadequacy, poverty, a victim mentality, or unworthiness. You can't work your way to feeling worthiness or relieve guilt with rituals to return to "holiness." Attempts to pay for alleged transgressions can cause codependent regression. Humiliation is not humility or humbleness, and it sure won't lead you to wholeness.

When actions or decisions are guilt based, choices you make could be further self-punishing behaviors, and you may not be aware of them. They may feel like "the right thing to do," or you may hear yourself saying, "I don't want to be a burden to anyone." Because it is shame based, the person seeking relief may never know how much punishment fits the "crime." That never-enough feeling is difficult to dissuade. Note any ways your religious background taught you to "pay" for misdeeds and how this invades other areas of your life or defines any conflicting factors.

I was born to a Catholic mother who dabbled heavily in metaphysics. She was a first-generation Italian American. My father was a Methodist, from the deep South, who seldom attended church but quietly read his Bible every night. Dad quit going to church because his family was in church when his brother called the preacher, asking him to send them home because he was suicidal. The pastor preached his sermon and never told them. When they got home, they found him deceased by his own hand. Though my father didn't attend church anymore, he did believe in God, just not in the same way as the men who talked about him.

Both sides of my family thought the other side was going to hell. I went to an Episcopal preparatory school with cohorts of all faiths, and the school required us to take world religion classes. I saw more similarities than differences in all the beliefs. Most are love based and encourage generosity. Most use bells to worship, and all incorporate some sort of high moral code. Ceremonies for births, weddings, and funerals are pervasive in most all beliefs.

It's the various practices of alleviating guilt that are significant to codependent recovery. Guilt fuels the self-limiting belief. Taking on the false guilt or over-responsibility of others is more self-denial and an attempt to recompense some vague need to make something right when you didn't do anything wrong. The weight of guilt for self and others hinders the ability to feel happiness. Your body, mind, and spirit are not built for guilt. Guilt is a crushing force, and when severe, it can cause suicidal ideations or inconsolable emotional pain.

When I was a child, I had to confess my sins for the first time. I was only eight, a pretty good kid, and didn't have many "sins." I rehearsed three "sins" for the priest:

1. I talked back to my mother.
2. I hit my brother.
3. I had an impure thought.

I had committed none of these things. I felt guilty for not feeling guilty, so I had to come up with something! It never occurred to me that lying to a priest was a sin. Wearing a white dress and veil, I sat in that scary dark box and confessed things I didn't do and did my penance outside in the cathedral. What a revelation of a codependent conditioning! Many adult Catholics have shared with me that they did the same thing. It's humorous now, but when you're a child, you take it seriously if you're a people-pleaser, and you have to make up lies to comply with a ceremony. Maybe this is where the little white lies saying came from; I was dressed, head to toe, in white lace.

This is not to pick on any one religion. In my childhood home, it was an eclectic belief system and very difficult for me to adapt to with any sense of truth. By the time I was twelve, I had broken my nose, collar bone, arm, and leg. Confined to a wheelchair for over a year, I asked my mother why so many accidents happened to me, and she said it must be karma. She explained I had probably broken people's bones in a past life, and this was my debt. I will never forget the feeling of that moment. Wow! Not only was I guilty in this life, but I was also in past ones. Didn't I have plenty to handle in this life?

Check to see if your faith upbringing caused you to feel fear, shame, or a false sense of responsibility. Once you do that, you can rewire impairing beliefs. You may have done this as a child by rebellion against your family of origin's faith or by finding ways to compensate for the skewed reality in the context of spirituality. Journaling about this can set your spirit free.

When I was in a wheelchair, teaching myself to play piano eased the boredom and also the guilt because it was an accomplishment. Teaching myself to play an instrument was early meditation, though I wasn't aware of it. Later in life, I had a cowboy music ministry and wrote songs both in the secular and gospel genre. After my second divorce, a woman in church said, "No one will want you to sing now that you're divorced again." She had been married twice but had laid on me judgment, guilt, and little compassion. I quit singing that day, and ten years later I sang for the first time in public at a domestic violence benefit and loved the irony and symmetry of it. In retrospect, I was in a cowboy ministry because my ex wanted me to project his Texas image, and when I had a revelation that this ministry was built on codependence, it was time to exit. Many cowboy pastors, in addition to regular ones, knew I was physically and financially abused by this man. When I asked for help, I heard the same version of the "Obey. Stay. Pray" message. There's an old saying that guilt is the gift that keeps giving, and it was time for me to be relieved of it.

I quit the music industry, became a counselor, and now help people of all faiths, cultures, and belief systems without judgment or any agenda. It was and is an authentic calling. Seeking your personal spiritual truth is essential for your recovery as well as for accepting the beliefs of others. Controlling codependents sometimes feel the burning desire to convert everyone to their faith and in doing so chase others away. Beliefs are intensely personal, and the more you try to change someone, the more they may push away. I don't share my full beliefs with others, but I always encourage others to seek their truth. We are all seeking asylum from suffering, be it guilt, fear, or loneliness. We are all reaching for fulfillment, meaning, and purpose.

Seek your spiritual truth with diligence, and you will not have to impose your beliefs on others, nor will you be influenced to believe something that doesn't sit right with you. Believing what is true for you may raise the vibration of all those around you. Dare to explore your spiritual life authentically and fearlessly. Being scared neglects the sacred and may keep you trapped in a system that doesn't serve you or the people around you.

Servanthood Versus Servitude

Being *of service* is servanthood, is voluntary, and is the opposite of being *in servitude* that is inflicted by the demands of others. Codependents struggle with this blurred semantic. It is fine to serve, but you must have a reserve to do it well. Understanding you deserve to have a good life may help you keep a picture of the word *DE-Serve* in mind. It will lift your spirit to help those you really want to serve and not the ones you feel you *have* to serve with your time, talent, or finances.

Cultures have long intertwined money and faith. Compassionate giving does relieve the suffering of others, and that's what higher giving is all about. However, it should not cause you to suffer immensely or become poor yourself. I've had so many people come to me for help who were financially ravaged from giving to a church or organization who took their time, talent, and money with little gratitude or restitution. When the supply runs dry, they are rejected—which was what they were trying to avoid by their giving. I was one of these people, and I understand the dynamic. It makes you feel accepted and appreciated for a while but tossed aside if you have nothing left to give. This is the same use-you-lose-you cycle that occurs in narcissistic abuse.

A long time ago, I joined a church, was in the choir, and felt good about myself until an arduous fundraising campaign. I gave sentimental, valuable items to the auction because we were told it would bless us if we did. Right there, I was off-kilter and vulnerable in my giving. Because my ex had driven us so deeply into debt and loss, I would have done anything to relieve the financial pressure. For several nights, they told the congregation, "You are blessed to be a blessing." As I was new to this type of flamboyant faith, so vastly different from reverential Catholicism, I placed items on the altar worth thousands that sold for forty-one dollars. I felt more guilt as most of these possessions were irreplaceable gifts from family and friends.

Later, I recognized and reframed the losses and chalked this up to experience to bring wisdom first to myself and now to others. I learned not to give through coercion or empty promises of great reward. It hurt the people who gave me these gifts when I told them, and when I confessed, it was a good thing because it relieved the real guilt, not the one imposed on me. My real friends and family were supportive as they knew my heart was in the right place, but my wallet was not. From private deep study and soul searching, I deduced if I wasn't giving cheerfully, I was giving out of coercion and undue influence. I needed to suspend giving and check my motivations and intentions while being sure I wasn't acting out of obligation or guilt.

Recognize anything in your faith or family system operating in your financial life. To get their children to eat vegetables, many parents say, "There are children starving all over the world, and you're lucky to have food on your plate; now eat it!" That's way too much guilt to place on a child, and no wonder as adults some of us may have an aversion to vegetables or we overeat. We may feel guilty if we don't clean our plate. Guilt is an appetite suppressant, and gut reactivity, along with other vital organs, can come from the vagus nerve. If you're a parent, use guilt as a motivator sparingly because it creates a sense of unworthiness or disingenuous, accomplishment-driven behaviors.

When you see the messages of the past infiltrating your present, you'll learn to give as an act of love and not coerced codependence. It will be conscious, gracious, fearless, and genuine generosity. It doesn't detract from previous generosity to question the past; it stimulates happiness when you see where you gave by exercising freedom of choice and compare it to times of obligation or fearful giving from religious ritual. If science is more palatable to you than religion, there's empirical evidence to support why giving freely makes us feel better.

> Because the need for autonomy is satisfied when people feel that their actions are freely chosen, the emotional benefits of prosocial spending should be stronger when people have a choice about whether to give. In one study, participants inside a scanner exhibited stronger activation in reward areas of the brain when they freely donated to a local charity compared with when they were required to make a donation.[1]

There is a more energizing way to think of giving, and that is bestowal. Bestowals are gifts that are mutually honoring. You won't feel taken for granted or become resentful, as this kind of giving is meant to produce joy, not sorrow or worry. Creating your own spiritual messages can lead you out of guilt-driven codependent giving into authentic bestowing.

Individuation: How Carl Jung's Concept Applies to You

You may be experiencing residual resistance or feel your spirituality is being attacked, and this is not the intent. If you're angry with this subject being approached, it may be that someone hurt you with religion or you find hypocrisy in it. The discomfort, irritation, or agitation are there for a reason. Finding out why may expose hidden spiritual roots of codependence. These examined beliefs may create new thoughts so you can act accordingly, liberated and independent from a new perspective.

A father of psychiatry, Carl Jung, did extensive work on what he termed "individuation." Part of this process incorporated personal spiritual beliefs. He studied many different faiths and developed theories on the importance of an individual's beliefs and how faith was essential to the person and the collective consciousness. As he lived in the time of the Holocaust and was of Jewish descent, this made perfect sense. In his therapeutic work, Jung often used mandalas which are circular patterned works of art. These are incorporated as mindfulness and self-exploration in recovery settings today. Jung shared his beliefs but didn't force them on others. He encouraged others to forge their spiritual path and not blindly walk on a culturally imposed one. He didn't want to deprive anyone of their faith or beliefs.

> We do not sufficiently distinguish between Individualism and Individuation. Individualism means deliberately stressing and giving prominence to some supposed peculiarity rather than to collective considerations and obligations. But Individuation means precisely the better and more complete fulfilment of the collective qualities of the human being, since adequate consideration of the peculiarity of the individual is more conducive to better social achievement than when the peculiarity is neglected or suppressed.[2]

This means the more you understand and act on the beliefs you discover yourself, the greater you can be of service to others and vice versa. Many people fear they will go to the dark side if they delve in other beliefs, and if you do, you can come back to your light at any time. It is your process, and for a codependent, this may hold some residual fears. Fear is one of the darkest forces. Jung often asked if we don't embrace our entire self, the darkness and light, how will we know who we are and what our purpose is? We can be taken offtrack by ignoring ourselves, which could be directly interpreted as self-ignorance. Ignorance of your own dark fears may be holding you hostage.

Jung exposed and expounded the importance of knowing our shadow selves, which are repressed characteristics. When you keep your shadow self in the light and become self-aware, you can no longer be set up or brought down by it. Codependent conditioning won't sneak up behind you, and this may mean acknowledging that you may give from fear of abandonment or judgment, not genuine generosity. When we fearfully give from ego, we're not connecting with others spiritually. When we give freely and fearlessly from our spirits, we forgo the ego, and miracles and synchronicities appear. Happiness happens, and you'll be better able to find your individual healing and guiding force.

The word *namaste* translates as, "The divine consciousness in me acknowledges the divine consciousness in you." It interconnects us. Jung dove deep into the oneness of people, and you are part of the collective consciousness, even if you are unaware of it. Einstein was right about how we all breathe the same air in one rotation of the Earth. It only took ninety days for Covid-19 to threaten the entire planet. We are connected and affected by one another now and in the future.

The more you model codependency to those around you, the more you're exhibiting this to generations who follow, and it will not serve anyone well to continue this tradition. Yes, we really do need to give to one another, as greed in society is getting out of hand. However, you can only do so much with what you have on hand.

Many codependents are great operating from some version of the Golden Rule that tells us to do for others as we would have them do for us. You understand this concept but only the side that says to do for others. If you begin doing for yourself as you do for others or allow others to do for you, such as learning to ask for help when you need it, you'll find a greater and more powerful benefit for all. It's gracious to accept acts of kindness, as others want to bless you and don't want to be deprived of helping you. Finding other codependent types for support in this area helps. Even Mother Teresa had to ask for resources and is a prime example of how you can't go it alone when you give. It is psychologically, physically, and spiritually rewarding to look at how and why you give, and if it needs changing or tweaking, use your mind to enhance your recovery.

Rationality and Spirituality

Albert Ellis, a mental health pioneer, created Rational Emotive Behavior Therapy (REBT).[3] He believed people were neurotic because they were doing what they *should* do, *ought* to do, or *must* do without question as a result of enculturation. Ellis labeled this, "The Tyranny of Shoulds and Oughts" and referred to it as "*Mus*turbation," believing we *must* do something because that's the way "they" have done it for centuries. Who are "they"?

Rationality is an impetus for reconditioning as it liberates your spirit from antiquated tradition, thereby squelching neurosis. Expressing true desires will lead you to seek fulfillment, unfettered by self-conceptions of unworthiness. When codependents say, "I'm used to being treated like this," they are expressing conditioning. You have become "used to" external forces of sublimation, and this is not something you want because it will cause you to feel used. Silencing personal fulfillment is passing judgment on ourselves by thinking we don't deserve as much as others. Repression of needs can stymie or break the spirit. In a positive sense, pausing to occasionally silence ourselves is an effectual tool of meditation. Being silenced by someone else is ineffective and keeps you attached to their beliefs and leaves no room for you to achieve individuation. If someone or something is silencing you, find your voice and make choices through your rationality and personal ideas about spirituality. Combined, this expedites insights and foresight without judging yourself or others.

I had a dear, departed friend, Hiroshi Tagami, who would get upset if he heard anyone judging others. He was a revered Hawaiian artist and refused to judge art shows because he didn't believe personal expression should be judged. If he heard me or anyone being judgmental, he would say, "May they all be so perfect as us." Ouch and thank you, Hiroshi! The truth heals, and his message has been a guide long after his passing. His meditation practice brought mine to a heightened sense of universal kindness.

Removing Blockages Through Meditation

My father taught me meditation and self-hypnosis in my teens, and his biofeedback equipment was fascinating. The machine immediately reacted to how thoughts affected my body. Science and spirit are not so far apart as you might think. When I neglect to meditate, I feel a heaviness of spirit, and my thoughts spiral from an accumulation of unprocessed negative emotions, words, or actions. As a therapist, it's essential to keep myself cleansed and buffered from negative things I take in all day, and it is the same for you to recover from codependency. Blockages to personal growth may occur without some sort of meditation or mindfulness practice. Meditation expedites codependent healing, and though it sounds mystical, it is practical because it works, and science has proven this on many levels.

Mindfulness is another form of being self-aware and present, but it is a foreign concept to codependents who live in a constant state of busyness. Mindfulness is really effortless mindlessness. In moments of doing "nothing" and being present, momentum occurs. You may still be resistant to joining your conscious and subconscious brain waves, but once you do, you'll find clarity and inner direction leading you to a happier life.

Connecting with Spirit Through Nature

If spirituality continues to turn you off, perhaps nature will serve as your guide. Walking quietly in nature, basking in the light and the shadows created by it, you realize you are part of it, and it is part of you. When you immerse yourself in a natural setting, the wind through the trees, the chirping birds, and your footsteps bring you closer to your core. Nature is a great teacher and powerful therapist. There are meaningful metaphors in nature, and its nurturing power is undeniable. Many cities have been incorporating green spaces to bring organic elements back to life from the concrete. It restores healthy air and mental clarity.

Notice the air you breathe, as it is the core of meditation and mindfulness practice. It will get you out of your head and into your spirit through the restorative power of nature. Fully attuned and grounded, barefoot if you like, be in nature and it will remind you that we are all interconnected to everyone and everything in the universe.

John Muir, a famed naturalist and known as the father of our national parks, was severely punished as a child for not adhering to the strict religious beliefs of his father. Scolded for his curiosity and love of nature, he could easily have allowed the lashings to deter his spirit, but he did not. Muir became one of the great preservationists and sought solace in nature. True interdependence can be found when you allow nature to be your teacher and take note of where you feel best in it. It may be in the mountains, near the water, or anywhere in between where you feel the most at peace with yourself.

At fourteen, I earned a SCUBA certification, and coral reefs became colorful cathedrals. Rays of light pierced the water, and I called them God's fingers. They were reaching from the skies of heaven into the sea, and I would swim into them to become enveloped in the ethereal, silent sanctuary. Like meditation, I focused on breathing and the upward drifting crystal bubbles. A regulator has a lovely sound and is your underwater life source. I marveled at the adaptation of creatures in the ocean, including me. No one could tell me what to do or who to be down there. I was purely, silently me. I worked hard, saved much, and traveled the world doing this. Meeting others from different cultures was another spiritual soaking. Connection is of far greater spiritual value than any tangible item.

Find nature that nurtures your spirit and seek its healing power. It is a great way to recharge from codependent crisis or compassion fatigue.

*En*lightening Your Stress Load

You may find yourself spiritually and mentally connected through grand architecture. Antoni Gaudi's La Sagrada Familia Cathedral in Spain doesn't have formal services but is a cathedral of the people still under construction, and it towers over Barcelona. It was conceived as an invitation to gather under an expansive interior inspired by nature. Translated as the "sacred family," it is a testament to how powerful it is when people, nature, and spirit combine. The light inside the building is colorful and the intricately constructed ceiling is made to look like giant trees. It opens the heart and mind as you have to tilt your head as far back as you can to see the arches at the top of the cathedral.

I went there with friends on Mother's Day and let go of much codependent conditioning. I'm so grateful for my friends, Michael and Danny, for sharing this space on this day when I decided to honor my mother, realizing she did the best she could with what she had to give. Hanging on to anger would disable me from joining with my friends in this spiritual "familyship." The cathedral had a section where silence was required for prayer and meditation. We partook in it and shared our individual experiences. Interdependence is supported by silent meditation: one with all. Finding like-spirited people and respecting one another's individuation is also a profoundly healing connection. Create or go to sacred spaces for yourself and invite others. Turn on healing music and listen to songs that uplift you.

Music ushers you into your subconscious, connected to all of creation. The word *Om* is translated as the sound of the universe. Omniscient, omnipresent, and omnipotent are derived from this word. If a song makes you sad, don't listen; if you feel good, listen often. Slow down and enjoy your own mind reflected in your spirit and share these songs of the heart with others. A recovered codependent can become an instrument of great healing for others once they learn the cadence and frequency that helps them remain in synch with themselves. Music combined with a steady meditation practice according to your belief system can attune the frequency of your life into better living and giving. No matter what your beliefs are, your brain is your most powerful weapon against codependent triggers.

The Commonality of Spirituality and Science

Attend and stay attuned to think about what you're thinking about. Your thoughts affect your spiritual life just as much as they do your emotional and physical life. You may have a hidden savior or messiah complex as some codependents do. Your beliefs become thoughts, then words and action. Thoughts and beliefs matter, and meditation and creative visualization change the brain. Many schools of thought concur with this as fact.

Jesus said, "As a man thinks in his heart, so is he."

Buddha said, "What you think you become."

Cognitive behavioral therapists say, "When you change your thoughts, you change your behaviors and life."

Scientists say, "What you think about changes your brain."

Paying attention to your thoughts and focusing on positive processing of your emotions increase the ability for learning and memory, and decrease the fight/flight/frozen reactivity of the amygdala, limbic system, and vagus nerve. Turning off your wandering "monkey brain" of anxious thoughts reduces depression and worry. Meditation can sometimes replace medication but check with your doctor first.[4]

The power of suggestion is stronger than you think. James Gordon at the Center for Mind Body Medicine[5] has an exercise that you should do before you proceed to the revision exercise; you can keep your eyes open. Below is a condensed adaption:

1. Pretend you are holding a big juicy lemon in your hand.

2. See yourself putting it on a cutting board while taking a knife and cutting it in half.

3. Smell the tangy, acidic citrus scent.

4. See yourself taking a big bite out of the lemon. A great big, juicy, sour bite!

5. Are you salivating?

Probably so, and this will teach you the power of your mind. You can retrain your brain and reduce codependent anxiety without dismissing your beliefs. Incorporating a meditative practice that suits you will help you enjoy a more peaceful, purposeful, and happier life.

There are many parts of your brain that work together to help you become what you think. With that in mind, focus on a new life of living and giving well, and your brain will set out to motivate your spirit and body to manifest it. It never fails unless you give too soon. Like exercise, it requires daily practice. Your mind will thank you for it, your life will change, and you can reprogram negative impulsivity simply by using your imagination and the power of suggestion.

Revision Exercise

Envision yourself in a position of abundance, giving lavishly and compassionately without fear. Regard yourself as a wise steward of your resources. Practicing this allows your spirit to lead you to how you really want to give. See yourself sharing peak experiences with your familyship or real family. If you don't have people like this in your life, imagine some, in detail. Notice how your body feels and any individuation experiences that may occur as you bravely branch out from the way you have been nurtured to give. Find your true nature, perhaps in nature, and apply this as a metaphor to think of new ways to independently and interdependently give from a place of peace. Composing these new thoughts in your journal will further enhance your healing.

AFFIRMATION: *I am developing sacred spiritual beliefs aligning with my true self and in an interdependent connection to others. I am worthy to receive and find fulfillment. I give according to promptings in my spirit and not out of fear, coercion, obligation, or guilt. I am an individual with beliefs that may be contrary to my past but are complementary to my future. I am able to give to others and receive from authentically conscious and collective sources with purpose and shared compassion.*

LIFE LIST

On the left, write how spiritual beliefs may have a role in your codependency. On the right, express what you desire that fulfills you personally, philanthropically, and authentically. Take time to reflect on covert conditioning and what you would like to feel and believe in the future.

Spiritual Codependent Conditioning	My Desired Spiritual Beliefs About Giving and Living
1. I must sacrificially give to feel worthy.	1. I am worthy and free from self-punishing guilt.
2.	2.
3.	3.
4.	4.
5.	5.
6.	6.
7.	7.
8.	8.
9.	9.

CHAPTER 8

Covert Codependents

The unexamined life is not worth living.

—Socrates

Are You One?
Uncover and Recover

C odependency, as you've learned, is a spectrum of extremes, but there are also subtle nuances of this personality type that present over an unexpected and broad array of characteristics. Though covert codependency is more difficult to detect, it is every bit as debilitating in the long term. Gaining a sense of worthiness through vocation can be accomplishment driven at the core. The codependents who "hide" in these categories may not be easy to spot as they are very adept at adapting. Their positions and careers may be honorable and praiseworthy. They may be shrouded behind white coats, uniforms, suits, costumes, or organizations with all the trappings of success and may be too busy to notice they're suffering until it's too late. You may not be one of them, but you will relate to all of them in some way.

People in these categories are not, by any means, all codependents. In fact, it may be completely the opposite. The difference is in the motives for success and the ability to enjoy life while caring for others. Healthy, successful people and covert codependents alike are often found in prestigious professions. They may be admired leaders, professionals, or volunteers. Some have exemplary talents, skills, or specialized training. The difference between the codependent and their healthy cohorts is their psyche. There is an invisible, incessant looping message of "I don't ever think I've ever done enough, so I have to prove myself and go above and beyond the call of duty all day every day." What we do isn't who we are.

We have all heard heroes say, "I was just doing my job. I don't feel like a hero at all." That isn't quite the way a codependent feels, but it's a similar frame of mind. A healthy hero knows when and how to rest, but a codependent never stops.

The covert codependent often works on overdrive, and if you didn't know better, they could pass for a narcissist. Narcissists also don't feel good enough, but they insist other people validate them without being deserving. They would embrace and take ownership of being called a hero. The covert codependent is the opposite, and they go overboard to validate and accommodate others while shying away from the hero role. They can also appear to be independent, flawless, fearless, calm, and happy on the surface, but underneath the façade brews a concoction of repressed anger, resentment, or pervasive sadness. These are but a few of the main ingredients of burnout. The categories here are not exhaustive, but they represent how codependency may occur invisibly and insidiously. It will also simplify how you may relate to these attributes so you can think about what you want to do to change.

You don't have to be a professional first responder to be a closet codependent. You may be the first responder in your family or circle of friends. If you are, it's imperative you practice self-care. When I was working full time and caring for my parents, I was surprised when I discovered an emergency room nurse knew my name. When I asked how she knew me, she said, "You're in this ER so often you're going to end up as a patient yourself." She also reminded me that when my parents were in the hospital, they were being cared for, and it was time that I could use to rest. It was as if I needed her permission to ask for help. I was grateful she pointed out my hypervigilance to be there every time a minor incident occurred. As a caregiver, I lived in self-imposed crisis and survival mode.

If you ever were to experience a crisis, and most of us do, who is there to help you? It's a good question to ask yourself before reading this chapter. If you have no one or very few in your life who would meet your needs in a crisis, you may qualify as a covert codependent. You may be leading others to believe you are their rock. Under enough pressure, a rock of any size will crumble. High-pressure positions are often where covert codependents are found. They are the ones who work tirelessly, but at some time in their life will be forced to self-care. This revelation usually comes through burnout or stress-related illnesses. Self-care is as difficult a thing for the overextended professional or volunteer as it may be for you. Let's pull back the covers on the lives of these codependents and take note of what advice or support you would give them about self-care. It's exactly what you probably need to do too. Codependent, it's time to heal thyself!

Healthcare Professionals

Doctors are often touted as being callous and criticized for their lack of bedside manner, and there are some like this. However, many doctors work within a corporate clinical system of having to see one patient every fifteen minutes or less. They are inundated with health complaints and often have to deliver horrific news to people and then are instantly forced to make notes about it in a computer, which is fragmenting. They witness many patients pass away, helpless to save them despite their training. Hospice nurses, emergency room doctors, and anyone in a high-stress area of healthcare are particularly at risk for burnout, and they receive little empathy.

A friend of mine is a thyroid physician and professor at a university. He is a philanthropic man who performs pro-bono surgeries in remote jungles. He would not want to be recognized for this or considered a hero. One day I saw him for a lump in my neck. He was surprised when he opened the door and saw me there as a patient. He sat down, sighed, and tears welled up in his eyes. He said, "I'm grateful it's you because I have to take a break. I just told four people back-to-back they're dying. It breaks my heart, and I have to be strong for them." He was suffering and needed someone to listen. I couldn't fix anything, but I could listen, and having compassion doesn't require effort. It may be good for some of you to know that your doctor may not be cold at all, but they are trained to regulate their emotions. This type of repression over time can cause them to become ill.

Doctors and nurses alike are exposed to intense pain and fear from their patients. They may become irritable or overworked, and many choose to become closet drinkers or pill poppers from the constant negative input. No one comes to see them when they are well, and few patients thank their doctors for helping them to become well. Does this sound like your life? Are you helping people, in your professional or personal life, who only call when they need you? Thankless jobs, no matter what the pay scale, are often where coverts shine, but it can harm them long term.

An X-ray technician sits in a dark room most of the day and never knows what kind of injuries they may encounter. The screaming of someone in agony takes a heavy toll on the mind. Any type of diagnostic testing professional can feel fear and pain but can't show it. They're not allowed to discuss anything with a patient. This can hurt them as much as it does the person they're serving. Double compassion fatigue, when a healthcare worker has their own life stress to deal with in addition to their practice, is common in the healthcare profession.

I will never forget shopping with my father in three major grocery stores for the only brand of canned tuna packed in olive oil my mother would accept. When we had exhausted our efforts, I told Dad we would have to buy another brand. In the middle of the grocery aisle, he broke down sobbing. He was in his seventies, and because of my mother's strokes, he had to do most of the shopping and errands in addition to his stressful psychiatric duties. He was overwhelmed with fear about how my demanding mother would react when we brought back the wrong brand. No one is exempt or immune from double compassion fatigue.

If you're a caregiver of any kind, you know exactly how exhausting this can be. Caregiver syndrome is serious and can cause physical, mental, and emotional complications. Respites or some form of pleasurable activity and social connection are necessary. Coverts often don't do this and feel guilt or shame if they ask for help. They may become afraid to leave their loved one for any length of time. If this goes on for months or years, it can result in dissociative states or many other negative emotional issues.

Therapists can also be coverts, and many of my colleagues, myself included, can become overwhelmed after a day of hearing the traumatic events in people's lives. We are the shock absorbers for people's emotional pain. Like the springs of an actual shock absorber, our resilience wears thin when we take on too many tough stories in rapid succession. We need to recoup and regroup, as everyone does. We do our best to serve those who need us, but it is imperative for us to take a break, or we will need therapy. Now you know why people make jokes about doctors playing golf. I hope my doctor and his staff are well rested. You need to take vacations and find respite—guilt free.

Do you relate to this kind of guilt? Do you ever feel anxious or hide your need for a break from those who need you? Have you ever longed to go for a short drive or on a long cruise or do self-care but have neglected to do it? The military mandates rest and relaxation (R & R). You can't be on guard or on call all the time.

Military and First Responders

At the time of writing this, over twenty-two United States military professionals commit suicide a day. Yes, a day! The stress of combat is more intense than your worst nightmare. The men and women who serve their countries witness atrocities. The phrase *war is hell* is valid. No one goes into the service thinking they will become a statistic, but service professionals have a dangerous duplicitous life cycle of "deploy then enjoy." They are deployed to war zones, then return home to resume "normalcy" and enjoy their lives after being "debriefed." Debriefing is very brief and usually done at times of extreme fatigue or immediately upon arrival home. Many of these men and women have witnessed friends pass away and experience survival guilt when coming home to their families. Each deployment reduces their ability to see life as something to be enjoyed. It can chip away their sense of safety with post-trauma reactivity.

The motto of the Marines is "Leave no man behind" along with "Semper Fi," which translates as "always faithful." These are wonderful sayings meant to keep unity and morale, but they are difficult to live up to when battles end with tragic loss. Their families notice a loss of their ability to feel happiness or enjoy life. They need help to process their trauma. Many are embarrassed or reluctant to open the wounds. Their secrecy causes covert suffering and dangerous isolation. Asking for help seems impossible for people who were once so strong and healthy.

First responders have a similar experience. They are called to horrific scenes, and the images may play over and over in their heads. Many never feel they have done enough to save a life or rescue someone. I see many of them, along with military members. These professions are full of valiantly brave but covert codependents who weren't prepared for the toll it would take on them to go into battle or to save lives. They often develop post-traumatic stress disorder (PTSD). Many don't process their pain or ignore it until it becomes an insurmountable emotional hurdle.

Many (but not all) first responders and military members tend to come from families of some sort of dysfunction or trauma. They reenact their past to gain mastery through service and rescuing. At some point, they need to have someone serve and rescue them from their memories. Their past can't go away, but it can be processed toward a better future by focusing on good things that happened when they were deployed. When they focus on what they have to live for, they think less about what they have lost and can dare to find happiness again.

Do you feel like you're being deployed or dispatched in your life by being of service to others? If so, take time to rest. If you continue to take on more than you can handle, a need to withdraw may overtake you. People who give help find it difficult to ask for it, but when they do, they are able to find a way to enjoy life again.

Service Professionals

Many flight attendants are a perfect example of a covert codependent. They may look like all they are doing is serving soda and snacks, but they are trained lifesavers. They're also hypervigilant to notice anyone who may compromise the safety of the flight. It's amazing to watch a flight attendant taking abuse from a passenger yet never lose their smile or ability to remain calm. Other service professionals such as nannies, day-care workers, housekeepers, restaurant employees, and concierges are also examples of covert codependents. When a bell rings at a hotel desk, the concierge will bend over backward to care for any odd demand with nonjudgmental discretion. You may have had this happen in your life when someone rings your front door or phone and asks you to immediately meet their needs. Think of other service professionals and how it feels to be ordered around with a smile on your face and a twinkle in your eye. It's not such a genuine feeling, is it?

Bartenders and servers may also fall into this category. They have to keep track of orders with a semblance of ease, or the tip they heavily rely on will reflect how the customer feels. Those serving customers who demand their full attention tend to be very irritable at the end of their workday. My father often said bartenders, hairdressers, therapists, and psychiatrists were all in the same business. People don't just come for a drink or a haircut, they tend to unload their personal life on service professionals.

Actors, Performers, Musicians, and Artists

There's a reason they call stories acted on a stage "plays." It is fun to pretend to be someone else. Many actors come into the profession to escape difficult childhoods. Every opening question on *Inside the Actor's Studio*[1] is about childhood trauma. We say entertainers "give" a performance and they do. Many do this for little or no pay. They want a break from their real life and to be in collaborative group to play. Irving Berlin's song says it best: "There's no people like show people, they smile when they are low."[2] As I used to be one of these, I know it's true. The stage, studio, or set is where codependent compartmentalization takes over, and the performer becomes a vehicle of entertaining others.

Actors, particularly females, are expected to be the perfect size and shape and remain ageless. Somewhere in between too fat or too skinny, a celebrity was the right size, and no one seemed to notice. Many develop eating disorders to please their audience. The same is true of being ageless, and no can be expected to retain their youth forever. How many Marilyn

Monroe–type tragedies do we need to see to show how seeking love from the masses to compensate for no lasting or close relationship can have devastating results? Celebrities attempt to stop time, push themselves to please an audience, and sadly, most of the time the audience turns on them, looking for a "fresh face." Suicide or accidental overdose often makes the headlines, but it happens with those who aren't famous too. Codependents often self-medicate from feelings of unworthiness no matter how much they accomplish. Have you felt this way, and if so, how has this played a role in your life and how can you exit putting on a show for others?

Countless performers, male and female, have been in abusive or codependent relationships. They endure public scrutiny and rejection, which further spirals them into lacking self-worth. You can probably think of many celebrity examples. They may look shiny on the outside, but they feel tarnished inside. After any public humiliation, they often go into hiding and reinvent themselves. If the new persona is authentic, they make their life better and lead others to happiness through their stories.

Can you relate to this in any roles you play in your life? Have you attempted to be a certain weight or keep up appearances out of fear of criticism? Have people turned on you no matter how perfectly you performed? It's good to be your personal best but not if you are externally motivated by what the other person wants. The desire to care for yourself must come from within, or it won't be sustainable. Perfectionism is a form of self-punishment or abuse. Pay attention to anything you do that might result in fear-based perfectionism.

In the studio in Nashville, we used to say, "The only thing wrong with perfect is it's not quite good enough." When I look back on this time in my life, I didn't realize I was a covert codependent, morphing myself into a country girl when this was far from the reality of my beach raising. Playing roles to receive love and attention can cause a disconnect from the true self. Think of ways you have done this in your life to garner attention you felt you desperately needed through achievement or success.

Applause, accolades, and awards are wonderful payoffs for performers, but they're fleeting. Think of how many entertainers you've seen on the news hospitalized from "exhaustion," which is a public relations term for burnout. All entertainers aren't necessarily codependent, but they do drive themselves to please, and it can prove to be an impossible task. They often isolate when they get out of the limelight. I have interviewed and worked around famous people most of my life, and there is a pervasive sense of feeling unworthy of such fame—or they say they were "just lucky." Like a reluctant hero, they don't want to brag and feel like they were just doing their job. Though many went into show business because they didn't get loving attention in their youth, they find it less satisfying than what they would have experienced with proper love as a child.

A handful of entertainers are enormously successful and give back with benefit performances to help raise funds for charities. They couldn't do this when they were starting out, and they had to work hard to receive fame and prosperity in order to give back. This is healthy giving when you work hard to make something of yourself and give back from a place of pure gratitude. Artists of all kinds give to charities and find it rewarding. They are often expected to give of their resources, and some feel selfish if they don't. They also give of themselves in another way as they reveal personal details of their life to remain connected to their audience. It has proven disastrous for some. Maybe you have felt obligated to overshare and had it backfire on you too.

Have you ever felt like you had to be "on" to make others happy when you felt badly yourself? Hopefully, you see that it's okay to have times in your life when you work hard to make yourself successful so you can give from a place of peaceful prosperity. There truly is a time to reap and a time to sow. We replenish agricultural fields this way, and this means to RE-Plenty. Think about how you can make changes in your perspective about the delayed gratification of giving from a place of restful abundance.

Legal Professionals

People make jokes about attorneys, but being one is no laughing matter. Not all attorneys are codependent to be certain, but like all the professions mentioned here, they can be quite the opposite. However, attorneys prone to codependency can become overworked. Litigation of any kind is stressful because somewhere in it is a fight. Staying in fight mode all the time can reduce a person's capacity for empathy from the constant barrage of vicarious trauma.

Attorneys who work in personal injury cases see people in pain. Legal Aid Society members experience the effects of abject poverty and desperation in their clients, very similar to immigration law. Divorce attorneys are married themselves with their own issues, so their work can literally hit home. Bankruptcy attorneys have to guide people through the loss of everything they worked for, and it is much like elder care law where people are losing loved ones. All of these things are what an attorney may encounter in their personal life.

I'm a family court mediator as the state I live in encourages mental health counselors to become involved in dispute resolution. We are trained to be neutral, but because we are human, it requires putting your feelings aside and compartmentalizing them to aid parties to reach an agreement. Sometimes children are involved in messy custody battles, and though rewarding, it can hurt to be "Switzerland" over the long term.

Have you had to fight for the legal rights of an elder or child with little thanks or assistance? Have you taken on the role of mediator with your family or friends? How did you handle the disputes? Were you able to remain neutral, and if so or if not, why and what was the outcome? More important, how did that outcome affect your feelings? What amount of time did you devote to it? Did you experience vicarious trauma? Getting in the middle of squabbles may be what you innately "enjoy," but learn to curtail this dynamic, particularly if you are the "fixer" kind of codependent.

The Privileged and the Impoverished

There is a French royal term, *noblesse oblige,* which means nobility is obliged to help those less fortunate. It's a magnificent concept, but perhaps you can think of those with a great deal of privilege or wealth who didn't feel good enough. Princess Diana was one of the most generous people with her time and charity work. She was a champion to the underdog and at times remarked how she felt unloved, so she related to the suffering on an intensely personal and emotional level. She often spoke of being uncomfortable with all the cameras pointed at her and set out on a mission to take the photographers to places they would never otherwise go. She said, "Anywhere I see suffering, this is where I want to be, doing what I can."

Sometimes the greatest leaders do their best to ease the suffering of others, but no matter how noble, wealthy, or powerful, one person can't take on all the pain in the world. Those who have more can do more, but they can't do it all. You may feel the same way. If you have more resources than others, do you ever find yourself feeling guilty or feeling intense obligation? You may have worked hard for your ability to give to charity, and by all means do. Philanthropists are noble in leadership and aren't motivated by guilt but genuine compassion. We discussed the concept of the synergy of philanthropy and how enlisting or combining time, talents, and finances collectively for the greater good may be how your giving will best serve others. Does this make more sense to you now as you read about covert codependency?

Conversely, impoverished people feel like they're not good enough, and you may be or know of those who give all their time and talent for free to prove worth and value. This can be a guilt and fear-based need to get rid of wealth from a false sense of unworthiness. Allowing yourself to realize you can be of the most benefit when you have more yourself will take time, but it will free you to become of greater value to others from a place of abundance instead of lack.

There is no shame in being rich or poor, but those with covert codependency may feel this way. It's lonely at the top and at the bottom and in between, but you can change the perspective when you realize your intrinsic worth just as you are.

Loving Parents

The best was saved for last as these are the least likely suspects of codependency. Loving your children and wanting to give them the best of everything are wonderful goals. Fearful "helicopter" parents have their child's safety at heart, but this can cause anxiety and phobias in children. Conversely, an extravagant parenting style creates expectation of immediate gratification. Narcissism is thought to be a learned trait, and one of its criteria is a sense of entitlement. If you give your child everything when they are young, they'll expect it from others as adults. This will not bode well for them in the future. If you don't teach a work ethic, kindness, or conscientiousness, you're running the risk of raising a conceited child. Parents who overindulge their children may think they are showing them love, but in truth, it's a veiled way of keeping them attached to you through material expression or excessive doting.

Counterintuitively, this creates a child who feels unworthy but overcompensates with grandiosity and a lack of empathy as they get older because they have not been afforded the one thing they need the most, which is the development of healthy maturity. Without being held responsible for chores, education, ideals, or values, a child doesn't develop into a healthy adult. Ask any parent who has given much to their child only to have more demanded of them. It's a frustrating cycle to break if you wait until your son or daughter reaches adolescence. Being a loving parent doesn't mean to overindulge or to deprive; it finds a healthy balance.

Add Your Category

There are many other categories of covert codependency than can be explored, but these will get you started to see how it relates to your life. Add whatever category you fit in as a closet codependent. The process of healing covert codependency is knowing yourself and your motivations. Like overt codependence, there's a root cause for the behaviors. It takes bravery to shine a light in the dark places of your heart, but once you do, the shadows don't follow you anymore. You will become a confident, well-rested leader, better equipped to help others to help themselves. This is what interdependent, healthy professional and personal relationships are all about.

Revision Exercise

1. *Discover:* List in your journal or make mental notes of covert ways your codependency may manifest.

2. *Uncover:* Check your motives and be honest with yourself about why you may overindulge or overdo in ways you never thought of as being codependent. These will be things motivated by guilt, fear, or feeling not good enough. Write these down as a reinforcing visual aid.

3. *Recover:* Apply honesty and write or think of ways you can reduce your covert codependent behavior. You may decide you want to keep giving to the same person or causes, but your expectation of return and motivation will be modified and less draining on your wallet, watch, or abilities.

4. With a few moments of self-compassionate silence, open the "closet" door of your codependency. Declutter and discard ulterior motives.

5. Forgive yourself out loud with a statement, such as "I forgive myself for not noticing how much harm I was doing to myself by caring for others above and beyond what I could handle or perform."

AFFIRMATION: *"As I come out of the darkness of any covert codependent ways I may not have recognized, I give myself permission to uncover and recover my gift of giving. I am not driven by fear-based perfectionism or self-sacrifice to feel good enough. I am enough. I look for ways to avail myself to others that are energizing and make me authentically happy. It's okay to ask for help when I need it, and it is acceptable and essential moving forward."*

Uncover any closet codependent tendencies you may have. List how you want to change them.

LIFE LIST

Closet Codependent Tendency	Cleaning Out the Closet
1. I define myself through my occupation and position.	1. I am not defined by what I do.
2.	2.
3.	3.
4.	4.
5.	5.
6.	6.
7.	7.
8.	8.
9.	9.

CHAPTER 9

Emerging Authenticity

To be yourself in a world that is constantly
trying to make you something else is
the greatest accomplishment.

—Ralph Waldo Emerson

Everybody Is Somebody

When you keep trying to be somebody else or lots of somebodies, your identity can become diffuse or eclipsed. We are all someone with something to offer, and no one is a nobody, including you. You've come a long way on this journey to dissecting, connecting, and intersecting your past, present, and future. You may have found missing pieces of your life and developed positive new traits. Take a moment to reflect on the most powerful ones and breathe in the potential of your future. Exhale and rest in the knowledge you are okay today, just like you are. By accepting yourself, you're fully present and don't have to worry about anyone else. You can simply deal with what is truly important in the moment.

We are all capable of occasional relapse. Taking a step or two backward is often necessary to revisit, revise, and move forward in your transition from being codependent to independent. Continue to look forward. Is there any other direction you can go? Forward is the only way any of us have to go. Even if you are living in the negative past, you are doing it in the present, and it will have a negative effect on your future. You live here and now. You can't go back, but taking positive action to create a better future by using the power of your mind will keep you on track. When what you think aligns with wanting a happier life, you'll naturally and vigorously become your best ally. When you become your best friend and are loving toward yourself, anything and everything is possible, probable, and immensely favorable.

Zero Tolerance = Infinite Possibilities

You are moving away from caring for others in chaotic states of urgency and emergency and reaching what medicine refers to as a state of equilibrium of interdependent elements, such as body temperature and hydration. There is much physiology to this, and psychology adapted this term to mean the human psyche also seeks equilibrium. In a word, it is balance. If you do the work of codependent recovery, you will tip the scales from codependent to independent and find the peace of homeostasis. What once was a compulsion for you will turn to repulsion and expulsion of the thoughts, feelings, and behaviors.

You are headed toward emergence as your genuine self, connecting to wonderful people. You're probably experiencing shifts in self-perception and have learned to heed physiologic warning signals with more accuracy. You're replacing negative thinking patterns with positive, expanded self-awareness. This creates mental clarity and opens your heart to affirm infinite possibilities. Remain receptive as you learn to enjoy the freedom of being yourself.

What you do for others is probably the same support you desire. It's your turn to be happy. Yes, you may continue to struggle with feeling unworthy of happiness at times. Relapse is part of reconditioning, but it will occur less frequently. Going backward into codependent relapse and collapse will no longer be an option if you're applying the life lists you wrote for yourself. You may make fallible decisions at times, but these can be reframed as teaching and motivating moments. You can reevaluate your choices without reverting back to self-punishment or deprivation. Take it easy on yourself. You have a gift to help others not repeat mistakes, without beating them up or judging, and you can do that for yourself too. It's good to know you weren't really codependent as soon as you chose not to be. You've seen this doesn't mean your personality changes, but your motives have been enlightened to receive and give more genuinely and joyously.

When I was coming out of giving too much to the wrong people, I didn't get greedy or selfish. I kept giving but in unique ways. If I noticed a hotel housekeeper, restaurant server, cab driver, or anyone who met the needs of others with little pay, I would tip them a great deal extra, within my means. It would give them hope, and it satisfied my need to help the underdog without getting bitten. You don't have to give up your gift of giving, but you may have to cull certain people out of your path, according to what is helping or hurting yourself or others.

Pay attention to any gift you possess that comes from a place of pure intention, with no expectation of your giving being returned. The list below contains genuine qualities to help you maintain independent thinking, giving, and thoughtful doing. You haven't given up your wonderful traits. You are just perceiving them in a new light so you can have more of yourself to give.

- Empathy
- Compassion
- Caregiving
- Problem Solving
- High Intuition
- Trustworthiness
- Benevolence and Generosity
- Peacemaking
- Mentoring

If any of these traits trap you into overdoing, note it and work on reducing the effect. Zero tolerance for things that deplete you gives you the energy to enjoy life. When you no longer consent, justify, or rationalize being used, abused, sublimated, or dominated, you will have infinite ways to live a happier life. Fear will no longer be part of the equation, and you will enjoy exponential freedom.

Fun and Faith Are Antidotes for Fear

Fear produces toxic physiologic reactions, but you can face it with faith to find freedom. This takes time and practice, requiring trial and error, but again, errors are merely reset places. Errors made from the subconscious are like a default on a computer; it may take repetition to change it permanently. You may have to turn the computer off and let it rest and reconfigure the program. Former codependents, like computers, may default to past programming from time to time, and it's okay. Codependent default is not your fault. You have to make connections before you can break them. You might have to take time to reboot and upload new thoughts before moving forward.

Breaking traditions creates transitions, but the rewards are endless when you systematically establish healthier relationships. Changing the default can be done with a fun little exercise that can reap immense transformation. Fear produces toxic stress chemicals in the body, but fun reduces them and increases healthy physiological responses. Have fun with your recovery and learn to laugh at yourself if you catch yourself slipping back into codependent reactivity.

The Ugly Jewelry Challenge

I developed a humorous exercise for myself to break codependent behaviors, and I've used it in my practice with similar results. I ask clients to go out and find a piece of jewelry they hate or wear a ring on a finger that bothers them. This is much like tying a string around your finger to remember something. The ring I chose was a big silver ring that looked like rope, and I wore it on my index finger, which annoyed me.

The jewelry has to be a piece you can see. The bracelet or ring needs to be inauthentic to your own aesthetic but unobtrusive so no one will ask about it. This is your intensely personal recovery tool and not show and tell. It works well with people who say "I'm sorry" or ask permission too much. When you catch yourself, stop the behavior, and become increasingly authentic, the ugly piece of jewelry can be discarded. Then you can reward yourself with jewelry or something you really like. This is not the same as the thought-stopping rubber band exercise of the past, when you punished yourself with a snap. It actually made anxiety worse. The ugly jewelry is a less punishing and more rewarding exercise.

Fun and reward create dopamine, serotonin, and oxytocin and result in more happiness and hopefulness. As you allow yourself to have fun, you'll be amazed at the healing power. We have a pleasure center in our brain, and the apex of it is in the ventral tegmental area. It seeks love and happiness, and when it finds it, or thinks it has, other parts of our brain and body give us feelings of excitement. Remember, fear creates the same physiological sensations as excitement but with opposing emotions. Your brain will now seek to connect with people who make you feel good while you do the same for them.

Take a chance to make a change, and if you're afraid you'll make a mistake, don't worry; you will! If you don't like the ugly jewelry, you can devise your own such, as wearing socks you don't like. Choose whatever will work for you in a tailored method. Do what's fun and compassionate for you that doesn't upset you. Remember it's a visual aid, not a punishment. When clients ask me about "fine jars," I say they are fine if you use the money after the behavior has changed to do something nice for yourself. When you apply loving self-kindness in your quest for authenticity, others will see it in you. When you are good to yourself, great relationships and true love won't be elusive anymore.

You can't live happily without love, and if you don't have it right now, dare to begin looking for it, incrementally and fearlessly. There may be extenuating circumstances preventing you at the moment, but everything evolves. Look with fervor for what you want and settle for nothing less than happiness. It may not currently be possible to do things in a big way to change your life, but you can take micro steps that will result in big advances.

While going through a divorce, I was caring for my ill parents, and this was a necessity. To seek some pleasure, I visited the free section of Disney World near my home, which touts itself as being the happiest place on earth. I felt alone but didn't want to date as the divorce wasn't final. I had unresolved issues with family and wanted to make peace with the fact I couldn't make peace with one of them. It was at this time I recalled every Disney movie began with traumatic parental abandonment. The main character emerged victorious by pushing through fearful wilderness situations. They then made unusual but powerful connections and, together, began believing anything was possible. Think of Bambi and Thumper or Mowgli and Baloo, the bear. This is healthy, reciprocal interdependence! Think of any unusual friendships or connections you have or can make to help hold you *responsible* for seeking more joy in spite of circumstances. You need more people in your life who protect you and don't correct you.

Realistically, I wasn't having "fun" at Disney World, but it was resetting my brain by vicariously seeing families enjoy themselves so it would ease my traumatic situation. Empathic responses work to the positive too. Instead of being jealous of happy families, I visualized being one of them someday. It manifested many years ago, and I have enjoyed many happy days at Disney since then with family and friends.

Use your empathic skills to soak up happy energy, and you'll be led to the beginning of enjoying your life to the fullest. Go to nice places near you. No one has to know you're taking a moment to refresh yourself. Don't be afraid to talk to safe people around you. More important, ask for help when you need it. You may have to go through wilderness experiences, but you don't have to do it alone.

What script writers know will help you emerge as your own hero with greater understanding and a renewal of being able to give from imparting wisdom. Almost every major film about the hero's fight against good and evil is based on the works of philosopher, Joseph Campbell.[1] However, Campbell didn't invent the hero's journey; he observed it from great people, fictional and real, and then compiled and applied his revelations with new insights. When someone is called to use their life for a greater purpose, they are resistant at first, and this pushback is almost always about fear. Codependents are already extraordinary in their ability to empathize and meet the needs of others. The ordinary world you are leaving is one where you are codependent and are not facing your greatest fears. Campbell's model was about hearing the calling, being catapulted out into a lonely wilderness experience, meeting mentors, making unlikely allies, going through trials, and emerging victorious, wiser, and transformed into an extraordinary person. The wonderful news for the emerging codependent, is the hero returns from the grand adventure back to their starting place, sharing the "elixir" with others for the greater good of all.

Adapted from Campbell's Hero's Journey model, this is what the codependent version would look like:

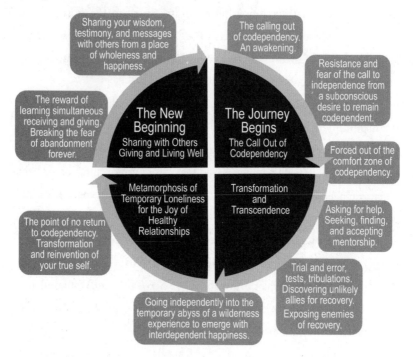

The caveat in the turning-back point in recovery is the temporary lonely wilderness experience. This is why it is so important not to let guilt or fear create a setback. If someone tries to get you to go on a guilt trip, decline the ride. If fear persists, push past it. Carl Jung said what we resist persists. When you're called out of your ordinary world, the resistance is immense and reluctance intense. That said, something usually forces a hero out of their ability to stay in their comfort zone, and you are no different or you would not be reading this. What forced you to move out of codependency? Your catapult might be exhaustion or rejection, and you are forced to move on to a new brighter life that may begin from a dark place of your soul. Remember it, but only as a reminder to propel you to move away from the gravitational pull of it.

"Suzanne" came to me in codependent crisis because she had gone to an attorney to file for divorce. This was a marriage of over twenty-five years, and even though she was verbally belittled and demeaned every day, she was afraid of being alone and felt guilty for going behind her husband's back. She had the calling to live up to her full potential, but fear stopped her. She felt pushed by her friends and family to "just leave," but again, she was doing what others told her to do, not what was right for her. She was relieved when I told her she was allowed to do whatever she wanted, when she wanted, and not what others said. She agreed slowing down felt right. In paralyzing panic, sometimes the best thing to do is nothing. Allow yourself to feel the pain, and the panic will subside. Then you can begin to move again incrementally, consciously, and confidently.

A year later, going at her own pace, Suzanne found peace and prosperity on every level. Her fear of being alone became a sanctuary of solitude and freedom. The false guilt she felt was gone, and she wondered if it was okay to feel a little guilty for being so happy. She barely remembered the codependent person she once was and loved the independent person she had become. It takes time for the reconditioned you to feel real. It's okay to feel whatever you want as an emerging codependent.

You may occasionally be drawn back to familiar negative feelings, but the "withdrawal" symptoms won't last as long. They are part of the process, but you don't have to regress; you can digress away from them expediently and purposefully. Suzanne has blossomed, and in doing the hard, dark work, she set a shining example for everyone around her and for those in her new life coaching practice. She became afraid to be afraid and knows how to deal with it if it pops up in her life again. She didn't change or leave her old self behind; she became her authentic self—the one she was born and meant to be. You are doing this now.

It takes courage to face the familiar fear of abandonment or leaving "home," whatever that means to you. Some form of temporary loneliness will most likely be a part of the battle toward living up to your full potential. When you run toward fear with faith, you gain freedom and more. Fear looks to the past through old mental data and calculates risk. This is when stagnation occurs. Pay attention to fear. It's there to teach you something, but move through it a little more every day by being good to yourself. Faith looks ahead to a brighter future and motivates you to your higher calling in spite of the fear.

You have this calling, or you would never have been able to become codependent. Without unselfish people like you, who desire to live and give from purpose and meaning, society would crumble from avarice. Anyone with a heart to serve humanity or who has a natural gift of giving is here to keep the world a safer and more loving place to live. There is room for you to enjoy your life too. The trick is knowing how to answer your call and not become eclipsed or knocked off the trajectory of your true purpose. Answering your calling is your call. No one else can answer it or be your hero but you. If you refuse to go into the abyss required to help you help yourself, you may remain the way you are. Is this an option anymore? Please, say no—a resounding no! Bravery begins when options and situations push you into adventures.

Anxiety has no place in the life of a hero. Fear is tormenting, and it can rush in like an invisible tsunami of pain and panic when you least expect it. The definition of courage is being afraid and doing it anyway. You have so much to offer to others. You have words of wisdom. You perform random acts of kindness. You will always be this way, but it's important to find your way first. If you choose to do nothing for too long, don't be surprised if circumstances or life-altering events force you to face your fears. Interventions happen all by themselves, and they are the most challenging but also the most rewarding. Interventions usher in reinvention. You'll know when the time to go arrives, and you won't be able to ignore it.

The Codependent Expiration Date

As you are well aware, codependent anxiety is literally toxic, and it also con-taminates your authenticity. When the fear of leaving a negative situation is surpassed by a desire to change, your expiration date has arrived. Hope-fully, you are closer to it now. Somewhere in the back of your mind is a time you foresee independence. When is it? Think for a moment about how much longer you can tolerate what is going on in your life. Stop and deeply ponder how much longer you can live like you are now. Then ask yourself what is keeping you from beginning the process to change. Money? Age? Fear? Anger? What are you afraid of and with whom are you angry? Anger and fear are traps. Acknowledging them and vowing to no longer act on them releases you.

Expedited healing occurs when your expiration date is in the forefront of your mind. Long-suffering is another quality of a codependent, but do you really want to spend another moment in codependent suffering or trying to please toxic people? You can't dwell on the past at the expense of your future. That's emotional atrophy, and exercising your free will can make you stronger and allow you to live a longer, happier, healthier life.

Self-reliance is also learned by trial and error. Never lose sight of your ideal life. Think about it and take steps toward it. If you have an image of something you want, find or buy a token or talisman of what you envision. Place the object where you can see it, and no one has to know what your token is. If you want a new car, you can go to a home improvement store and pick out a key and place it on your key ring. No one will know. Then drop by a dealership and take one for a test drive, even if you can't afford it right now. It will get your brain out of park. Suspend the fretting of not being able to afford it and just enjoy the ride in the moment. Your brain will set wheels in motion when you do things like this. Vision boards and journaling work well too. Journal these things and what you would tell someone else to do if they were you. Then read back your own advice out loud as if you are hearing it for the first time—and heed it.

Any increment toward your authentic desire is one step closer to manifesting it. Doing something mindfully and with a clear vision creates uplifting hope. *Not* worrying about the future also helps you to appreciate the present. Gratitude for what you have now is a way for your brain to reset, and we'll explore this in depth at the conclusion.

For now, look around you and give thanks for what you have. This builds a platform to step out of lack and into abundance. Complaining and pessimism keep you stuck. Optimism clears the path for you to seek positive outcomes, and many will come to you. Your brain responds and recalibrates to your beliefs as self-fulfilling prophecies. It believes what you tell it and sets out to receive it. What's keeping you from thinking positively? Push past the impediment and do it anyway. You probably won't receive everything you want, but you won't get anything if you do nothing.

When your expiration date is up, self-sabotage is no longer an acceptable or viable option. Experiment with optimism, even if you have to force your brain to think about good things. It's like learning a new language: to become fluent you must practice, preferably with others.

Scripting Authentic Communication

Emerging from codependency requires new language skills, and proper semantics are essential for recovery. Scripting is a valuable tool for authentic, fearless self-expression. Choosing the right words in advance and rehearsing them will help you when someone toxic catches you off guard. Positive conditioned responses will help you avoid conflict before it starts. Do you say, "Nothing's wrong," when asked if something is bothering you to avoid conflict? You rehearsed the phrase many times, and you can use the same skill to rehearse the opposite. You don't have to say, "Nothing's wrong." You can be honest and express, "I feel hurt and would prefer not to have a discussion about it."

Controller codependents enjoy starting confrontations to get the person they're trying to change to see their point of view. They lecture or inject opinion and don't listen to the person they're attempting to change. Most codependents prefer to avoid conflict, but some of them jump in offensively or defensively to prove a point. If you don't take the offense, you won't have to go into defense mode. You also won't overexplain or overshare. Scripting keeps conversations less inflammatory, more succinct, and less self-sabotaging. Here are three mantras for quick fix remembering.

- Take no offense; give no defense.
- When you're prepared, you won't be scared!
- Be self-aware before you overshare.

Like an actor, you can reduce reactivity with rehearsed responses. When you practice scenarios of saying what you really mean, you'll reach liberation through language. You can say no, yes, I don't know, or maybe with truth, conviction, and confidence. You'll be respected more and more as you take back your power with what you articulate. Diplomatic language is a great boundary maker.

I help clients with this in practice. Often, controllers ask them what we discussed in sessions. Though sacredly confidential, controllers don't respect the therapeutic relationship. This is one place where they don't want to be the center of attention because they can't control the conversation. Scripting answers maintains safety. If we've discussed exit strategies, we script we're working on "better communication skills." It's authentic. We are working on communicating their needs in the future. The controller hears this as compliance and not as a threat. It buys time but not forever.

Ultimately, it's your choice to decide if you want to remain in toxic relationships. If you decide to stay, you need to diplomatically learn to calmly and confidently speak your truth. You can't do this with someone who constantly stirs up strife. Benign statements to verbal attacks, such as "I see your point" or "I understand," leave little room for argument. As we discussed earlier, do not ask questions if you know someone will reply with a version of "It's your fault!"

Asking questions invites hurtful answers, but making statements keeps you safe. Responding calmly and saying something like "I won't be pulled into this heated discussion" is healthy and true. If they continue to confront, walk away or leave. It disengages you from an exhausting battle you won't win. Fighting or trying to prove a point is futile and may cause dangerous repercussions. There is no excuse to give or take abuse. Your emergence depends on your ability to speak freely and fearlessly. Shrinking back or arguing won't be possible when you know what you want to say and simply state it.

Self-Advocation

Like an addict in denial, codependents only *think* they can't confront. It's a conditioned *feeling*. A filter or gateway to healthy dialogue that has been adapted from and attributed to many ancient philosophers and spiritual leaders is an excellent way to think before speaking to anyone about anything. Ask yourself:

1. Is it true?
2. Is it necessary?
3. Is it kind?

If someone is hurting you, it is true and necessary to confront them. When you do it kindly, even if they don't honor you, you have communicated wisely and independently. If you are at someone else's beck and call, you cannot be true to yourself. Self-discipline in communication and in all areas of your new life will help you to be true to yourself. It's okay to let people know you love them, but make sure you let them know you love yourself and think you are every bit as important as they are. If you love yourself, you won't allow yourself to be used or hurt. Discipline takes practice. Learning to value yourself in conversation is gratifying and powerfully charged with positive change. I assign clients to view diplomatic relations between diametrically opposed leaders. They meet in summits (higher ground) to reach agreements. They take photos, smile, and shake hands. They sit in cozy chairs in front of soothing fireplaces flickering with the hope of reaching a positive agreement for both sides. A lovely table with flowers creates a calming aesthetic and distance between them. These staged and rehearsed confrontations avert global disasters. They are most often scripted by advisors. You can do this in your personal life, and you will no longer cave in to tyrants or chaos creators in your life.

Peaceful Is Powerful

When you retain peace by staying out of ridiculous battles, chaos creators can't target you. Your limbic and parasympathetic nervous systems and techniques such as autogenic training[2] are important to achieve peace. Paying attention to tension is essential to recovery and can be achieved by practicing emotional self-regulation through progressively relaxing your muscles. A quicker technique is to tense up your entire body, including clenching your fists and tightening your jaw as you inhale. And, as you exhale, concentrate fully on releasing the tension in your muscles while opening your palms and stretching your mouth open.

Mindfulness is also helpful as you employ your five senses. You can imagine places of peace in real time, and when in conflict, superimpose this scene like a filter in front of your adversary. It is invisible to them and powerful for you. If someone is yelling at you, see and feel yourself on top of a lovely mountain overlooking the sea. Serenity will increase and involuntary fight/flight/frozen responses will decrease.

Your mind is powerful, and you learned that with the lemon exercise. You may have instantly salivated remembering it. Thoughts are powerful beginnings of creating a new reality of your independence. You don't have to vehemently declare your independence with many words or explanations; you just have to confidently and peacefully project it.

Yes, sometimes you have to fight for peace in court or other important issues but choose battles wisely or walk away entirely. If something doesn't matter in the big picture of your life, let it go. Most codependents' number one wish when they come out of the past is to have more peace and less chaos. Before giving someone a piece of your mind, get peace of mind first, and all these things will be available to you. PEACE is an acronym I developed to help you understand the importance of keeping strife out of your life.

Power

Enjoyment

Abundance

Clarity

Energy

You have the ability to harness the power of peace as you find it within yourself and connect with others who wish you wellness and wholeness, the same way you wish for them. You are learning to enjoy abundant relationships and gaining clarity of what they feel and look like. The energy you emit from now on will draw the people you want in your inner circle.

Mentors and Metaphors

When you diligently seek supportive people who have your best interests at heart, they will show up in ways you never expected. They also need you to pass on the wisdom they learned from their hero experience. None of us have lived a moment of our lives in vain when we share what we've learned with others. Inviting reciprocal and restorative conversations will help you establish happier relationships.

It's said, "When the student is ready, the teacher appears." Mentors usually aren't friends, and at times they can feel more like tormentors, but they're actually inspiring and encouraging you. They intersect your life exactly when you need them, and you usually see them in retrospect. When you open yourself up for guidance and allow mentors to impart wisdom to you, the exchange can radically alter the course of your life. One of mine came on a wing and a prayer.

For some reason, I've been close to professional pilots all my life, and they taught me great metaphors. My life partner, Tommy, flew over forty years as a veteran Air Force pilot and airline pilot. My father's best friend let me fly his plane when I was very young. He could take the yoke at any moment, but he put his hands in his lap while instructing me how to keep the plane level. He taught me confidence from a very literal, uplifting perspective. Another pilot mentor was my friend Leslie's aunt, Dora Dougherty McKeown. She was a decorated Women Airforce Service Pilots (WASP) pilot during World War II. She trained men to fly B-29s at a time long before women were considered competent to do such things. I spent hours asking her about her life, gleaning her analogies and metaphors. She told me about her mentors, and she shared that when someone didn't support her, she distanced herself from that person and found someone who was supportive.

When she was no longer needed by the WASPs, she earned a PhD in Psychology and Human Factors and designed cockpits for Bell Helicopters. She said, "If you design it, they have to let you fly it." She didn't allow anyone to clip her wings and taught me the same. When breaking my solitude after my divorce, I told Aunt Dora I was dating a pilot. She gave me the best advice of my life: "Let him be himself...and make damn sure he lets you be yourself!" In that moment, this seasoned, intrepid woman taught me how to become independent in all my relationships.

When Aunt Dora passed away and her family opened her Bible, there was only one scripture underlined: "In quietness and confidence is your strength" (Isaiah 30:15). Pause and think about that. She was the most independent and creative person I've known. She learned many things the hard way, including going through a divorce and widowhood, but she spoke softly, humbly, and confidently. Listening to her wisdom helped me find my true self.

Former codependents (which you are by now) have much to learn from those who fly. There are attitude and altitude instruments on a plane. Awareness of attitude is essential for taking off. Altimeter instruments measure the altitude of the plane and keep you aware of its position on the horizon. A balance of the forces of lift and thrust is required for optimal takeoff and for reducing drag. Apply this metaphor to your life, and it will reduce who or what drags you down.

Like codependents, pilots can become task saturated. They practice flying and crisis procedures in simulators because it's crucial to remain calm and nonreactive. You have been rehearsing calming skills through meditation. Formation jet pilots practice guided imagery, called "chair flying." The squadron rehearse together in real time with their eyes shut. It's a marvel to witness them feeling themselves flying in chairs. When they have completed this mental exercise, they leave the chairs and immediately hop in real jets and take off independently. They meet interdependently in the air, nearly wing to wing. Keeping safe boundaries becomes instinctual through practice and a tiny mirror reflecting from the ground as their guide.

You can become instinctually interdependent with guided practice too. Planes don't have rearview mirrors or go in reverse. They only go up or forward. Don't let your past drag you back to your former behaviors.

Seek your own mentors and metaphors. Simply showing up for a class you're interested in could be the twist in the plot of your life and broaden your perspective. You will probably become a mentor yourself. Helping others is what you love and are meant to do, but you must know when to allow others to teach you. Journal about mentors who imparted metaphors to you. Metaphors stir your spirit to metamorphosis. This is the opposite of morphing yourself for another. Like time in a cocoon, you may feel lonely as you struggle to find independence, but it's worth the transformation. The struggle is where the muscle strength is developed to fly, and you can't hurry the process. Ask any butterfly!

Revision Exercise

Emotional Self-Regulation

An expedited way to avoid ineffectual conflict is to visualize yourself arguing, trying to prove a point, or attempting to convince someone to get help when they don't want it, and then visualize doing what is best instead of what doesn't work.

1. Close your eyes. See yourself in an argument or trying to change someone or prove a point. Take a moment and note how you feel mentally and physically. Agitated? Frustrated? Pointless? Briefly hang on to this feeling and note where you feel it in your body.

2. Rewind the vision and see yourself at peace, calmly responding. See yourself walking away if the other person continues to be confrontational. How do you feel? Calm? Peaceful? Powerful? Note any expansion or lightness of being in your body. Hang on to this feeling. If it becomes difficult, go back to the negative feeling and you'll crave the catapult back to the peaceful scenario.

3. You can do this many times with limitless possibilities of conflict and resolution. Jumping back and forth between negative and positive feelings keeps you conscious of your subconscious through rehearsal and reversal techniques. When you're in "real" life, your brain will default to positive choices more intuitively.

A note on this exercise:

Keeping the peace is not a weakness, nor is it surrender. It's taking back your power. It takes more strength to hold your temper than to lose it. The meaning of temper in an object is the ratio of hardness and elasticity. It is the same with codependents in the recovery process. Controlling codependents can become increasingly harsh and punitive. The doormat codependent can become so elastic they snap without warning.

We say we "lose" our temper when we explode. We use terms like peace*keeper* and *losing it* for a reason. When you keep your peace, you circumvent the collateral damage anger inevitably creates. Codependents hold their anger in so long, they blow up or melt down. Think of your anger like lava in a volcano. When it slowly lets off pressure, all is safe, but when it blows from too much pressure, it self-destructs and harms everything around it. Letting off steam, methodically and with good intentions for all, without raising your voice, enables you to confront without blowing up or melting down.

Anger is there for a reason, and it needs to be addressed as it arises, so you won't regress. It's not to be "put on the back burner" of your mind, simmering until it catches on fire, creating an emergency. When you are emerging, everything may feel like it's an emergency, but it's not. Bring any anger you have forward with light and love in your conversations. Even if the other person isn't receptive, you've said your piece with peace, and anger won't overtake you. The debilitating and destructive guilt that ensues in the aftermath will never haunt you again. It's okay to be angry. It's not okay to wait until you're ready to explode to express it.

Anger fueled by anxiety is often the last phase of the codependent to independent transition. Emergence is a transcendent process. Ease into it and you will come out renewed, restored, and at peace with yourself and others. Your list will be your personal guide to address residual traits and to write about the progress you want to make.

AFFIRMATION: *There are infinite possibilities when I develop zero tolerance for abuse. I am no longer tethered to past conditioning. I am restored with peace and power. I am fully showing up in my life and allow mentors to show up and give me metaphors. I listen and apply the lessons. I meditate on the positive so I can easily mediate and mitigate the negative. I am becoming independent and fulfilled with interdependent relationships. Connected and protected, I am emerging more authentically upward and onward every day, peacefully and powerfully.*

LIFE LIST

Residual Codependent Traits	Emerging Independent Traits
1. Proving I'm right.	1. Enjoying the peace of quiet confidence.
2.	2.
3.	3.
4.	4.
5.	5.
6.	6.
7.	7.
8.	8.
9.	9.

CHAPTER 10

Quick Fixes for Codependent Relapse Prevention

As a single footstep will not make a path on the earth,
so a single thought will not make a pathway in the mind.
To make a deep physical path, we walk again and again.
To make a deep mental path, we must think
over and over the kind of thoughts we
wish to dominate our lives.

—Henry David Thoreau

Your journey has been one of compassion and progressive self-awareness. You've been reconditioning and repositioning yourself from triggers of former codependent behaviors. Isn't it nice to hear the word *former*? Even if you're not there yet, when you refer to yourself as a *former* codependent, you'll become independent sooner than you imagine. Words change your brain as well as those who are around you.

They notice the difference, and it will take time for them to catch up to your new boundaries. Stay the course, and they will.

My friend Leslie remarked how she was proud of me for learning to stand up for myself and asked how this happened. I said, "You know that thing I wrote about codependency?" She nodded and I added, "I read it too." Read your journals and refer to your Life Lists, often making additions as you evolve.

Practicing what you preach speaks much louder than words. I understand the principle of twelve-step programs that make you stand up and say, "Hi. I'm John. I'm an alcoholic," but I don't agree with it wholeheartedly. Dr. L. told me that I should never call myself a codependent again or I would stay one, and that is a truth to me. You're conditioning your brain to believe you're only in remission, ready to relapse at any second, instead of cured. You can be cured of the addiction-like symptoms of codependency.

"One day addiction programs will change," Dr. L. said. "They will no longer say, 'Hello, I'm John. I'm an alcoholic.' Instead, they'll say, 'Hello, I'm John and my brain once craved a substance that was killing me, but I am recovered now.'"

Remember the importance of positive "I am" statements and how they imprint the brain.

You would say, "Hi, I'm _____, and I'm cured of codependency. I used to want to rescue others because my brain made me believe it was better to care for others than myself, but I am practicing self-care so I can care for others better." Your brain craved to nurture others to the point of neglecting yourself. It's more like a one-step program to realize this and do everything you can to establish positive neural pathways. Though you may relapse, it's part of the process to help you remember why you sought recovery in the first place.

The trigger for relapse is usually anxiety driven. You can relieve it, short term, by taking care of someone or allowing someone back in your life that you know has the propensity to mistreat or shame you. You may want to believe the best of all people, but deep down, you know this isn't healthy. So, what do you do? Quick fixes can help.

Contingency plans are necessary when the urge to relapse occurs. You can crack the code of codependency when you're in crisis, relapse, or regression. Staying the course is possible, but don't expect support from those who don't want you to change. They may even ramp up the chaos to keep you stuck. Like exercise or any healthy lifestyle change, it requires self-discipline, delayed gratification, and allowing the anxiety to ebb and flow without caving into its demands. Free-floating anxiety is often a symptom of codependency. Like a riptide that runs parallel to the shore, acknowledge the current feelings. When you relax and don't fight them or try to fix them, you'll end up back on shore in safety. You've come a long way to be free of guilt and feeling the need to be needed. Remember, it's healthy to want to be wanted, not needing to be needed.

But what about those times when you're caught off guard and you feel like going into full codependent relapse mode? You can't think about metaphors, meditate, or speak an affirmation on the spot, nor can you deny yourself authenticity. You can be prepared and remain as self-aware as possible at all times. Being aware of others is your more innate style of relating, but by focusing on yourself, equally and compassionately, you will have an increased ability to regulate harmful relapses.

Recognize and Neutralize

You may feel a bit of residual knee-jerk reactivity with codependency all your life. I do. We are born with generous natures, and it's not that you can't continue to give lavishly or lovingly. You can and must, as generosity is one of your many wonderful traits. It's to whom and how you gave that may have tripped you up in the past. When you recognize regressions, you can neutralize them easily. Be patient with yourself as you make the transition from codependent to independent, and be ready with these quick fixes that are based on a four-step process to recognize and neutralize traits: embrace, face, replace, and erase:

1. **Embrace** the fear or negative emotions. Briefly feel them. If you repress them, resentment and anger may build. Catch and release feelings by denying their right to take up residence in your body, mind, or spirit.

2. **Face** the emotions. Courageously recognize what you want to neutralize. Discard guilt. Accept responsibility, and reach for authenticity.

3. **Replace** the emotions. Challenge negative thoughts with positive ones. Your feelings catch up later, and then peace will override the anxiety. Make a choice to change, exercise that choice, and remain steadfast to it. Wait expectantly for an emotional breakthrough of confidence.

4. **Erase** the emotions. This will naturally occur with practice. When you change thoughts and actions, your life changes. Fear gets extinguished. This is systematic desensitization, and you'll be able to lead yourself out of codependent exhaustion into healthy, interdependent, energized relationships.

Generalized relapse preventions are presented here, and all may not apply to you now, but they could in the future. Adapt, devise, or journal specific things tailored to your vulnerability. Think of your own quick fixes. Write and speak your own mantras and create your own affirmations after each one supplied to you below. You're ready to help and heal yourself now!

Loss of Self

"What happens to a codependent when they die? They see someone else's life pass before their eyes."

How did you feel reading this joke? I hope it made you a little bristly. I also hope it makes you want to live *your* life. You may feel lost, but it's only a feeling, and feelings are fickle. If you depend on others for validation to feel good, it's never enough. Anxious fear creates an empty emotional tank that seeks fuel. You can feel good independently by ceasing to look for external validation. How others feel about you runs through their filter about themselves. Free yourself from other people's opinions. Seek deep reciprocal relationships with people who naturally add value to you and you to them, and you won't become lost in appealing to others while forgoing your own personal rights. If you do something nice for someone even if they can't reciprocate the gesture, don't forget to do something nice for yourself too.

When I feel good about me, it removes the fear, and I'm free!

Your affirmation: _____

Self-Limiting Beliefs and Self-Fulfilling Prophecies

You can tear down old beliefs and manufactured limitations and construct new ways to think. Self-fulfilling prophecies work to the positive too. Keep telling yourself, *I am.* "I am" statements are powerful. Say, "I am independent. I am authentic. I am able to enjoy great interdependent relationships." Say these aloud to yourself. Do this often and add your own. It may not be your belief system, but there's a Bible story that illustrates this concept well. Moses asked the name of the presence he felt. The answer was, "I am who I am" (Exodus 3:14). Simply *I am.*

Let's take this concept to a humbler level.

Remember Popeye? His character was introduced in an animated feature titled, *I Yam What I Yam.* It was his mantra. He wasn't a perfect hero, but he was beloved for what he was and how true he was to himself and loyal to those in his inner circle. You are who you are: an evolving human being with strengths, frailties, and the ability to know what fortifies you. For Popeye, it was spinach. For you, it may be time away from toxic people, getting a good night's sleep, exercise, meditation, or spiritual practices. Whatever your source of strength is, make sure you have it readily available.

If you make it too complex or daunting, codependent identity disturbance may trap you. Whatever makes you feel stronger, simply do it!

True to me is all I have to be! I am what I am.

Your affirmation: _____

Neutralizing the Fear of Being Alone

No one wants to be or should be alone. Releasing unhealthy connections and establishing healthier ones is the key. Fear of losing friends or family causes resistance to recovery. Break the addiction of unhealthy connections and the need to be needed. Walk away from those who suck the life out of you or expect you to be their ego supply. When you become part of another's entourage, you lose sight of your need to breathe and take up space too. You may feel falsely guilty when you begin to honor yourself. Get off the hook of craving the "love" of those you know aren't good for you by transforming self-sacrifice with self-compassion. Insulate yourself with people who make you feel good, and you will never feel isolated again. This is not your shallow entourage, but a deep pool of friends who watch out for one another and have one another's best interest at heart. No one has to be the leader or follower; it's all about being in peaceful flow with your relationships.

I no longer crave those who make me feel bad.
I am brave to honor and seek the love I desire
and have no need to follow anyone's lead.

Your affirmation: _____

Silencing Your Inner Critic

Codependents speak about themselves in ways their worst enemy wouldn't dare to do. Would you call someone a clumsy idiot if they dropped their keys? Of course not, but we all do it to ourselves. I have. You may say things like this about yourself. Silencing the inner critic is not ignoring it; it's there for a reason. Find the root of who planted this weed in your spirit. The voice of negative self-talk is loud and persistent, and you can resist it by "talking" back to it like you're defending someone you love. Replacing the inner critic with inner praise eradicates it.

Occasionally a controlling codependent may outwardly criticize others or talk behind someone's back under the guise of wanting to help them or make them change. I have when I was at the end of my rope living with a narcissist. Beware of the inner critic projected on to others, and *if you can't say something nice about yourself or someone else, don't say anything at all.* This isn't just good advice; it is time-proven wisdom. What you *don't* say won't hurt you or anyone else inwardly or outwardly.

Self-deprecation and criticism diminish.
Self-appreciation and praise replenish.

Your affirmation: _____

Curing Self-Sabotage

Many codependents *almost* finish school or *nearly* get the career of their dreams. They become entrenched in being what others want them to be or helping others be what they want to be. We looked in depth at this in the financial chapter. By living for others, you turn away from what you want and deeply regret it later. It's what you *don't do* that hurts you. Vow to not create elaborate rationalizations for missing your calling. Climb back up to your dreams and do what you can do to retrieve them and achieve them. I went back to graduate school at forty-five. It's never too late to return to your calling in some way, shape, or form. After I beat myself up for not getting a PhD or becoming an MD or JD sooner, I researched alternatives and found a master's program that was a good fit. Do what you can with what you have, including time, money, and talent, and you will recover much of what you only thought was lost. If you focus on what you didn't do or can't do, you will stagnate in the self-pitying, muddy water of doing nothing. Make some waves and stir your spirit. Use your internal compass that you so readily give away to others to give you direction and then take action.

I won't camouflage or self-sabotage. I dream it, wish it, and do it!

Your affirmation: _____

Over-Apologizing

Saying "I'm sorry" too much is subconsciously conditioned. In the future, apologize only when you need to truly make amends. Selfish people seldom apologize. They say things like, "I'm sorry you feel that way." That's blame-shifting and is a twisted tool of the narcissistic and sociopathic type personalities. Taking ownership of what we are truly responsible for is a virtue, whereas taking the blame or feeling shame for what others impose on you is codependent transference. For example, if someone has a headache and complains, do you say, "I'm sorry"? You didn't give them a headache. A more authentic and less codependent response would be "Oh, headaches are awful. I feel for you." This is not taking blame but expressing compassionate empathy, which is what you are naturally good at doing.

Another way over-apologizing can manifest is in everyday life. For example, if you're in a grocery store aisle getting an item, and someone pushes you out of the way or encroaches on your space, you might catch yourself saying, "I'm sorry," and move for them. They are the intruder; an "excuse me" would do well for each person. If it's not your fault, saying I'm sorry is not only disingenuous but insidiously dangerous. Buildup of false apologizing can turn into resentment and anger, and you could blow up or melt down when you least expect it. This happened to me, and I said, "Saying excuse me would have been so much nicer than pushing my cart out of the way." I couldn't believe I said that out loud to a stranger, but when I did, I realized it was festering in me. It was a genuine statement but was not dignified and could have started an unwanted altercation. The last straw is never one you see coming.

The ugly jewelry or accessory exercise you learned is a tactile, visual aid to recondition this behavior. In fact, when writing this, I was wearing an ugly bracelet to break an old habit that could lead to relapse. We're all works in progress, including me. You can expedite healing by coming up with, or scripting, more genuine responses than apologizing. The humorous bracelet or ring is an effective reminder. When you cease the behavior, you can choose how to ceremoniously release the object. Like a talisman or touchstone, the visual reminder quickly embeds a neural pathway to positive behavioral transformation.

I will apologize less and not repress my feelings.
In doing so, I won't get depressed or digress. My dignity and
self-respect help me interject my truth with confidence.

Your affirmation: _____

Minimizing

Codependents minimize to the max! Minimizing is a great interim defense mechanism. It's the opposite of catastrophizing and awfulizing. However, this is denial of a need for your full attention to your truth or pain. Like all mechanisms, no matter how well you care for them, they age and become impaired over time—or become useless. Minimizing is fine for speaking to acquaintances or for maintaining good boundaries with nosy people but not with those in your close relationships. If you're not fine, you don't have to say you are. It's not up to you to be "up" for others. Every jolly person is allowed to have bad, sad, or mad days. If someone asks you how you're doing, you have the right to say, "I'm doing well under the circumstances," or something truthful for your situation.

When I was in a grieving process and people asked me how I was, I didn't say, "I'm fine." I told the truth and said things like, "I'm in the healing process. I have good days and bad days, but I'm doing the best I can." It was honest, and I didn't attempt to evoke sympathy from others or to linger too long in negative conversations. When you feel the grip of the negative energy, release it by changing the subject or saying what is true for you with brevity. It sets an invisible but powerful boundary. It's a conversion process of finding balance between letting people know you have some pain to process but not talking about it too much. Minimal words aren't minimizing. You're speaking truth without dwelling on the negative too long or minimizing your pain, and in doing so, negative neural pathways won't be able to imprint as easily.

When I minimize, I deny the honest expression of myself.
When I am real, I heal as I deal with the truth.

Your affirmation: _____

Comparing and Unhealthy Competing

Comparing and competing unhealthily with others is self-rejecting your uniqueness, value, and purpose. It's also a common sign of envy, which is difficult to accept. Being envious is a trait no one likes to admit, but to the positive, envy is a sign of deep desire. It can be used for fuel to get what you want. Crushing desires are there for a reason. Cherish them and go for them head-on, full force, and with fervor and joy. Depriving yourself of aiming for your dreams keeps you stuck in the torment of comparative envy, which further stagnates cycles of comparing and competing.

You may have learned unhealthy competition from your parents, classmates, or siblings. Perhaps, like me, you were taught to be an extension of your family image. If so, has this made you compare yourself to others? Becoming completely your authentic self is out of the question in families with this dynamic. Often, siblings, cousins, or other relatives are pitted against one another to be the best family image maker. No one can win this race, including the enforcer, because good is never good enough. As a child, you don't have the knowledge or vocabulary to protest this invisible starting gate with no finish line. You're incapacitated to become your true self. This may result in an inability to pay or receive compliments because both require self-actualization.

I noticed a sign of codependency in an adolescent when she gave away a prize she had won to another adolescent who looked sad. I noticed this because I did it so often at that age too, and throughout my adulthood. She, like me, admitted she hated competition because someone had to lose. She would rather forfeit her prize so the other person wouldn't feel sad. This is really to relieve the pain of seeing someone else sad at your expense.

The most insidious form of unhealthy competing is allowing someone else to win. Similar to taking a fall for someone, when you lose on purpose to make someone else happy, thinking they will like you more, you're subconsciously learning to like *yourself* less. When you become totally selfless, you are self-*less*. If you feel guilty because someone else has to lose if you win, it's time to stop. I have done this, not only as a child, but as an adult and watched others do this to keep another person happy. It is really relieving subliminal false guilt imposed on you. A doormat kind of codependent often does this when competing.

Conversely, the fiercely competitive controlling type of codependent gets furious if they don't win. They are similar to the doormat in that they're both trying to exhibit worthiness. The doormat needs to lose so others can be happy, and they will be known for respecting the feelings of others. The controlling type *needs* to win instead of wants to win to gain respect as a "worthy" opponent. The better they do, the more they think others will listen to them. If only they would listen to themselves. Neither extreme is healthy. It's okay to win. It's okay to lose; just be certain you're doing your personal best and competing with integrity and authenticity of emotions.

All codependents are genuinely competent at many things, but rarely toot their own horn. They let other people take the credit, and this also causes resentment of self and others. There will always be someone better or worse at whatever you do. Most of it is subjective and not reality based. Comparison and competing to be better than someone can cause extremes of disturbances, such as grandiose pride, inferiority complexes, or other ego-driven identity stealers, such as dumbing yourself down. Being self-deprecating to be liked is self-betrayal.

Becoming your personal best breaks the maladaptive behavior and doesn't strive for perfection but rather for contentment. Content people are those of substance. Competing with yourself is ideal, and this is what personal best means.

A quick fix for comparing yourself to others is to take a digital detox from social media. Few people post their internal strife or emotionally bad days. You don't post an average day at work, but you do post a cruise or good days. Removing yourself from social media will help you reduce unhealthy comparison or competition. After a few days, you'll notice the difference, and you can return when you stop comparing yourself to others. You may also want to limit exposure to other things in your personal sphere, which trip you up in this area. Quick fixes in this area are all about reducing the feelings of inferiority on one end of the spectrum, and the other end is a need to control, prove worthiness, or be right.

I'm at my personal best when I don't compare
or compete in unhealthy ways. I will implement sincere
compliments and receive them graciously and confidently.

I can enjoy my life without internal strife.

Your affirmation: _____

Perfectionism, Overdoing, and Over-Giving

Having everything "just right" releases a rush of dopamine, but the reward is fleeting. Faultfinding begins its cycle in the mind of an overdoer. The invisible fault line running underneath perfectionism is hidden anxiety, resentment, and anger that never seem to be appeased or abated. The more you do, the more you find there is to do, and it can snowball beyond your ability to stop or control the resulting exhaustion. Think ahead to how exhilaration quickly fades to exhaustion when you overdo, usually because someone talked you into doing something you didn't want to or believed you should, ought, or must do. You may also be the pushover type, who allows others to coerce you. The perpetrators often use flattery, such as saying, "No one bakes as well as you do!" Custom bakeries do, and you can send your pushy person to one you recommend. Over-giving sparks the same quick rush of happiness when you see someone receive a gift. This is great but only if you are meeting your needs, wants, and desires as well.

The adage, "It's the thought that counts," is a quick fix with a twist. Think before you give. I made a rubber band bracelet for clients that says, "It's the thought…that counts!" Much like the ugly bracelet, an observer won't know what the ellipsis means. Those three dots mean think and count to three before you buy something you can't afford to give. This reduces codependent impulsivity.

If you have an ungrateful recipient who makes you feel badly about your gifting, cease being so extravagant to them. When shopping, did you ever feel a dopamine buzz when you saw an item? "Oh! So-and-so would *love* this! I must get it for her!" But "so-and-so" is the one who never appreciates you. Put the item back or buy something you like. It's the thought…that counts!

Being self-indulgent isn't selfish, though it may feel that way at first. It will boost your confidence and reduce your getting hurt by someone who doesn't appreciate you. Narcissists usually find fault with what you give them, and it hurts. Robbing them of the opportunity to gaslight you will make you feel better.

Flattery is another tool narcissists and con artists use. The words feel good for a moment, but it's an emotional blackmail tactic, veiled by praise and a smile. No one will notice how straight you spread the frosting or if you put just the right amount of baby's breath in a table centerpiece. Another adage is "The devil is in the details," and this is so true for a perfectionistic codependent. Change this to "The angel is in the big picture."

The little things you obsess about can cause mental disturbances. When someone asks you to do more than you want to, remember the gratitude sandwich and say, "Thank you for thinking of me, but I'm overextended. Thank you for understanding." Period. No commas, no excuses. The other person may not like it, but they will respect you more and ask you to do things less. No longer will you be controlled by their expectations that feel like heavy obligations. If someone constantly pushes you and won't take no for an answer, limit them by not being so available.

Being perfectionistic isn't realistic.
I am not overdoing or over-giving; I am living well.
I vow to not be a pushover anymore. I can diplomatically but
emphatically say no without feeling guilt or anxiety.

Your affirmation: _____

Compassion Fatigue and Burnout

Clients have expressed anger toward me for not crying with them. I explain that if I move to the couch and cry with you, it's sympathy. It won't help, and you would feel really creepy. I add that if I listen to your expressed emotions and help you process them, that's empathy, which will help you. Cathartic tears are trauma seeking resolution, and I do get teary eyes sometimes and experience countertransference. As an intern, I went to my supervisor, beating myself up for having too much empathy with some clients. He said, "Let me be the first to tell you, you're human! I would worry about you if you didn't care or experience transference or countertransference."

He taught me how to process this, and I found that taking time to self-care was more helpful to everyone. Therapists who work harder than clients burn out quickly. You may relate to this yourself as a "therapist" to your friends and family. All empathic people are at risk for burnout and must self-care for well-being. Compassion fatigue leads to toxic chemical dumping in your body. Your brain and immune system go offline. The prefrontal cortex and executive functioning in the brain become impaired. You become forgetful, irritable, and are at risk for fender benders, mistakes, and mishaps great and small. Compassion fatigue doesn't pass; it gets worse if you don't deal with it.

Yes, you have to care for ill or helpless people in your life. No, you don't have to kill yourself doing it. The best way to fix this is to check in with how you feel physically and mentally before taking on anyone else's pain. For example, if you're going through a divorce, don't take on helping a friend with her dating issues, as this would be too painful. Most things you think are urgent can wait a bit. Many times, with time, a crisis resolves itself without your immediate intervention or attention. You truly can't help anyone else if your reservoir of compassion has run dry. If you know you'll be drained by a situation, remove yourself from it and gain your power back before tackling someone else's needs. Sometimes you need to disconnect the phone and take a break before you break down or blow up from the repressed anger compassion fatigue creates.

Caregivers need respite care too. Take a breather or a moment. Five minutes locked in a bathroom in silence is better than nothing. A walk outside in nature or listening to music can restore the body, mind, and spirit quickly. By now you are aware of the value of meditation, even if you remain resistant to it. It is immediate relief to sink into soothing solitude and lift the vibration of your attitude. When you feel overwhelmed, you can retreat to your own mind, which wants you to be well and free from being overburdened. Meditation is like medication or a massage for the brain. A few moments of breath work will bring in oxygen and release toxicity. Moderate, not intense, exercise is also good for adrenal fatigue and restoration. Do whatever you feel is best and right for you.

A good cry also releases the toxicity of trauma and compassion fatigue and returns the nervous system to rest. Whether you walk it out, talk it out, or cry it out, take a break. You must come off the battlefield of caregiving every now and then to be healthy. This quick fix will insure you don't have long-term repercussions from compassion fatigue.

Self-care requires me to be self-aware.
I take time out, so I don't burn out.
I don't have to set myself on fire to keep everyone else warm.

Your affirmation: _____

People-Pleasing and Approval-Seeking

Remember the simple way to stop saying yes to please someone that you learned earlier: If anyone asks you to do something magnanimous, ask yourself one important question. *Would I ask someone to do this for me?* If the answer is no, say *no!* I learned this from a friend who is a successful engineer, and I love the logic of it. He said I don't need to go overboard by over-giving, defending, or justifying a need to say no. It's not natural for a codependent to say no, but you can practice ways to say it and stop any coercive conversations by asking yourself the previous question. Developing your own diplomatic but emphatic vocabulary will also give you more confidence, which will result in less people-pleasing.

Approval-seeking follows the same course of communication. When you say, *"I'll be glad to help,"* are you really glad? Do you agree with someone, when you really disagree, just to keep the peace? If so, you can reset to get back in alignment with your authentic beliefs. To do this, you can silently and mindfully ask yourself another question: *Is this something I want to do or feel like I have to do?* If it's the latter, refuse politely, again, without defensiveness or excuses.

If you're bombarded with more coercion, ask for time to think and, as soon as you feel comfortable, politely decline by a brief phone call, text, or e-mail to reduce the visual neural input and feelings of false guilt that arise from being in front of a persuasive manipulator. You can say, "I won't bore you with a list of my present obligations, but I simply have to decline." Preemptively script other answers, such as "I used to be able to help, but I'm spread thin and can't now." These are authentic but not guilt produc-ing, and they leave little wiggle room for the other person because they are statements. It's humbling to learn to say no; however, in no way, shape, or form do you have to conform or confront harshly. You can agree to disagree with kindness and without feeling defensive or guilty. Heated discussions are other approval-seeking triggers. You can say, "I don't talk about politics or religion with anyone because I love to remain peaceful."

Instead of agreeing with others when you don't mean it, say, "I see your point," or "You've given me a lot to think about." These benign statements don't say you're agreeing; you're merely keeping the peace, which is what most codependents like to do anyway. It surpasses the extremes of subju-gated people-pleasing or adamantly disagreeing. You may have collateral codependent fallout of feeling guilty for a while, but at least you won't feel guilty *and* exhausted. You may feel some pushback but keep pushing through. People seldom applaud your newfound ability for refusing their requests but the payoff of having more time for doing what you really want or are truly obligated to do will be your reward. If you still feel exhilaration from the need to be needed, think and ask, *Are others* enlisting *me or* including *me?*

Eliminate one-sided chaos creators. "I feel so much better after talking to you" is what you hear from these relationships. It's wonderful to hear, but if they never reciprocate and you feel drained after talking to them, stop availing yourself so frequently. Allow no more refills from the oasis of your kind heart unless they return the favor when your well is dry.

Please seek your own approval. In doing so, you'll have a clearer filter to say what you really mean without the gnawing anxiety of feeling rude. The controlling codependent will also benefit from this filter. You won't be trying to fix anyone, and you'll sound supportive instead of critical. No matter where you are on the spectrum, people-pleasing and approval-seeking are exercises in futility and rob you of precious authenticity.

> *Giving into coercion is self-desertion.*
> *When I placate others, I negate myself.*
> *I release the disease to please and enjoy a life of flow and ease.*
> *True friends don't enervate; they reciprocate and elevate.*

Your affirmation: _____

Intervention for Rescuing Behaviors

This is the most challenging of codependents to treat. They take deep offense in counseling when it is pointed out that they are on Karpman's Drama Triangle. Defensiveness is displayed with interruptions and assumptions. They don't listen well, and many begin telling me how I should feel about their situation. I tell them I'm not correcting them; I'm protecting them. As they are trying to control someone, such as an addicted family member, I tell them to practice the same principle of correction versus protection. Nothing is effectively enforced with an invisible badge of superiority. Teaching a "fixer" codependent to protect those they love as opposed to correcting them helps. This is a skill you can learn by listening to yourself, especially through tonality and semantics. Are you loud or harsh? People run from that. Are you using words that sound punitive instead of supportive? Take note if you see any defective or defensive modalities in how you relate to others.

Recognize when you are about to perform futile exercises and stop. When you discover how little you are actually in control of, it liberates you from manipulative emotional calisthenics. Remember no one is in control of anyone. Evidence of this are things like major catastrophes such as the Great Depression, 9/11, or Covid-19. When things like this happen, it's a wakeup call for you to know you can't control unforeseen events on a global scale or in your own life. During Covid-19, many codependents called and reported, "I feel lost because I can't see my family or do things for people." They, like the planet, were forced to rest and reset.

You can control your controlling behavior. Before you even think about saying, "If I were you, here's what I would do…," stop! You're not them. It is okay to say, "If you need help, I'll be there," but don't insist on giving advice or get angry if they don't listen or heed it. They may not be ready, and it is possible you may not be right. Even if you are right, the timing may be off, and it's off-putting.

It's emotional extortion to say, "If you don't go to rehab, I'm leaving you!" Instead, say, "I can't live with your addiction. I wish you'd get help, but I must do what's right for me." That's healthier. You're not correcting the other person; you're protecting yourself and leaving them to make their own decisions.

If you really can't stop controlling, do what counselors do—explore options and help others find their best answers. It may be projection if you tell someone what they need when they don't want to hear it. No one can predict anything for anyone. The variables are too numerous, and people you want to "help" may view you as overbearing. Reduce your compulsion to self-avoid and fix by working only on yourself.

You can humorously ask yourself, *What would I do if I were me?* You know the answer!

I don't impose on others what I think they're supposed to do.
I take no offense and give no defense. It's liberating to know I'm not
in control of anyone or anything. Others will come closer
to me when I'm protective and not corrective.

Your affirmation: _____

Morphing, Chameleon, and Splitting Behaviors

Shakespeare's Hamlet, the Prince of Denmark, couldn't make crisis decisions very well. Indecision is also evident in codependents as they second-guess themselves, overthink, or seek external reassurance. Hamlet was the character who spoke the soliloquy beginning with "To be or not to be, that is the question." This suicidal ideation was never carried out, but he felt hopeless and voiceless after his father's murder. He wanted to avenge the murder, but the killer was his uncle and his mother married him. (That's a lot of family secrets to keep.)

When circumstances force you into feeling like someone else for a long time, you may feel like you don't want to continue living. Many codependents secretly contemplate suicide, and it's important to be true to yourself to preempt this lonely, existential crisis. Loneliness combined with a crisis can be disastrous. Seek the help of professionals if you feel this way.

Morphing behaviors, such as changing mannerisms or speech patterns, may result in losing sight and sound of your true self. You may be able to blend in everywhere but feel you don't fit in anywhere. It takes exemplary emotional intelligence to read others, adopt mannerisms, and adapt to beliefs, but it can damage your psyche.

Remember, a chameleon blends in for safety, but there is vulnerability in the transition of changing colors. Stability is knowing and being who you are all the time. You may feel pulled out of your true image, like how mirrors in a fun house make you look. It's not funny to be bent out of shape. Removing masks of any roles you may be playing might cause you to feel vulnerable at first, but it's a powerful action that will change your life for the better.

Look at yourself directly in the mirror. Who do you see? Do you like who you are? Do you recognize yourself as who you want to be? Do you love your life? Why or why not? Question yourself as you gaze intently and gently, using your own mirror neurons to reflect what you're projecting. Be mindfully present when doing this introspective exercise. Shift your thoughts from what you see to who you want to see in the future. Say affirming words to yourself. Notice how any of your expressions change or if you feel any oppression lift. Note all your emotions and physical symptoms. To be yourself or not to be yourself, that is the question.

Looking at photographs of yourself will help you see what image you project and how to protect the real you. This is an expedition into your inmost evolving soul. It's good to take a few seconds to do this every day. When you see yourself daily and get honest with what it will take, without pressure or judgment, to be who you want to be, a better life will manifest. You won't have to ask the big questions anymore. You will become more self-actualized, and the momentum will continue.

As I remove masks of codependent roles I play,
I become self-actualized, and I realize who I really want to be.
To my own self I will be true!

Your affirmation: _____

Taking a Fall or Covering for Others

Taking responsibility for things you didn't do in order to stay connected with someone is self-betrayal. Doing this will cause the most detriment in your life, as it did in mine. The detriment comes in delayed, severe regret. Some of the ways people do this are

- Hiding abuse (Having shame in allowing it. Not wanting to get the perpetrator in trouble. Fear of loss of partner, income, or life being threatened if you tell.)
- Cosigning notes you know won't be paid
- Calling in sick or making excuses for hungover partners, spouses, or children
- Covering up for someone's illegal activity or con artistry

You didn't create the chaos; why should you fix it? There's no shame in being a victim. Bailing out others can leave you in an emotional prison. When I was much younger, I remember thinking if I hid the truth for someone in my family or overlooked large betrayals in some friendships, people would love me, like me, or appreciate me more. The opposite was true. Because I took falls and covered for others, they didn't want to see me as much. I reminded them of their misdeeds, even though I said or did nothing to make them think I would reveal their secrets. I'm not saying to become a tattletale, but don't lie or take a fall for anyone—ever! I carried this into adulthood, and it made my moral compass feel very rusty and inoperable. I had to change directions and decided to confront the facts to get back on course.

Later, when confronting these people in my life, it was the same. They didn't want to see me if I hid the truth, and they didn't want to see me if I spoke the truth. I learned the hard way what I'm teaching you now. Taking a fall or covering for others is fictionalizing fact. You are negatively bending reality. Think of the disclaimer on things based on truth: "The names have been changed to protect the innocent." As a codependent covering for someone, the facts have been changed to protect the guilty. The doormat type of codependent is more likely to engage in this clandestine murder of the truth. Seek counsel if you need to unload any false guilt or any facts you've fictionalized for so long you can't bear the regret anymore. I couldn't.

The last time I did it, I lost respect for myself and vowed to never ignore my internal compass or take a fall again. If you ignore it, it won't go away. The root word of ignorance is to *ignore*. Don't ignore your own truth to benefit those who have no intention of rewarding you for your kindness, no matter what they say or do to repay you. You may have been acting in innocent ignorance for a long time, but now you are educated and liberated.

The only quick fix for this is to stop. Stop taking falls, hiding facts, or making yourself look crazy by protecting harmful people or perhaps criminals. Return to your innocence and have common sense. Stop protecting those who ask you to reject your truth, moral compass, or authentic self to protect them at your expense.

If I take a fall, I may lose it all. My moral compass is the only guide I need to know what's right or wrong for me.

Your affirmation: _____

Setting Yourself Free from Attracting Users, Abusers, or Controllers

Codependents often find themselves instantly attracted to the dark side of others. The film, *A Star Is Born*, has been remade three times. Elements of intense codependent relationships resonate in the story. If you remain attracted to addicts, narcissists, or sociopathic people, professional help may be vital to your recovery. You may have even struggled with addictive self-medicating habits to relieve the pain of living with someone who is dependent on a substance. You may have participated with someone's substance abuse to keep them happy if they pressured you to join them, which often happens, and then you feel more phantom guilt.

When the term *codependency* originated in the 1950s twelve-step addiction model, it referred to a person in a relationship with someone dependent on a substance. If they tolerated or enabled the behavior, they were called codependent. The term has long since been expanded in meaning because codependent behaviors reach far beyond being in a relationship with an addict. Codependent relationships can be ones where there is no substance abuse but there may be abuse or family conflict of other kinds. This is best explained by the adage "misery loves company," as dysfunctional or clinically disordered people tend to gravitate toward one another.[5]

Many disordered people feel good when you feel bad. *Schadenfreude* means someone takes pleasure creating or witnessing another's pain. These people often criticize by projecting their misery onto others by saying things they subconsciously feel about themselves. If they call you stupid, they may feel intellectually inferior. They don't know *why* they're doing this, but they know *what* they're doing. Though this may seem irrational, it is intentional. They know how to hurt you and enjoy it. They set you up to get you upset. Has anyone provoked you to lose your temper, or got you to raise your voice by talking over you only to get calm and call you crazy for screaming? That's classic gaslighting. If you repeatedly fall into this trap, it can cause complex trauma symptoms. This rhyming and opposing word game will help you recognize and rid yourself of toxic and dangerous relationships.

Gaslighting and crazy-making behavior "work" within this pattern. They . . .

- **Interrogate** you under the guise of wanting to get to know you.
- **Infiltrate** your life by systematically taking control with false kindness or "love."
- **Isolate** you from family and friends.
- **Annihilate** your true self and leave you discarded, abandoned, or living in cycles of abuse.

You break the pattern this way:

- **Educate** yourself about narcissistic, borderline, and antisocial personality disorder traits.
- **Extricate** yourself from anyone in your life like this (exit strategy).
- **Insulate** with family and friends.
- **Elevate** your mind and spirit, and
- **Celebrate** your freedom.

I am no longer attracted to those who don't have my
best interests at heart. I am able to stop crazy-making behavior
in its tracks. Gaslighting no longer confuses me, and
no one abuses me. I am confident and competent
and free of the fear of being alone.

Your affirmation: _____

Poor Boundaries, Oversharing, and the Ability to Say No

What do you call a codependent who says no and doesn't feel guilty? *Healthy!*

When you respect your boundaries, others do too. When I had horses, I learned fences were not there to keep people out, but to keep the horses in and safe. Very few people knew about the secret locked gate in the back, which was only meant for emergencies.

You hold the keys to the gates of your heart and mind, and no one can bring chaos into your life unless you invite it. You alone retain the right to allow people to come and go as you feel safe, and trespassing on your life is unacceptable. Make your boundaries known to those who expect you to allow them to take advantage of you. This may be something you wrestle with daily. If so, kindness and diplomacy are great catalysts for boundary setting. Remember to use the filter:

- Is it true?
- Is it necessary?
- Is it kind?

This is lovely in theory, but boundary busters don't take no for an answer so easily. If diplomacy fails, then boundaries must become unbreachable and unreachable borders. You may have to lock the gate, unapologetically. Boundaries are not about building walls but creating safety in relationships. Gain greater understanding of developing and maintaining healthy boundaries, and you will feel less stress for the rest of your life. Saying no isn't rude; it is self-advocation.

Taking inventory of your emotional and physical reactivity helps with boundary setting and prevents being waylaid by people-pleasing relapse. Negative emotions are processed in a different part of our brain than positive ones. Negative emotions take up more space and linger longer, hence, making it more difficult to break a bad habit. Think of it as replacing an old habit with a new one. It will feel like you are speaking a foreign language at first. No one is accustomed to you saying no, but it's imperative to learn. It's also important to learn not to overshare when you say no.

Oversharing is a general boundary flaw with codependents, particularly when saying no, and is a faulty defense mechanism. Codependents overshare out of desperation for interaction, and it can put them in further risk of personal safety and boundary violation. People used to ask me so many personal questions when I was in show business and especially the part of my life when I worked with celebrities. This is how Dr. S., my supervisory professor, called me out of the closet of codependency when a fellow student inquired about my life among the rock stars. When I began to answer, she intervened and said, "Mary, don't answer that question, and see me after class." She admonished my classmate for breaching boundaries and told me not to be such an open book. She taught me to regain my privacy rights that had been compromised by working in the public eye for so long. I didn't have to be withdrawn, but I did have to be less emotionally available for the curiosity of others.

You can keep your boundaries from being breached too. A codependent is often a celebrity in their hometown, place of worship, or family. Be conscious of your anxiety if you feel the need to overshare and relax your vagus nerve. You can come out of the negative neural vortex of oversharing private or negative things about your life. Con artists love hearing them because they are testing your tolerance for bad behavior. One way they can hear this is if you complain about how much you do for others, and no one helps you. They know they have a sucker when they hear that you keep doing things for people who don't appreciate you.

Complaining also keeps you stuck focusing on problems and not solutions. Set boundaries on your own complaints and murmuring. Self-pity is a pit as it concentrates and perpetuates itself by deepening negative neural pathways. You may have done something, such as folding someone else's underwear, according to their demands. You may complain because you didn't have time to fold yours and threw it into a messy drawer. Stop complaining and quit folding their underwear. Fold your own underwear!

Doing silly little things like this quickly elevates positive thinking and boundary setting. Boundaries feel bold when first practiced, but when you set intentions to make them and keep them set, you'll lose the fear and gain respect from others and yourself.

There is abundance in setting boundaries.
I am the gatekeeper of my life. I can say no and let guilt go!
I enjoy the safety and sanctuary of healthy boundaries.

Your affirmation: _____

Remaining Resistant: If All Else Fails!

Remember reactance theory? That's when someone desires something with more intensity when they're told they can't have it. In evolutionary terms, it's all about autonomy and not allowing anyone to take authority over us.

In modern science we have many pills to cure many diseases, but we don't have a pill for the desire to quit a bad habit. If the desire to stay the same outweighs the desire to change, nothing changes unless a rock-bottom consequence occurs. However, rock bottoms are better places to push upward from than soft sandy ones. For a quick fix, instead of the ugly jewelry, put a stop sign on the home screen of your phone. *Stop* doing too much or rescuing potentially dangerous people. There are many safe ways to help others. You have to have self-preservation skills and a deep desire to change. Without desire, you may remain in codependent addictive cycles of being there for everyone but yourself.

If you remain reticent, resistant, or convinced that you're appointed or anointed to self-sacrifice and all else fails to get you to self-care, then the last resort is to go back to your codependent ways. Go back to over-giving and overdoing for at least a week and see how you feel. Do you feel exhausted just thinking about it? Is the reverse psychology working with reactance in a positive way? I hope so. I hope you feel angry when you think about reverting because denying the higher self is not the answer.

Perhaps a bit of philosophy from someone long ago will tell you codependency is not a new problem; it just has a new name. This quote from Friedrich Nietzsche's book *Human, All Too Human* encourages us all, codependent or not, to self-care and explains why many of us don't.

> *Traffic with one's higher self.* Everyone has his good day when he finds his higher self; and true humanity demands we judge someone only when he is in this condition, and not in his workdays of bondage and servitude. People deal very differently with their higher self, and often act out the role of their own self,

to the extent that they keep imitating what they were in those moments. Some regard their ideal with shy humility and would like to deny it: they fear their higher self because, when it speaks, *it speaks demandingly.*[5]

When codependency is no longer an option and you have a visceral desire to change, daring to do what it takes to give and live well demands you become brave and focused. The fear of abandonment will be replaced by the fear of staying the same. You have entered a personal revolution to find solutions.

Re-solution for your issues is by trial and error. Relapse can be your best teacher instead of your worst punisher.

Continuation of Affirmations and Meditations

Affirmations are powerful to maintain recovery as they internally make *firm* your externally spoken words. They are proclamations and declarations that transmute into invocations and invitations for a new life. Words are powerful, audible vessels for recovery, and though some people make fun of affirmations, they are of great value. When you say, "I am" instead of "I'm trying," the semantic is dramatically different. Trying implies struggle and failure. Saying "I am" implies you're dedicated and resolute to bring your affirmation into fruition.

Affirmations also engage the brain through auditory sensing of emotions. They create a shift and an emotional barrier to any future assault on your newfound independence. Through affirmation, you are reconditioning your reward circuits and changing the future on how you allow yourself to be treated.[5]

When you have a detailed vision, you're able to reach it more easily and sometimes it can be effortlessly through synchronicities. Neuroscience is exploring empirical evidence on thought changing that creates positive outcomes. It is how preparation meets opportunity, and when you prepare to be happily independent, your brain sets out to guide you. If you're a spiritual person, you may see this principle as one of guidance from a force greater than yourself. If you are a person of science, the psychological term for this is a self-fulfilling prophecy but no matter what your belief system, intentional positive thinking about being your happiest self sets you on a path to achieve it. Your brain will not take no for an answer, and you will find yourself better able to set boundaries when you think abundantly about your goals.

Meditation increases your emotional intelligence and ability to self-empathize. Your brain has the ability to create more folds and this is referred to as *gyrification*. The greater the folds, the more capacity a brain has for change, memory retention, and growth. When you meditate with positive reflection, more brain folds are generated. This improves your life and allows it to unfold in flow and ease. Everyone around you will benefit from your ability to give from a place of greater well-being. Meditation and affirmations of what you want will keep your conscious and subconscious connected and protected and will dispel the fear of being rejected.

Revision Exercise

For just a brief moment, shut your eyes and go back to your worst codependent day or time. Think about staying this way forever. Think about it a little more until you feel the desire to change deep in your body and mind. Now think about living free of codependency and how that feels. Deeply inhale new air and exhale the thoughts of exhaustion. Feel the centering peace and physiologic momentum to move toward an interdependent future.

AFFIRMATION: *I am no longer allowing the fear of abandonment to overtake me. I am a work in progress, and self-compassion keeps me moving forward. I am no longer giving power away or seeking approval from anyone. I approve of myself and gain power to help myself and others from a place of energized authenticity. I am able to diplomatically say no to others and yes to myself without guilt or fear. I am attracted to people who are good for me and I am good for them. I am honoring and respecting my boundaries, and in doing so, others respect and honor me. Relapse is part of the process, and if I have a setback, it is setting me back up to become more aware to self-care.*

Your affirmation: _____

_____

_____

LIFE LIST

On the left side of the list, write down any negative behaviors that are persistent and pervasive in your life. On the right side of the list, make opposing statements that begin with "I am."

Negative Persistent Behaviors	Opposing "I Am" Statements
1. I feel selfish and guilty if I don't do what others ask of me.	1. I am finding the healthy balance of giving and receiving.
2.	2.
3.	3.
4.	4.
5.	5.
6.	6.
7.	7.
8.	8.
9.	9.

CHAPTER 11

Continuing to Establish Independent and Interdependent Abundance

Life doesn't make any sense without interdependence.
We need each other, and the sooner we
learn that, the better for us all.

—Erik Erikson

Healthy Interconnectedness

This book has been all about learning to care about yourself and to like yourself as much as you want others to like you, just as you are. Self-like may be a term you'll feel more comfortable with than self-love, and that's okay for now. When you like someone, you understand and accept that they aren't perfect.

Accepting your imperfect humanity sometimes means having to admit frailty or a weakness, and this isn't natural for a codependent. Finding others who have been or are codependent is beneficial because you'll watch out for one another. You'll know the joy of becoming interdependent, which is retaining your independence while having healthy relationships with people you can depend on and they can on you. We are social beings, hard-wired for connectivity for safety. We also need autonomy, but this doesn't mean being alone. Science tells us loneliness is dangerous and can lead to an early demise. Loneliness has been found to be as detrimental as smoking or alcohol abuse; the good news is good social-connectedness buffers us in old age and protects and improves our brain and memory skills.[1]

Buffering our brains as recovering codependents is essential in relapse prevention. It is also crucial to our physical health. An emerging field of medicine is called *psychoneuroimmunology,* which is a big word that encapsulates how your own body is interdependent with itself. You need healthy relationships for immune support.[2] Finding others of like mind to be reciprocally supportive will keep you healthy and help you live a longer, happier life.

When you develop a false sense of safety through loving those who are less than the best for you, you may lose touch with your real self and diminish your true calling to give from a place of wholeness. You need love returned, and this began at birth. As you've learned, babies are born to be cared for, and a fear of abandonment isn't innate. Babies expect love, and if they don't get it, fear and helplessness become a learned trait. Facing fears imposed on you can be more frightening than feeling the fear itself, but once you begin the process, there's no turning back. The culmination of all your fears can be assimilated into a new way of gathering information for establishing better life, without self-sabotage or self-doubt.

You have learned the core essence of giving out of love and not fear.

Some say those two things are opposites. I don't know if they are or not, but I do know fear is crippling, and if you love yourself enough to embrace it, face it, and fight it, your intentions will shift away from what impedes a well-lived life. You will be well-loved. You will! You are free from the tyranny of obligation, perfectionism, and people-pleasing. When you're ready to do what it takes to rip off the shackles of codependency, or to allow someone to help you, creative juices will flow and your authentic journey will begin. Rewriting your story isn't easy, but it is never too late to be unapologetically and happily you.

Your obligation is to obtain healing for yourself, and then you can give it to others.

Oddly, I was writing this sentence during the Covid-19 quarantine. I had been helping others through telehealth. I was hearing revelations from those being forced to stay home and not doing for everyone. Easter dinners weren't cooked. Parties, egg hunts, and all events were out of the question. It was as if all my codependent clients needed an excuse as extreme as a pandemic to allow themselves permission to say "no" guilt free. They were experiencing the freedom of saying no, but it was so unfamiliar, it was rocking their world. A few expressed anger we couldn't meet in person, but I was honoring the health department guidelines. I didn't need an excuse to keep everyone safe.

The crisis brought me back to a time on the KISS tour when I had respiratory failure, went Code Blue, died, and was revived. I was in the ICU for eight days in New Jersey, and my parents never came. Only Gene Simmons's bodyguard "Big" John Hart visited. If the people who contracted Covid-19 only knew how it felt to suffocate and drown on dry land for weeks, they would have stayed home as health officials warned. Thus, I asked all my clients what they learned from Covid-19, and the major consensus was some version of "we are not in control of anything." I knew this from the Code Blue experience. This did not make controller-type codependents happy, but it did make sense. Those who did everything for everyone felt some relief, but it took some time for them to move from frustration to resignation. I hope it makes sense to you. Dying to your old way of doing things is far more rewarding than dying emotionally from the fear of abandonment. It is what a metamorphosis is all about. You must die to a dysfunctional way of life to become who you were meant to be.

It's time for your life to be resuscitated and resurrected. Adversity is the ugliest but best teacher you will ever have. Learning the lessons from your history gives you wisdom to not repeat it.

- What have you learned from your codependency?
- What has it taught you to do and not to do?
- What have you learned about fearful controlling?
- What do you want to do about it?

Doing nothing is no longer an option. Complacency is the enemy. Finding love for yourself and others with reciprocity is an alliance in alignment with your true calling.

Habituation and Adaptation Decoded Forever

Habituation is self-explanatory, but some exploratory work to unravel the remainders of your codependency may help. It's more than a habit that needs to be broken—it is breaking you. You have been fighting your brain that derives vicarious pleasure from giving to others to make them happy. We've reiterated this many times to hammer home what you need to do going forward. Your limbic system, which includes the reactive amygdala, has been controlling your fight, flight, and frozen reactivity and is the operating mechanism creating a resistance to change. You can outsmart it!

The reason your codependency may have escalated over the years is that your brain adapted to one level of pleasure and it needed more of the same "substance" to create the same "buzz." This is an example of the adaptation level phenomenon.[3] The neural stimulus is something we adapt to until it becomes our new norm. When mistreated you have probably said many times, "I'm used to it." You weren't used to it; you were being conditioned to be used by it. When you kept the peace or acquiesced, the pleasure center in your brain created a feeling of false happiness. You're actually overloaded and saturated, unable to find the real happiness you seek. Ask any addict. You're no different. The more you enjoyed helping others, the more normal it felt. The more you did, the less you were able to receive reward from it, so you did more and more to the brink of disaster. Are you there yet? Have you been there more than once? I sure have. As a codependent, the pleasure centers of your brain become saturated when you've overdone it for too long. If you're a saturated codependent, you're an exhausted one.

You've had many epiphanies and now it's time to apply them. See the bigger picture, alter your perception, your consciousness, and, more important, your ego. You don't need the camouflage of a needy entourage anymore. It's time to build on your strengths and not allow a subconscious victim mentality to overtake you anymore. People with a victim mentality have a duplicitous battle raging within them. One side says, "I'm entitled to everything," and the other says, "I'm worthy of nothing." This creates codependent rage if left unchecked. Finding another recovered or recovering codependent person will help you to influence each other to stay true to yourselves. You may have to begin the process with a therapist, but you will find strong interdependent relationships when you concentrate on healthy living and giving.

When we give and receive in our relationships, there's balance. You can live in a state of internal peace and rest by being attuned to your mental, physical, and emotional needs. Hopefully you have been gaining momentum each day that inspires you to continue moving forward. Attending to your emotions is important to keep flowing in healthy directions, and you are no longer an emotional contortionist to make others feel good. You have been too good for your own good for too long. Just saying no to others isn't the end game. It is the beginning of saying yes to yourself. Stagnation won't be possible when you stir the waters of what's possible.

In physics, Sir Isaac Newton's first law of motion, also known as the law of inertia, may help you to see how important it is not to be distracted in your codependent recovery. The law states, "An object at rest stays at rest and an object in motion stays in motion, with the same speed and in the same direction unless acted upon by an unbalanced force."

There is nothing more unbalancing to a codependent than being acted on by the negative pull of someone else imposing on you. In review and preview of the rest of your life:

- Repetition creates a foundation of long-term potentiation.
- Take ownership of the past.
- Have a vision for the future.
- Habitually work on it.
- Adapt moderately and purposefully to stay on track, and you won't go back.

You can and will love and be loved *with* someone who treats you well and who appreciates your kindness and returns it. Your resolution creates space for your desires to come to manifest with wholeness and happiness.

Remaining Buoyant and Resilient

Sir Isaac Newton also discovered the force of gravity. We are pulled downward by an invisible force, and this is another metaphor for you. When you're recovering, there will be those who will attempt to pull you back down, and you may feel an intense urge to revert. Remember the bucket of crabs phenomenon, and you will keep reaching for your personal best, unhindered by those who wish you to remain trapped. It is more difficult to be buoyant and resilient when someone or something you have been conditioned by is tugging with invisible intensity and has an agenda to get you off course—but stay the course.

Yes, we are born to help one another. No, we are not meant to do it alone. Reciprocity is paramount to healthy interdependent safety and resilience and will guard you from slipping back into the pathological altruism model of severe codependency. Science hasn't studied much about the negative outcomes of too much empathy. It is not a condition to be ignored. In the microcosm, users will manipulate your empathy to get you to part with things that are meaningful to you. Let's also not forget that Ted Bundy would hitchhike with a cast on his arm or leg near college campuses to evoke sympathy. His victims were kind people who felt sorry for him.

In the macrocosm, millions of people have been killed by genocide that arose from a call to false altruistic beliefs, and this goes on today when societies accept or overlook atrocities. We need more empathy in the world on a level that will change it, not become a victim of it. More studies need to be done on the suffering of those who fearfully comply to despotic regimes.[4] This may sound dramatic, but the scientific community needs to give credence to the dangers of extreme and pathological codependency. Some have tried to include codependency as a disorder in medical diagnostic manuals for years, but there has been a lack of consensus for precise criteria. It's not a one-size-fits-all diagnosis or recovery process.

Learning to replace fear-based compulsions will require self-compassion, discipline, and perseverance. Transforming fear as a motivational tool can assist your recovery. If you live to be one hundred years old, you have 36,500 *days* of existence. That's about 5,200 *weekends*. How many more days do you want to spend as a codependent? None, I hope. If you fear you have wasted time, you haven't. Giving from the heart isn't a waste when you learn from it and pass the wisdom on to others. You now have a sense of urgency to use what you've learned to help others in more authentic and productive ways.

- Forgive yourself right this very moment!
- Do something nice for yourself today!
- Treat yourself the way you would want your soulmate or best friend to!

Being kind to yourself will help you take ownership and responsibility but not guilt or shame. When you make decisions based on guilt and shame, they often result in choosing less than the best. Choosing what is good over what is *best* is what you have done in the past. That person doesn't exist anymore. Be grateful for wanting and allowing yourself to become the real you. You may have weak moments or relapse, but you will bounce back sooner and wiser. Sympathy tugs won't compel you to rescue without thinking it through.

- You're no longer in survival mode, you're in revival mode.
- You no longer need to be needed; you want to be loved.
- Approval-seeking and people-pleasing are behaviors of the past.
- Feeling selfish or guilty for not meeting the needs of others is gone.
- Feeling not good enough, "too much," or "too little" is over.
- Diminishing yourself to lift others isn't an option.
- Being everyone's "go-to" person is over.
- Rescuing or fixing others has lost its luster.
- Giving ultimatums, unsolicited advice, or nagging to keep others out of trouble ceases.
- Covering or taking a fall for others will never happen again.
- Self-limiting or self-sabotaging beliefs dissipate.

This is the new list for your life. One of a codependent's greatest strengths is tenacity for helping other people. Now you are using it with audacity and bravery to rescue and restore yourself.

You haven't lost yourself sacrificing for others; you're finding the healthy balance between selflessness and selfishness. You're more than independent; you've made decisions and taken steps to become healthily interdependent. There's nothing "wrong" with you. Allow the information you've learned to become revelations to elevate you. Think about what's *right* with you. Focus on the future you do want, and watch it unfold with ease. This isn't about working on yourself; it's about restoring effortless playfulness.

Imagine you're holding three helium-filled black balloons with the words BLAME, SHAME, and GUILT on them. Release them and let them go up past a black cloud over your head and into the stratosphere where they will pop under the pressure. Hear the sound of them in your mind. Then grab one last large black balloon labeled CODEPENDENT. Send it up there and wait for the boom.

Now imagine sunshine beaming down on you from where those balloons pierced through the black cloud and feel the restorative warmth and peace of being in the moment, appreciating yourself for all the days you spent learning and all you have left to enjoy. Breathe in the rejuvenating air and return to innocence and hopefulness. You widen your innate capacity to uplift others and love greatly when you allow yourself to be uplifted first. There are two more things that will help you maintain emotional buoyancy and resilience.

The Transcendent Power of Forgiveness and Gratitude

The idea of forgiving people who used you or hurt you isn't difficult for most codependents. In fact, some of you have done it too quickly or blindly. Forgiveness doesn't mean forgetting or letting the same people hurt you time and time again. Forgiveness doesn't let the offender off the hook. It keeps you from being hooked by remaining attached to them. Forgiveness detaches you from those who hurt, used, or rejected you. Resentment can't hide in your subconscious.

The most important and difficult person to forgive is yourself. You have allowed people to hurt you in the past, but you can vow to not repeat this cycle. Uniquely transformed gratitude will bring you to a place of liberating, true forgiveness. Thankfulness empowers forgiveness in three major phases. It's more than conditioned forgiving from the belief that it's the "right" thing to do or the thing you "must" do. It's wise and redemptive when done according to your truth.

1. Look back to a hurt. Feel the pain momentarily. Suspend it.
2. Find the lesson(s) it taught you. Say or write, "I'm thankful because this taught me _____."
3. Feel how wisdom facilitates forgiveness toward others and yourself.

Coalesced thankfulness and forgiveness raise your vibration from fearful to powerful. Fear dies as the self reaches beyond acceptance into transcendence and atonement. Forgiveness works best when you're ready, not when you're forced. Self-forgiveness holistically renews you. I've forgiven myself for allowing others to hurt me. I am thankful for the learned lessons that sustain me. Wisdom shared between others like you brings healing from compassionate understanding.

Repeat this process whenever you get stuck. Think about a hurt. How did you feel? What did you learn? Find the lesson. Give thanks. Move on with wisdom. Don't get burned by holding grudges, carrying unresolved anger, fear, or fatigue. With self-compassion, and through seeking daily recovery, you can be resurrected to the life you were born to enjoy. It's time to light your way out of the darkness of self-neglect.

Ascendance from the Ashes

You may still have doubts or wonder how you can truly release your fear of abandonment and live in abundance. You really can. You can't get rid of fear. It's always there to remind you to be safe, but you can conquer and control it with courage. You don't have to live in codependent burnout. You can rise like a phoenix from the ashes of it.

There is a plethora of stories about the mythical phoenix bird. Most all have the commonality of resurrection and ascension messages. Many describe that after living in Paradise over one thousand years, the bird begins to feel age and fatigue. This is burnout. It builds a funeral pyre, eats nourishing spices, such as cinnamon, and waits for the sun to set it ablaze. It appears to be its demise, but the phoenix rises restored from the nourishing ashes rekindled, ascended, and stronger than before. It is a ceremony and celebration of the cycles of life. This is much like being codependent and coming full circle to the independent person you were born to be.

Let's bring this concept into reality.

A long time ago, I took letters from my mother to a therapist. I let her read the "I love you, but…" letters. They all started with, "You're beautiful, talented, wonderful, and creative, but…" Pages of criticism and shaming followed. The therapist advised me to go home to my farm, put the letters on the burn pile, and ceremoniously watch the flames dissipate and the ashes fly away. She said it would be cathartic and therapeutic, and it was. It felt good for a while. Yet, there was more work to do.

I had been keeping journals that were filled with complaints about my abusive husband. Some were prayers begging God to fix him, my family, and, of course, me. It became apparent that complaining was a damaging stronghold. I thought writing how I felt was a good thing. Isn't that what a journal is meant to be—a place to put down your innermost thoughts? Yes, it is, but there is a greater good in writing what you do want instead of what you don't. (I hope you have seen this entire book is helping you do just that.)

One cold day, I decided to burn those diaries. I was crying and lighting the pages inside my fireplace. A friend walked in unannounced. She often entered my house without calling or knocking. She knew I had poor boundaries!

"What are you doing?" she asked.

"I'm sick of complaining about being abused and abandoned," I said. "This pile of diaries is now kindling. The kindling is building a fire of kindness. I'll find a way to get away."

It didn't happen overnight, but when I set fire to the negativity and began taking positive action, I resurrected.

Like the phoenix, life is about cycles, seasons, and epiphanies. Becoming your true self is sometimes an arduous task, but the peak experiences are splendidly worth it. You will feel better physically when you release what is causing you to emotionally burn out. Put to ashes things you can't change for anyone but yourself. It's good for your mind and body and connects you to your transformative spirit. Are you ready to begin the ceremony? When you are, proceed with love for yourself.

This Phoenix Ceremony will be done with your Life Lists. Prepare a safe and sacred location, such as a fireplace, where you can burn the negative left side of your Life Lists. This is best done in solitude so you can independently make requests or vows to your renewed self without hindrance. This is your sacred event to release the past and rise up out of codependent loneliness to the blessings of happy interconnectedness. Light a fragrant candle, sage, or put spices on your lists. Salt and cinnamon are healing. You choose. If a fire isn't possible or safe, create your own ritual and cast your past away. You can scatter the ashes to the wind, water, earth, or trash can. Ash has nourishing qualities in cycles of nature. Do what will feel the most freeing and powerful and won't be harmful to the environment. If you have no place to burn anything, a shredder works well too, and you can think of this as making celebratory confetti.

All that will be left of your Life Lists is what is right for you! These are your validating lists of self-compassion and a promise that you no longer have to look beyond yourself to feel worthy of love.

Find a box or a sacred place to keep the positive lists. Refer back to them often. They are your personal guide to finding true happiness. They are your manual for independent living and interdependent giving. Let love overtake fear and live boldly in your newfound liberty of body, mind, and spirit.

Revision Exercise

1. Close your eyes and imagine one of the worst experiences of your codependent life.
2. Feel in your body where the tightening pain is manifesting and relax and release it.
3. Take three deep cleansing breaths and imagine the thing that makes you happiest or what you want to do to be happy. Be sure to imagine you are surrounded by loving, kind people who appreciate and admire you and who you appreciate in return. Imagine the best of friends, partners, soulmates, or people you work with who are collaborative and find you worthy. See scenes of sharing the limelight or being supportive. See someone bringing you a gift and receive it graciously and gratefully. See yourself giving a gift back to them and how they appreciate it.
4. Notice how your body feels. Buoyant? Relaxed? Calm?
5. Alternate for a few brief moments back to codependent exhaustion. Use these negative moments as momentum to move forward.
6. Take three deep cleansing breaths.
7. Go back to the vision of the new you. In doing this self-guided exercise, you will establish neural pathways to keep you out of the darkness of fear of abandonment and move you into the light of fulfillment and abundance.

AFFIRMATION: *I am free from the past. I am rising from the ashes of my former fear of abandonment into an abundant future. I am my true self and allow others to be themselves. I am worthy of love, and I am loved. I am no longer codependent. I am able to give and live well. I am independent and happily interdependent!*

Add your own affirmation.

_____

_____

LIFE LIST

Express thankfulness that you're a compassionate, loving person with an empathic heart and innate talents to help others. You now give with purpose, without pain or fear, to others and yourself. You learned to give and live well! Write your desires of what it is to:

- Exit codependency.
- Enter independence.
- Enjoy abundant and healthy interdependence.

These happy lists are your words and your story. It is your benediction to begin anew, refreshed, and restored. You can now share your story with others. Every hero's journey takes them to the wilderness of their soul, alone and abandoned, and it hurts at first but is worth the reward to come full circle, with the ability to recognize a relapse and get back on your path to freedom. Embrace the wilderness times of your recovery, and you will feel a reassurance you aren't alone and a resurgence in your ability to give out of love without fear. The benevolence you bestow upon yourself will enable you to transcend who you were. You will become who you want to be and attract who you want with you in your continued life's journey. Well done! Go have fun with your new life.

EPILOGUE

This has not been merely a self-help book, but one offered from personal and professional experience to lighten your load and enlighten your spirit. You will always want to keep helping others. I made a donation to a food bank recently. The gift was within my means to a local trusted organization staffed with volunteers and matching funds. It's good and fun to keep giving. You will do it because generosity is built into your personality. This is the upside to a codependent nature. Now you know how to do it with self-care and by keeping safe boundaries, so you can live abundantly too. The intent of this book was never to make you self-serving or self-righteous but to help you serve others in ways that energize you with a sense of meaning and purpose without neglecting your need to be served as well.

Make one last list. Write down everything you like about yourself. Add to it often with gratitude and remind yourself to continue on your life's journey with love and compassion for yourself as you maintain giving and living well.

Blessings to you for an abundant and overflowing life!

REFERENCES

Chapter 1

1. Rappoport, Alan. "Co-Narcissism: How We Accommodate to Narcissistic Parents." 2005. http://www.alanrappoport.com/pdf/Co-Narcissism%20Article.pdf. Used with permission.

2. Tronick, Ed. *The Neurobehavioral and Social-Emotional Development of Infants and Children.* New York: W. W. Norton & Company, 2007.

3. Burns, R. C., and S. Kaufman. *Kinetic Family Drawing (KFD): An Introduction to Understanding Children through Kinetic Drawings.* New York: Brunner/Mazel, 1970.

4. Bowlby, John. *Separation: Anxiety and Anger Attachment and Loss.* New York: Basic Books, 1976.

5. Seligman, M. E. *Authentic Happiness: Using the New Positive Psychology to Realize Your Potential for Lasting Fulfillment.* New York: Simon and Schuster, 2004.

Chapter 2

1. Bacon, Ingrid, Elizabeth McKay, Frances Reynolds, and Anne McIntyre. "The Lived Experience of Codependency: An Interpretative Phenomenological Analysis." *International Journal of Mental Health and Addiction,* 18 (2020): 754–71.

2. Linde, Sharon. "Brehm's Reactance Theory: Definition & Overview." *Study.com,* July 15, 2015. Retrieved from study.com/academy/lesson/brehms-reactance-theory-definition.

3. Karpman, Stephen B. *A Game Free Life: The Definitive Book on the Drama Triangle and Compassion Triangle by the originator and author.* San Francisco: Drama Triangle Publications, 2014. Used with permission.

4. Boyd, Bobby E., Jeff Hanna, Marcus Hummon. "Bless the Broken Road," Nashville: Broadcast Music, Inc., 1993.

5. Williams, Rhiannon. "Why the Fairy tales You Know May Not Be as They Seem." *The Telegraph,* 2016. https://www.telegraph.co.uk/technology/google/google -doodle/12093512/Who-was-Charles-Perrault-Why-the-fairy-tales-you -know-may-not-be-as-they-seem.html.

6. Drigotas, Stephen M., et al. "Close Partner as Sculptor of the Ideal Self: Behavioral Affirmation and the Michelangelo Phenomenon." *Journal of Personality and Social Psychology,* 77 (1999). Used with permission.

7. Rosenthal, Robert, and Lenore Jacobson, *Pygmalion in the Classroom: Teacher Expectations and Pupils' Intellectual Development.* Carmarthen: Crown House Publishing, 2003.

8. Shaw, George Bernard. *Pygmalion.* New York: Simon and Schuster, 1981.

9. Alan J. Lerner. *My Fair Lady*, directed by George Cukor. (Los Angeles: Warner Brothers, 1964).

10. Maslow, A. H. "A Theory of Human Motivation." *Psychological Review,* 50, no. 4 (1943): 370–96.

Chapter 3

1. Oakley, Barbara, Ariel Knafo, Guruprasad Madhavan, and David Sloan Wilson. *Pathological Altruism.* Oxford: Oxford University Press, 2011. Used with permission.

2. Hebb, D. O. *The Organization of Behavior.* New York: John Wiley and Sons, 1949.

3. Price, C. J., and C. Hooven. "Interoceptive Awareness Skills for Emotion Regulation: Theory and Approach of Mindful Awareness in Body-Oriented Therapy (MABT)." *Frontiers in Psychology,* 9 (2018): 798. https://doi.org/10.3389/fpsyg.2018.00798.

4. Davidson, R. and A. Lutz. "Buddha's Brain: Neuroplasticity and Meditation (In the Spotlight)." *IEEE Signal Processing Magazine* 25, no. 1 (2008): 176. https://doi.org/10.1109/MSP.2008.4431873.

Chapter 5

1. Fisher, Helen. *Why We Love: The Nature and Chemistry of Romantic Love.* New York: Henry Holt and Co., 2004.

2. Herrmann, Ned. "What Is the Function of Various Brainwaves?" *Scientific American*, December 1997.

Chapter 6

1. Dunn, Elizabeth W., Lara B. Aknin, and Michael I. "Prosocial Spending and Happiness: Using Money to Benefit Others Pays Off." *Current Directions in Psychological Science*, 23, no. 1 (2014): 41. https://doi.org/10.1177/0963721413512503.

Chapter 7

1. Dunn, Elizabeth W., Lara B. Aknin, and Michael I. Norton. "Prosocial Spending and Happiness: Using Money to Benefit Others Pays Off." *Current Directions in Psychological Science*, 23, no. 1 (2014): 41–47.

2. Jung, C. G., "The Relations Between the Ego and the Unconscious." In *The Collected Works of C.G. Jung, Vol. 7: Two Essays on Analytical Psychology.* New York: Routledge, 1966.

3. Ellis, A. *Reason and Emotion in Psychotherapy: Comprehensive Method of Treating Human Disturbances.* Revised and Updated (New York: Citadel Press, 1994).

4. Walton, Alice G. "7 Ways Meditation Can Actually Change The Brain." *Forbes,* 2015. https://www.forbes.com/sites/alicegwalton/2015/02/09/7-ways-meditation-can-actually-change-the-brain/#1345fadc1465.

5. "Lemon Imagery Exercise." *Suppers*, https://www.thesuppersprograms.org/content/lemon-imagery-exercise.

Chapter 8

1. Lipton, James. *Inside the Actors Studio.* New York: Bravo Network, 1994–2018.

2. *Irving Berlin's No Business Like Show Business.* Directed by Walter Lang, music by Irving Berlin. CA: 20th Century-Fox, 1954.

Chapter 9

1. Campbell, Joseph. *The Hero with a Thousand Faces*. Princeton, NJ: Princeton University Press, 1949.

2. *The Karate Kid*. Directed by John G. Avildsen. Los Angeles, CA: Columbia Pictures, 1984.

Chapter 10

1. Yin, J., and Q. Yuan. "Structural Homeostasis in the Nervous System: A Balancing Act for Wiring Plasticity and Stability." *Frontiers in Cellular Neuroscience,* 8 (2015): 439.

2. Nietzsche, Friedrich. *Man Alone with Himself*. United Kingdom: Penguin Books Limited, 2008.

3. Falk, Emily B., Matthew Brook O'Donnell, Christopher N. Cascio, et al. "Neural Bases of Affirmation." *Proceedings of the National Academy of Sciences*, (2015). https://doi.org/10.1073/pnas.1500247112.

4. Nietzsche, Friedrich. *Human, All Too Human: Revised*. Nebraska: Bison Books, 1996.

5. Knudson, Theresa M., and Heather K. Terrell. "Codependency, Perceived Interparental Conflict, and Substance Abuse in the Family of Origin." *American Journal of Family Therapy*, no. 3 (2012): 245–57. https://doi.org/10.1080/019 26187.2011.610725.

Chapter 11

1. Waldinger, Robert. "What Makes a Good Life? Lessons from the Longest Study on Happiness." Filmed November 2015 at TEDxBeaconStreet. TED video, 12:38, https://www.ted.com/talks/robert_waldinger_what_makes_a_good_life _lessons_from_the_longest_study_on_happiness?language=en.

2. Mate, G. *When the Body Says No: Exploring the Stress Disease Connection*. Hoboken: John Wiley and Sons, Inc., 2003.

3. Helson, H. *Adaptation-Level Theory: An Experimental and Systematic Approach to Behavior*. New York: Harper and Row, 1964.

4. Oakley B. A. "Concepts and Implications of Altruism Bias and Pathological Altruism." *Proceedings of the National Academy of Sciences of the United States of America, 110 Supplement 2* (2013): 10408–10415. https://doi.org/10.1073/pnas.1302547110. Used with permission.

ABOUT THE AUTHOR

Mary Joye is a licensed mental health counselor, life coach, and Florida Supreme Court certified family mediator. She is the author of popular courses for DailyOM.com, a monthly contributor of the Body, Mind, Spirit column for *Central Florida Health News*, and is a guest author and speaker for globally recognized websites, podcasts, and events. In 2019, *O, The Oprah Magazine* featured her journey out of codependency to authenticity. Raised on the Gulf Coast of Florida, Mary is the daughter of a psychiatrist and worked at her father's practice earlier in life. She then put herself through college as a stagehand and earned her bachelor's degree in technical and performance theatre. Her first job was as a makeup and wardrobe assistant for the band KISS. This stepping stone led to a twenty-year career as a professional singer/songwriter in Nashville for major publishing companies. She later earned her master's degree in counseling and discovered the depths of her codependency from a professor, and thus, her true calling. It became her mission to recover from severe codependency and help others do the same. In her private practice, Mary combines creative, traditional, and holistic modalities of healing and attributes daily meditation to her expedited recovery.

Mary loves saltwater activities, hiking, and traveling extensively to be with the people she loves. She can often be seen walking her dogs while looking at the sky and admiring the freedom of exotic birds wherever she goes. Inspired by nature, Mary sends herself messages with ideas that come to her and incorporates them into her work. She believes this makes her writing more conversational and relatable. This book began that way and she hopes it helps you find your own inspiration on your path of self-discovery and recovery.